Crime in Wartime

Crime in Wartime

A Social History of Crime in World War II

by EDWARD SMITHIES

London
GEORGE ALLEN & UNWIN
Boston   Sydney

George Allen & Unwin (Publishers) Ltd,
40 Museum Street, London WC1A 1LU, UK

George Allen & Unwin (Publishers) Ltd,
Park Lane, Hemel Hempstead, Herts HP2 4TE, UK

Allen & Unwin Inc.,
9 Winchester Terrace, Winchester, Mass 01890, USA

George Allen & Unwin Australia Pty Ltd,
8 Napier Street, North Sydney, NSW 2060, Australia

First published in 1982

British Library Cataloguing in Publication Data

Smithies, Edward
    Crime in wartime.
    1. Crime and criminals – Great Britain – History
    2. Punishment – Great Britain – History
    I. Title
    364'.941   HV6943
    ISBN 0-04-364020-6

Set in 11 on 12 point Baskerville by Inforum Ltd, Portsmouth
and printed in Great Britain by
Biddles Ltd, Guildford, Surrey

This book is dedicated to my parents

Author's Note

I wish to thank all those who have helped me in preparing this study. In particular I owe a considerable debt to my friends who have read and discussed parts of the book with me. Any errors that remain are entirely my own.

Contents

Introduction

The Second World War has arguably been the most decisive experience of British people during the present century. This study examines one aspect of that experience – the influence of the war on patterns of crime.

To illustrate how the war influenced the way people behaved, let me quote from four cases at random:

(a) 'In June, 1941, this woman's husband, to whom she was most devoted, was killed in the course of a bombing operation. The shock to her was a dreadful one, and she sought every possible means of getting away from herself, her loneliness and her sorrow. She sought out all the friends she could muster, so to speak, and entertained them, or travelled long, expensive journeys at weekends to visit' them with the result that she began 'to borrow' in a small way 'and so this wretched business started'.

(b) 'There were special circumstances in this case ... as a result of the war he had been living alone in a room, separated from his family. Bombs had fallen on each side of the house and his windows were broken by blast. All this had a serious effect upon him and he had been suffering from melancholia. He had now lost his job and his pension.'

(c) He 'had been badly wounded at Dunkirk' and was discharged from the Army as medically unfit. 'He had lost the sight of one eye while his left arm was partially disabled.' He 'had been reading a lot about fifth columnists dressed in women's clothing' and so 'he had decided to try it'. He 'had walked three miles before being detected'.

(d) 'A few days before the war began he met a refugee girl, who was unable to find any friends and was without any means. He and his wife took pity on her and kept her for about eight months when she left them to get married. As a result of their keeping this girl he fell into arrears with the instalments on his home, and furniture. He then lost his job at the railway and took a job as a stretcher bearer, at a greatly reduced wage. He then found himself very heavily in debt and committed these offences.'

The defendants in these four wartime cases were respectively charged with (a) falsifying entries in the wage sheets during the course of her work at the Treasurer's department, Chatham Town Hall,[1] (b) stealing postal orders from letters,[2] (c) importuning in the North End Road, Fulham, wearing silk petticoat, knickers and a brassière filled with inflatable balloons,[3] and (d) stealing eleven suitcases from unattended motor cars.[4] In common with many hundreds of other people who found themselves in court between 1939 and 1945, they attributed what they had done to the impact of the war on their lives. The war saturated the consciousness of the people who lived through it to the extent that they would seek to explain many peculiarities of behaviour by it. Maybe they were merely looking for a persuasive story to put before the magistrate, but it was to the war that they turned, the tribulations and horrors of which everyone, including magistrates, had shared.

To begin with the most immediate record, the statistics. In 1939 the police had known of 303,771 crimes;* in 1945 they knew of 478,394,* a rise of 57 per cent in seven years. In the previous five years (1934–8) the number had increased by only 21 per cent, so the war saw a marked quickening in pace.[5]

Of the persons accused of committing these crimes, 47,223 were found guilty in 1939, and 72,758 in 1945,* a rise of 54 per cent. Or, to express the change in a different way, for every 100,000 people, 149 were found guilty in 1939, and 223 in 1945.[6] Recorded crime and recorded criminals thus both increased during the war, and most alarmingly during its last two years.

The war has generally been regarded as a heroic period in the country's history; this study, however, is concerned with the underside of that achievement: the English people in their unheroic moments. Yet these two aspects of the country's experience cannot be separated from one another, a point that might best be illustrated by one contemporary who writes

* In England and Wales.

of a drunken party he attended: 'I thought I had better go to bed. I had had my fill and found it rather difficult to walk straight. As I was trundling along the corridor there happened to be four fire extinguishers in the way. These I did not see, partly for the obvious reason and partly because the corridor was dark. Anyway, I had the misfortune to trip over them and one by one they went off. I did not know what to do. First I tried to sit on them to keep the liquid from going on the corridors; that was no good. The stuff seeped through my trousers and then began to spray out again. There was no way out of it. Nearby was a large and ornamental door covered with glass. One by one I threw the fire extinguishers out, making a most horrible noise of tinkling glass and squirting extinguishers. Then I went to bed, feeling that I had done my best in difficult circumstances.'[7]

The author of this account could well later have found himself in court facing a charge of committing wilful damage to government property, or drunken and disorderly behaviour; whilst if his act of hooliganism had taken place at an armaments factory the charge might well have been sabotage, carrying with it the possibility of a lengthy prison sentence. In fact the offender was the RAF pilot and future war hero, Guy Gibson; nor did he escape punishment of sorts. He was 'impolitely informed' that he had been taken off drinking in the Mess for a month. Thus even war heroes had unheroic, antisocial, destructive moments: this study proposes to examine the behaviour of the English people at such times.

By 'crime' in this book is understood those acts which are punishable by law; the war itself caused Parliament to add considerably to their number, and this explains the topics that are examined here and the way in which they are set out. For example, the maintenance of public morale was a major preoccupation of the authorities, and those organisations which were identified as potentially disruptive soon found themselves the object of police attention. There was a wave of prosecutions for offences against 'morale' in the first eighteen months of the war and for a time they loomed large in court proceedings and newspaper reports. The wave subsided during 1941 as the authorities grew increasingly confident about the country's morale and as other forms of crime pressed for their attention.

The government had attempted to control the market, and as the rationing regulations made themselves felt with considerable thoroughness a black market emerged which rapidly began to influence other types of crime, especially theft. Pilfering from the employer; the professional robbery designed, for instance, to steal a lorry or break into a warehouse; and receiving – all expanded to meet the demands of the black market. And the techniques of professional robbery underwent a most significant transformation, as the emphasis shifted from stealing property (paintings, jewels, or furs) from the rich to obtaining goods in short supply (cigarettes, alcohol, consumer goods). Between 1944 and 1946 the black market reached its highest point of development, and theft and receiving flourished along with it. Involved actively in hastening the process were hitherto 'respectable' persons. Many businessmen, shopkeepers and tradesmen participated energetically in the black market, and connived at breaking the rationing regulations, while countless members of the general public co-operated with them over the counter and elsewhere. A similar process affected other 'respectable occupations' – most conspicuously the civil service and the building industry: 'white collar crime' emerged for the first time as a serious problem.

The black marketeers had a great deal of money to spend, as did the traditional 'leisured' classes (now confined to the island for the duration) and those well paid visitors, the United States and Canadian military. Many sought the usual outlets of gaming, unlimited drinking, the company of prostitutes; and racketeers were only too anxious to supply them. But they did so at a time when the authorities, with strong support from a substantial section of public opinion, were seeking to limit and control such 'action', partly because they wanted to concentrate energies on the war effort, but mainly because they feared that the dynamics of the war itself threatened the country's established code of morality. The young were identified as the most vulnerable, and also as advancing the trend: the law was thus introduced to try to halt the process of social change itself.

Running parallel with these trends was an alarming increase in violence which, however, had separate roots, but which also added to the impression of greater lawlessness in the country in the concluding stages of the war. The police were required to cope with all these developments at a time when their own resources were much reduced: by 1945–6 they were enduring severe strain, as their spokesmen did not hesitate to point out. The courts were in similar difficulties and in both areas policy needed to be adjusted to take account of altered circumstances.

Although the range of 'crime' discussed in this book is a broad one, it is not intended to be exhaustive. There is little discussion of prison and borstal in wartime, and less about the intervention of the law into, for instance, industrial relations. There are also geographical limitations. Even though many of the statistics refer to 'England and Wales', the social histories of Wales and Scotland differ markedly from that of England, as the nationalism of recent years has demonstrated. England should be studied as the national entity it is, while Glasgow (and perhaps Cardiff also) pose problems sufficiently complex and interesting to merit studies on their own account.

Within England, London will be seen to dominate. London was the crime capital of the country, especially where professional criminals were concerned. But this emphasis reflects also the documentary evidence available for the capital. Many of the policemen, lawyers or former criminals who published their memoirs were Londoners, or had spent the greater part of their professional lives in the capital. The reports of the Commissioner of the Metropolitan Police were (when they appeared) fuller and richer than those of his provincial colleagues. To this must be added the wartime complication that whereas the provincial big city press largely abandoned its interest in local affairs for the duration, not surprisingly preferring to concentrate on reporting the war, the local London press, and to a lesser extent that in the smaller provincial towns, continued to offer comment about and reports of court proceedings. This is vital for understanding the pattern of crime as it developed in the capital but it causes gaps where the great provincial cities are concerned – Liverpool, Manchester and Leeds especially.

The problem is compounded by the exigencies of the war itself. Even in their published form the statistics do not provide answers to a number of questions the social historian wishes to ask. They do not give clear indications of what was happening in the various forms of theft (especially pilfering) nor, for example, do they show the amounts stolen in robberies, nor how many robberies were accompanied by the use of guns or actual physical violence. The statistics concerning the black market lump together buyers and sellers, 'big' dealers and the trivial shopping offence which happened to be reported. Nor do they distinguish the social class or occupation of the offender, so it is not possible to estimate the extent of 'white-collar' and 'proletarian' crime. But, incredibly, during the war publication of the relevant statistics was in many instances interrupted. The most severe omission affects *Criminal Statistics*, suspended for the duration, but even the reports of the Commissioner of the Metropolitan Police ceased during the middle stages of the war, whilst reports for Liverpool were abandoned altogether. Even the police reports that continued to appear did so only in truncated form.

The greater part of the book, therefore, concerns *reported* offences, which represent, of course, only a proportion of the crimes actually committed. The 'dark figure' varies considerably from one type of crime to another – certainly very small for murder, enormous for the black market. It would be helpful to know the extent of police *suspicions* about offenders and offences which were never developed into prosecutions but, understandably, the relevant files are closed and will remain so until well into the next century. Unfortunately, closed along with them are all other police files, and my attempts to secure access to them have been totally unsuccessful. This means that it is not possible to follow the development of policy in such crucial areas as the relations between the Home Office and the Chief Constables, the character of the instructions relayed to the provincial forces, how these were translated into general inquiries, and how they affected the approach taken by the individual constable in the street. From time to time guesses have had to be made as to the broad lines of policy, but they can remain no more than that until the files have been opened.

CHAPTER ONE

Morale

In March 1942 in Hove, an elderly and impoverished American lady, living alone, happened to go into a café and sit at a table near a young army officer. The two began a conversation and, almost inevitably in that grim third winter of the war, they talked about politics. Or rather the American lady talked, for politics and the war were matters about which she held strong opinions.

'She said, among others things, that she was an American, but, owing to the war, could not return home. She told him she had travelled extensively in Europe, including Germany, and the Germans were quite happy working for the State. She expressed admiration for the German type of government now in existence, and said that in her opinion Germany did not want to fight this war . . . it was this country's fault we were at war. She admired Hitler, and considered he was a great ruler . . .'

The 'young lieutenant of infantry, in uniform', did not protest; indeed, he encouraged her, so much so that she invited him to visit her at her flat. She went on to inform him that Roosevelt and Churchill had 'Jewish blood' and produced a piece of paper on which she expressed herself in verse. She was, it seems, the kind of elderly crank, more pathetic than menacing, who sought out resorts like Hove as a refuge in wartime; but the soldier did not think so, nor did the police. She was prosecuted on a charge of having 'published a statement related to matters connected with the war which was likely to cause alarm and despondency'. She pleaded guilty and the magistrate sent her to jail for a month's hard labour, and fined her £50.[1]*

---

* 'Hard labour' at this time meant that the prisoner performed whatever labour he or she was medically fit to do, and also went without a mattress during the first fourteen days of the sentence.

To understand the motives of the prosecutors, and the view that such a person could represent any sort of threat it is necessary to recall the general atmosphere of the time: the invasion scare of 1940–1; the blitz; the uncertainty of final victory; and the German armies ever-present on the other side of the Channel. Even so, the response of the officer, the police, the court, and the local newspaper (which reported the case in detail) seem out of all proportion to the 'offence'. The courts were here clearly being used for a political purpose, to maintain public morale, and they continued to be so used throughout the war, though the type of activity penalised altered from time to time.

The first of several waves of wartime prosecutions began with the very start of hostilities, and concerned the blackout. Something of the tension of those first weeks of war can be recaptured from reports of the scenes which occurred when the blackout regulations were flagrantly broken. Crowds gathered, the police were summoned, windows got broken, and the culprits were threatened with violence. Old and 'eccentric' people (who may not have realised 'there was a war on') were particularly vulnerable. Police called to the home of an 83-year-old man in Hampstead found a hostile crowd assembled, shouting 'Smash the door down!' Lights showed in two front-room windows. The court fined him £2 (four times the weekly pension of a single man in 1939).[2] An elderly man in Highgate who burned a fire in his garden was remanded in custody for a week for a medical report. People in the 'large crowd' which collected 'wanted to assault' him.[2] Shopkeepers and businessmen who broke the law were heavily fined: £50 was by no means unusual. A Stamford Hill shopkeeper who left arc lamps burning in his shop was fined this amount: an angry crowd of between fifty and a hundred people gathered outside.[3] Such incidents reflected fears derived from the propaganda of the 1930s that the bomber 'always gets through'; indeed, devastating German air raids were expected within days of the declaration of war. As autumn lengthened into winter and the raids did not materialise, the public became more casual in its attitude and infringements of the blackout were increasingly regarded in much the same way as breaches of the traffic regulations – as not being real crimes at all. Nonetheless, 300,000 people passed through the courts in 1940 alone, and the fines imposed must have represented a considerable extra source of revenue for the exchequer. Court proceedings seemed incomplete without a batch of blackout prosecutions.[4]

In the first twelve months of the war the courts took very much more seriously another category of offenders: the political critics of the Government on the extreme left and the extreme right who advocated their views in public. The authorities decided that the British Union of Fascists and the Communist Party of Great Britain represented potentially dangerous centres of disaffection and were prepared to use the courts in an attempt to silence them.

The British Union of Fascists received the closest attention during the first year of the war, and from its very first day. One early prosecution involved a thirty-year-old clerk who spoke in London to a crowd of about 2,000 people, including, according to the police, about 100 Jews. The meeting actually took place on 31 August, but the case came to court after 3 September when war was declared. The clerk had said, when he mounted the platform, 'I feel very bitter tonight . . . the call is to revolt . . . If there is a War Chamberlain will still draw £10,000 a year, and so will Mr. Atlee [*sic*], the stinking traitor . . . The German people are led by a German, the British are led by a Jew, fed by a Jew, clothed by a Jew, pushed by a Jew . . . Don't think it [the war] will be a walkover. What a chance we have! Look at our Army! Look at its leader – Hore-Belisha! . . . Whenever I see this man's physog in the paper a horrible, revolting feeling comes over my stomach . . . Don't blame Hitler; blame the people who have brought us to this state of affairs. When you walk down the High-street show your common enemies what you think of them. You can show them in many ways . . .'[5] Not surprisingly, the clerk was charged with threatening a breach of the peace, and he was jailed for three months.

Such cases, where the evidence was clear, were comparatively easy for the courts; much more difficult were those involving persons who chose their words with some care. When Alexander Raven Thompson, 'the philosopher of British Fascism',[6] offered some of his philosophy to a crowd of 400 in Finsbury Square in January 1940, the police noted the following from his speech: 'The British Government is rotten throughout . . . the sooner we Englishmen rid ourselves of the filthy corrupt practices and the alien influences of the Jewish financiers, the sooner the War will end and England will be a better place to live in.'[7]

The problem the courts faced in sentencing in such cases was how far they could go without causing an obvious miscarriage of justice: Raven Thompson was found guilty of using insulting words and fined £25. The answer to the problem lay in the phrase often employed in bringing charges against Fascists and Communists: 'using insulting words and behaviour whereby a breach of the peace might be occasioned'. If a man or woman spoke to a crowd which did not like what it heard and showed it, then the speaker could be accused of having provoked them to a breach of the peace. It was a dangerous situation: strong language used by ministers in the government, which might well be regarded as insulting by some sections of their audience, rarely if ever resulted in the prosecution of those ministers. But, when an opponent of the war spoke out, then a prosecution could well ensue. The evidence in some of these cases looks very thin indeed. A 23-year-old clerk was prosecuted after addressing a BUF meeting in May 1940. His audience included men and women in uniform and presumably the most inflammatory section of his speech was held to be insulting to them: he said, 'My forefathers from Wales won five V.C.s at Rorke's Drift. They were then called heroes: but when they came back what did they come back to? Why, their dirty little villages and slime. That is what the soldiers of 1940 will come back to.' The police conceded that 'no one attempted to attack the accused' but added that 'it was evident that his remarks were disliked'. The court accepted this and the clerk was jailed for three months.[8]

On several occasions magistrates were able to expose the poverty of the propaganda of right-wing critics of the war. When a 25-year-old clerk was prosecuted for pasting bills on a wall, the magistrate asked him about the contents of the posters and the following exchange ensued:

Defendant: 'We were just publishing the names of those people who were trying to dodge conscription.' (The names were all Jewish.)

Magistrate: 'Then why isn't your own name on it, you've dodged conscription.'

Defendant: 'No, I haven't, I've registered as a conscientious objector.'[9]

However, according to the police, the defendant was surrounded by a 'very large and hostile crowd' shouting 'Lynch him!' and 'Let us have him for ten minutes!' Although the clerk pleaded that there had been no trouble till the police arrived on the scene, he had no witnesses, and the magistrate sentenced him to three months hard labour.

Such prosecutions took place against the background of the invasion scare of 1940. France fell in June 1940, and the coincidental sharp increase in penalties against persons convicted of using 'insulting words and behaviour' is striking. This was particularly so in London, where Fascists had found some measure of support in the 1930s, especially in the East End. When two members of the Imperial Fascist League (a minute organisation) were jailed for six months in June 1940, the extent of the evidence against them was that they had in their possession an army uniform and could not explain how they obtained it. The men claimed that they had been taking the uniform out to destroy it (they were arrested in the street carrying a brown parcel; the uniform was inside); the prosecution alleged that it belonged to a deserter.[10]

Although the courts, in imposing such sentences, sought to satisfy what they conceived to be the national interest, the prosecutors were imposing a dangerous strain on them – one that was to be clearly revealed during prosecutions of Communists. If it was necessary to put political opponents of the war behind bars, then better it be done by direct political act (18B) than by straining the country's legal machinery.

By late summer many active Fascists had indeed been interned under Regulation 18b and the rate of prosecutions thereafter declined. The Fascist organisations had been broken and people who now came to court were usually acting on their own. Many were eccentrics, but the authorities regarded them as seriously as they took themselves, as the presence of G. R. Paling, Senior Legal Assistant to the Director of Public Prosecutions, as prosecuting counsel in a typical case demonstrates. This, in February 1941, involved an eighteen-year-old youth, a clerk in Rochester Town Hall. He had been spending his leisure time inserting pro-Hitler pamphlets in newspapers at Chatham Public Library and in telephone kiosks. He was also accused of having sent the following message on a postcard to Chatham 'Chief of Police': 'This is to give you notice that from today onwards, a most vigorous National Socialist campaign is to take place in the Medway Towns, in order to prepare the way for the victorious German troops as they pass through here. National Socialist Britain is coming. England awake.'[11]

Great nonsense no doubt, but the case received front-page treatment under the headline 'Hard Labour for Corporation Clerk'. Such cases were taken seriously because the authorities – especially in the early stages of the war and being uncertain about the morale of the English people – were afraid that opponents of the war might be listened to. The impression is inescapable that police attended political meetings with the instruction to find something – anything – that would enable a prosecution to be initiated.[12] Three cases in the East End (where the Communist Party of Great Britain had some strength) illustrate the point.

In the first, in May 1940, a nineteen-year-old hat machinist was reported to have remarked in a speech that 'the rotten Government hold 390 million Indians in slavery'. The police also noted that he had copies of the following publications: *Daily Worker*, *Labour Monthly*, and a booklet entitled 'How To Be Safe in Air Raids'. The 'hostility of the crowd' to his speech was such that 'he was removed more for his own protection than anything else'; nonetheless he was jailed for two months.[13]

In July 1940 a 25-year-old presser was delivering pamphlets at a block of flats whose residents, the police stated, objected. This time a prosecution witness who was not a policeman appeared in court (which was itself unusual) and said that 'a leaflet was handed into his home. He heard several people say it should be reported so he went and called up the police.' Evidence was also given that the defendant 'was regarded by the Special Branch as an extremist of the Communist party'; perhaps, after all this, it is only surprising that he was jailed for a period as short as twenty-eight days.[14]

The third case, which came to court a few days after the

second, involved a housewife and a writer charged with contravening the Public Order Act. They had been distributing handbills which the police claimed caused anger among passers-by, so much so that they had been obliged to take both women into custody for their own protection. Counsel for the defence argued that the women were entitled to criticise the government and call for change: 'It surely could not be said that because people disagreed with certain views it was therefore insulting to express them.' And he managed to sting the magistrate into stating his own attitude to such prosecutions '. . . the Court was neither Communist nor anti-Communist . . . [he] suggested that the leaflets contained an attack on the recognised labour movement of this country at a time when both workers and leaders had earned the unspeakable [*sic*] praise and gratitude of every citizen for their contribution to the national cause . . . [The] case had given him an opportunity of expressing his intense appreciation and gratitude at the way in which the British working man was being led and the way he was conducting himself in the national emergency.' If so, one wonders with the defence counsel why the court felt it had 'the duty . . . to protect the labour movement from criticism' by Communists. The magistrate found both women guilty and bound them over to be of good behaviour.[15]

Simultaneously, in south London, a series of prosecutions of Communists was launched; the fact that they took place at the same time as those in the East End suggests that the police might have been acting on instructions from higher authority.[16]

Protestations by prosecuting counsel and magistrates that the political views defendants held were irrelevant in these cases[17] may be tested by comparing what happened when an anti-Communist set out deliberately to disrupt a Communist meeting. A retired railway official so objected to what a Communist speaker was saying that he 'went behind him and . . . lifted his stand at the back a few inches, and the law of gravity happened to precipitate him in front of his audience'.

Magistrate (Brodrick): 'What happened to the speaker?'
Defendant (pleading not guilty to a charge of insulting behaviour): 'He went over with the platform.'

The magistrate found him guilty and bound him over to keep the peace for twelve months. The defendant immediately announced that he would appeal and added: 'It is a matter for us to take up, whether these people should be allowed there. I will hire a vehicle and ride backwards and forwards among them.' So much for the promise to keep the peace; nor did the magistrate offer any rebuke to the defendant.[18]

Coincidentally with these prosecutions of Fascists and Communists went a wave of arrests for 'careless talk'. These divided into two main categories: the first concerning security and the second, remarks or behaviour said to undermine public morale.

In the former, courts were usually cleared, so it is not possible to reconstruct in full what happened. The main groups of persons involved seem to have been officials and workers on the railways and at ports (who were likely to know the details of ship and troop movements); civilian staff attached to military bases; and the workforce in armaments factories. Prosecutions were designed to warn the public as well as to punish the offenders, as counsel observed in a case in Brighton in 1942: 'The proceedings were brought as a warning to other persons who got information that they must lock it up in their own heads.' The defendant was a 54-year-old special constable; he was jailed for two months.[19]

How these offences might come to light is revealed in two cases in the Rochester district, a sensitive area with its important naval base. In the first a 24-year-old worker in 'a vital industry' got into conversation with an elderly man in the public bar of a hotel, but, unluckily for him, also present were two officers of the Intelligence Corps. They heard him 'discuss information he had obtained as a result of his work . . . not only did he say production was going well, he also talked about the destination of certain important components'. The prosecution argued that if this information had reached the 'ears of the enemy' the factories the man mentioned might easily have been bombed. The offence was not committed deliberately: it was 'the criminal folly of chattering'; nonetheless it attracted a two-month jail sentence.[20]

The officers in this case were doing their duty; but sometimes individual members of the public acted as informers. A consulting engineer was staying at an hotel in Rochester and 'entered into conversation with a gentleman . . . in clerical dress . . . to whom he was a complete stranger. He is a very eminently respectable Canon', but the engineer did not know that 'and he might have been anybody disguised as a clergyman. During that conversation he disclosed certain secrets to the Canon. They might be very vital to the enemy of this country . . . and he did it in such a tone of voice that he could be heard by other persons in the room.' Instead of asking him to lower his voice or turning the conversation, the clergyman informed the police, and the talkative engineer was jailed for three months.[21]

Motivating such prosecutions was the fear the authorities had that a 'fifth column' was at work in England, gathering information and passing it on to spies. In fact there seem to have been very few English spies, and those tended to be incompetent amateurs. A 28-year-old welder engaged on 'Admiralty work of vital importance' was jailed for seven years for cutting receiver cords in telephone kiosks in west London; while in Southsea, also in July 1940, a group of British Union of Fascists members with spying ambitions was rounded up. The principal figure was a German woman married to a Briton, who, with a fellow member of the BUF, tried to cause disaffection among troops stationed locally (conversations took place which were 'disloyal and pro-German'). They also attempted to obtain secret information, though what they proposed to do with it once they got it is not clear, since they had no links with enemy agents. The woman was jailed for fourteen years and the man for ten years, and they were trapped because they tried to recruit a young man who informed the police what was going on.[22]

Other cases involved people who already had a reputation for political eccentricity to which the war gave a criminal edge. A 31-year-old aerofitter, nicknamed 'squarehead' at the RAF base where he worked as a civilian, had been under observation for pro-German sentiments since April 1938, but he was not prosecuted until 1943 because assembling evidence that would stand up in court sometimes took a long time. He was found to have drawn up a plan of a military base 'which might be useful to an enemy' and was jailed for three months.[23]

Nervousness about the loyalties of such persons was probably justified – they had no doubts about which side they supported in the war. But the prosecution of another category of offender – those accused of making statements likely to undermine morale – demonstrates the tense atmosphere of the time. Even magistrates, who tended to see themselves as being in the front line when it came to maintaining public morale, had difficulty in knowing exactly how to respond as a motley collection of moaners, grumblers and defeatists was brought before them.

The press gave these cases considerable publicity. For instance, the *Leicester Mercury* of 5 July 1940 carried three separate items taking up most of the front page. The prosecution of two men on a disaffection charge at Preston was headlined 'No Bad Thing If Hitler Came'; a paragraph in heavy black type headed 'Five Years For Nurse' referred to a woman who had published and distributed postcards relating to German wireless propaganda; while an article, 'Foolish Curiosity', told about a ship's engineer who was fined £10 for taking photographs of a warship at Liverpool. In most of these cases the press attention given was out of all proportion to their seriousness in terms of the sentence imposed; while sometimes an extremely petty element entered into the proceedings.

A Czech Jew, who was found to have in his possession standard guides to London, Chester and Europe, was kept in custody during the four days between his arrest and appearance in court and then was fined £4. The guides were ordered to be forfeited.[24] In a case in Luton, the prosecuting counsel (E. G. Robey) endeavoured to shift the court's attention from the feeble nature of the evidence (a company director had photographed an RAF training plane, but when the police developed the film it was found to be over-exposed) by reminding the court that 'motive did not matter. It was common knowledge that fifth column activities were rife . . . the enemy was at our gates.'[25] It was presumably for this reason that foreign sailors who broke the 10.30 p.m. curfew for aliens were vigorously prosecuted. Nearly every week in the summer of 1940 the *Birkenhead Advertiser* carried a list of cases, sometimes on the front page. Typical was 26 June, when eight were taken to court. A Dane and a Swede were arrested 'on account of their foreign appearance' (and fined £15 each), while three other Swedes were 'discovered' at 11.10 p.m. by two soldiers. The arrest of two Greeks was a policeman's dream: they got lost and went to the police station to ask for help in finding their way back to their ship. Instead they were prosecuted and fined £10 each!

Nor did prosecutions for 'careless talk' cease with the passing of the 'Silent Column':* they continued intermittently throughout the war, and the police sometimes pressed charges surprisingly hard. For instance an Army major was prosecuted and fined in November 1941 for making 'defeatist statements' in a London pub ('Churchill is leading this nation to ruin . . . we have not the tanks to compete with the Germans . . . I was in charge of three . . . we should have had eighteen . . . we will never win like that . . . the country is rotten to the core') and, moreover, making them 'in a loud voice that could be heard all over the bar'.[26]

If the roles in this incident had been reversed – if civilians had made defeatist comments to military personnel – then a prison sentence would almost certainly have been the result. An artist was jailed for three months in 1940 for 'trying to seduce soldiers from their duty'. He was alleged to have remarked to two Canadians: 'Don't fight for England. The whole Government is rotten to the core' and to two New Zealanders: 'You don't want to get killed in this bloody war.'[27]

The risk to civilians, even to politicians, of participating in political discussions with servicemen – and of the difficulties courts faced in picking their way through this kind of evidence – was demonstrated by a case involving the Secretary of the South Hampshire branch of the Commonwealth Party in June 1944. He was distributing pamphlets entitled 'How to Win the Peace' in a pub one Sunday evening and apparently entered into a discussion with a group of soldiers. According to them (and this was the prosecution case) he remarked that the recent increase in soldiers' pay (by 6d a day) was not 'a fair crack' and suggested that 'they ought to pack up until they got more than that paltry —— sixpence'. The implication, presumably, was strike. The Secretary disputed this. 'There was a discussion among soldiers in the public bar', he said, 'about

---

* The 'Silent Column' was inaugurated in the summer of 1940 by the Ministry of Information to stop rumour and gossip, and thereby defeat the fifth column.

the miners' strike letting down the fighting services. He remarked that his party did not agree with strikes although the miners might have a grievance about pay. One of the soldiers said that the miners ought to be put on soldier's pay . . . He denied using the words 'a fair crack' or saying anything like 'it's time you lads packed up until you got better pay'. Luckily for him – whereas the prosecution was unable to produce any of its soldier witnesses, even on subpoena – a private testified in his favour, quoting him as having said 'I don't hold with strikes in war time. It is up to everyone to pull his weight and win the war.' According to this witness, his reference to pay was: 'If an American soldier is worth 10s. or 15s. a day, an English soldier is worth the same.' The charge the authorities decided to press was serious enough: unlawfully endeavouring to breed disaffection among H.M. Forces; but in the absence of the prosecution witnesses the magistrate dismissed the case.[28]

Refusal to perform military service caused another wave of prosecutions. For some conscientious objectors, the sticking point, which brought them into conflict with the law, was whether they should take the medical examination. A young pacifist who refused was fined £5 and ordered to be detained until he had been examined (although the magistrate told him 'you will have the satisfaction of living at the expense of your fellow citizens who are bringing in food from abroad at the peril of their lives. If you think that is a proper and worthy thing to do I cannot understand that state of mind at all').[29] On the other hand, Jehovah's Witnesses were often jailed. At one stage in April 1942 some two hundred of them were in jail.[30] They argued that they were ordained ministers in accordance with the National Service Act of 1939, and should therefore be granted unconditional exemption. Three who offered this argument in April 1942 were jailed for two months; two of them had previously been jailed as conscientious objectors during the First World War.

They pleaded that they were full-time Ministers of the Gospel who 'would suffer complete moral degradation and serious consequences in the hereafter [if they] broke their covenant with God', but it was an appeal that failed to move the magistrate.[31] These men were not of military age; they were jailed for refusing to perform work of national importance. Jehovah's Witnesses who were of military age and who refused to take the medical faced tougher punishments – nor was their 'stance' necessarily 'anti-social'.[32] One twenty-year-old told the court: 'I would like to express my deep regret at the inconvenience I have put officers to. But I do it, not in any spirit of stubbornness, but simply because it is my duty to do it.' He added that he had been working on the land for the previous five months and asked to be allowed to continue, rather than go to prison. But the magistrate was equally clear about *his* duty and the young man was jailed for nine months, as was another twenty-year-old prosecuted along with him.[33] It seems that the Jehovah's Witnesses did not possess the reserves of powerful political support (or any reserves for that matter) on which most pacifist and socialist objectors were able to draw.

One other group of persons whose offences the authorities related to the war was fortune tellers and (some) spiritualists. The records do not provide the numbers involved, but this is not the main point. The object of the prosecutions was to attract publicity by making examples, and one case in particular was very successful. This concerned a Mrs Helen Duncan, who was tried with three others under the Witchcraft Act of 1735. The prosecution argued that the defendants were ordinary common frauds and 'at this time when the dead are no doubt anxiously thought after and . . . sought after in prayer . . . to pretend to conjure them up when it is false and a hollow lie is nothing less than a public mischief'. Mrs Duncan was a well-known medium and two hours before the court opened (she was tried at the Old Bailey) queues formed outside.

She was able to produce numerous witnesses to testify to her honesty, including the journalist Hannen Swaffer. However, a retired captain in the Indian Army also gave evidence and, although he was speaking for the defence, touched on exactly the point that worried many people about some spiritualist proceedings in wartime. He told the court that 'at a seance with Mrs Duncan on January 13 [1944] he saw his son who was reported missing in May, 1940, and who had since been reported presumed killed in action'. Father and son had had, via Mrs Duncan, a conversation. It was this kind of revelation that the Recorder referred to when passing sentence of nine months jail on Mrs Duncan: 'There are many people,

especially in wartime, sorrowing for loved ones. There is a great
danger of their susceptibilities being exploited, and out of this
yearning for comfort and assurance there are those unfortunately who are ready to profit.' He pointed to the fact that in
only six days she had made £112. 'That being so, it is highly
important in the interests of the community as a whole that
these demonstrations should be conducted without fraud.'[34]

The jailing of a medium was unusual (Mrs Duncan had two
previous convictions); most defendants in similar cases who
were found guilty were fined. Nor was there a question of
fraud in every case. One woman, whose system was to pick up
articles and make comments about the persons they belonged
to, usually referred to matters of health, but she did include
the occasional prediction. She informed one customer whose
son was a prisoner-of-war that 'she would have him home
before the end of the year' and told another, whose husband
was missing, 'I can see him in a camp, surrounded by barbed
wire.' The prosecution drew particular attention to this:
'Never was it more appropriate for such offences to be
brought before the magistrates . . . the prisoner-of-war fore-
cast was particularly offensive. At fourpence a time, this
woman traded on the gullibility of people.' Even so, the magistrates were unable to agree and the case was re-heard six
weeks later.[35] This time the defendant was found guilty and
fined. In the next few months similar cases were heard in
Tottenham, Bath, West London and Hackney, and the fines
imposed ranged up to £20.

In the latter half of the war the pattern of prosecutions
for offences concerning morale shifted markedly as the
authorities became increasingly involved in an attempt to
maintain industrial as well as political discipline. The courts
only became involved in a minority of cases, when the
authorities decided that an example must be made. That they
were able to intervene at all in this way was a product of the
war. The labour surplus that existed during the first year
(there were still over a million unemployed in April 1940)
eventually dwindled until an acute labour shortage
developed. Inflationary pressures soon made themselves felt
as did the possibility that certain unpleasant or low paid jobs
would simply not get done. In 1942 the law was changed to
allow the prosecution of those who refused to work, and such

prosecutions were often carried through with surprisingly muted opposition from the unions. In part this was because they abandoned the attempt to defend chronic absentees and partly because the left, after the German invasion of the Soviet Union in June 1941, was almost unanimous in its support of the war effort. The Communist Party of Great Britain now had as little patience with 'slackers' as had management. Into the gap stepped the Trotskyists, but their organisations were too small at this time to have more than local effect and in any case they soon found themselves the object of police interest.[36]

From 1942 the 'workshy' came under increasing pressure from the authorities, even in occupations where there was a tradition of labour militancy and absenteeism, such as mining. During 1944 miners in the Leicestershire coalfield were summonsed at a rate of about one a month, and the penalties imposed included imprisonment. When two brothers aged twenty-two and twenty-five were charged in September, one had not worked since March, the other since May. The magistrate predictably compared their behaviour (lying in bed till ten in the morning and living off their parents) to the heroism of front-line soldiers when he sent the elder to prison for six weeks and fined the younger £7 10s.[37]

The courts were also employed to deal with absenteeism among dock and shipyard workers during 1943 and 1944. In Birkenhead between 20 February and 5 June 1943, twenty-nine workers at Cammell Laird's were prosecuted. The worst offender had missed thirty-five out of fifty-three working days (two weeks jail) but others had missed only three or five days (fined £6 and £3). The prosecuting counsel in one case declared on behalf of the Ministry of Labour ' . . . we are at our wits' end to know how to get these men to work'. Young men appear to have been particularly frequent offenders (as they were in the coalfields). Many of them offered as their defence their wish to join the armed forces: by being persistently absent they had sought dismissal in order to be able to join up. In one Birkenhead prosecution, four out of five men gave this defence.[38]

The magistrates threatened increasingly harsh punishments ('unless there was a more serious outlook among the young men of 19 to 25 years in connection with the importance of attending their work regularly the time would come when the bench would . . . make an example'),[39] and a climax was reached when a twenty-year-old shipyard worker was jailed for six months for a second offence. The magistrate told him: 'You are an absolute traitor . . . It is an absolute scandal that men like this should be retained in a sheltered occupation, while others are slogging about in Sicily and elsewhere. It makes my blood boil when our own sons are out fighting and young men like this go scot-free.'[40] It appears that where magistrates became aware that a problem existed – often as a result of reading reports in the local press – they responded by taking a tougher line themselves. This attracted more press attention and provoked a yet harsher sentencing policy.

Many unpleasant jobs had to be filled by the conscription of labour. The best publicised example was the mines, and some 'Bevin boys' objected to compulsory work in the collieries to the extent of going to jail, amid much popular press attention. Similar cases occurred affecting many occupations. There was of course a limit to how far the courts could go at a time of acute labour shortage: it was hardly logical to jail people for refusing certain sorts of work. Hence fines were preferred, though in extreme cases jail was used. A girl who ignored six out of nine vacancies offered to her was prosecuted three times between August 1943 and November 1944, the punishment rising from a £3 fine to one month's jail and finally to three months jail.[41] 'You are a thoroughly lazy young woman,' the magistrate told her. Some women found they were obliged to take on work for which they felt totally unsuited, but their protests elicited little sympathy from magistrates. A Chatham girl directed to work as a mobile crane driver at a railway goods depot told the magistrate, 'I don't think the work is fit for a woman – it's not a woman's job', but he retorted that 'there are lots of things you don't fancy in wartime and have to do. You have got to do what you are told.'[42] In other cases girls resisted being compelled to take on low-paid jobs even if it meant going to jail. A Strood girl walked out of domestic work, quit a job as a ward maid at a hospital (without 'apparently any excuse'), lasted only two days in a NAAFI canteen and refused point blank to go to another hospital ('because she did not like the smell'). The newspaper report implied that her problem was laziness, but the girl's sister may have been more accurate when she commented that the wage of 25s a week the hospital paid was simply 'insufficient for her'.[43]

Many workers were only too aware that if they could once escape from their current employer numerous better-paid jobs were available elsewhere. But they were prevented from doing so by the conscription of labour. So they endeavoured to get the sack. The trick lay in judging the correct balance between doing enough to be dismissed but not so much as to invite prosecution. It was a calculation that some discontented workers failed to get right, with the result that they found themselves in court on a charge of sabotage.

Cases in which a serious attempt was made to impede war production for a political purpose seem to have been extremely rare; when the details of the case are examined they usually reveal that the destructive behaviour did not have a political motive. A Stockton-on-Tees man jailed for three months in January 1942 was accused of 'wilfully stopping machines in a factory doing war work'. According to the prosecution, he had been refused admittance to the factory because he was 'worse for drink'. Enraged, he climbed over a fence into the works and proceeded to switch off a number of machines. That was the extent of the sabotage.[44]

Other cases appear more planned. In September 1941, four youths aged from fifteen to twenty-one were prosecuted for putting sand in die-casting machines in a factory in Hackney. Counsel for the DPP told the court that 'it was a charge commonly known as sabotage, which was . . . desperately serious . . . in wartime'. The machines broke down and could not be worked for 24 hours with the consequent loss, he explained, of 8,000 plugs and 6,000 flanges. However, it emerged that the two older boys had had a dispute with the employer about a bonus, while the younger ones had 'asked for their cards because they wanted to go to another job and get more money, but [as] this was of course controlled labour . . . they were quite properly refused'. The magistrate imposed fines of £5 and £10.[45]

Perhaps the most common offence against industrial discipline was the clocking-in fraud. This was endemic in English industry, but the war induced managements to tighten up. Sentences imposed by the courts varied considerably from one district to another. In Portsmouth, for instance, workers

were jailed, two for one month in April 1942 for an offence
that was 'widespread and chronic'.[46] In the neighbourhood of
the Ford factories in Dagenham, however, in March 1944,
workers were fined £10 and £15 for this offence, even though
a spokesman for the company declared that 'at the present
time there was a considerable ramp going on which was serious'.[47] Other workers in the area were also fined for this 'quite
familiar means of fraud'.[48]

The clocking-in fraud resembled another offence: that
ancient fiddle, pilfering from the employer. Not only was this
a serious problem in English industry, the war seems to have
produced a veritable 'crime wave' of thefts at the workplace.

CHAPTER TWO

Theft at Work

Nicholas Monsarrat's novel *The Cruel Sea* (published in 1951) describes the Battle of the Atlantic as it was experienced by the crews of ships engaged on convoy duty. The first part of the novel is concerned with the history of a corvette, *Compass Rose*, which in 1941, the grimmest period of the war, is laid up in a Liverpool dockyard for refitting. This brings its crew, and particularly the First Lieutenant, Lockhart, into contact with the shipyard workers. They do not like what they find. Lockhart, for instance, 'could not help contrasting the disciplined and cheerful crew of *Compass Rose* . . . with what passed for the war-effort among the dockyard workers . . . some of them worked hard and honestly, most did not: most of them jogged along at a take-it-or-leave-it pace, talked and shirked in corners half a dozen times a day, and knocked off with so great a punctuality that when the whistle went they were already streaming across the gangway, homeward bound. Many times Lockhart interrupted card games, down in the engine-room out of sight of the foreman: there was one hardy poker school which assembled every afternoon in the asdic compartment, locked the door on the inside, and played out time till five o'clock, deaf to everyone but the dealer . . .'

One day the coxswain takes Lockhart to examine the Carley floats, safety rafts equipped with paddles, a bag of water, and a watertight tin of provisions. The tins of food have been stolen. The coxswain is furious: 'Stealing food that might keep a man alive after he's been torpedoed . . . by God, I'd like to put some of them [dockers] on a raft in the middle of the Atlantic, and let them work it out for themselves!' Lockhart, however, has 'learnt a lot of things during the past few days' and knows that a complaint to the dockyard superintendent will make little difference. ' "They just haven't got the same idea, coxswain, and that's all there is to it," ' he says, 'with melancholy calm'.[1]

In October 1940, a 61-year-old docker was leaving a Birkenhead yard when he was stopped by a policeman who noticed that the overcoat he was carrying 'banged heavily against him'. The policeman found that the right sleeve of the coat was tied at the bottom and there was a bottle of alcohol inside. In May 1944, five dockers, aged from twenty-eight to fifty-three, were stopped in similar circumstances. Ties and handkerchieves were found concealed 'in various parts' of their clothing, while one had sixty yards of artificial silk wound round his body underneath his coat. A few months later, two dockers were spotted by policemen on motor patrol 'sitting on bulky packages covered by overalls, waiting for the bus'. Questioned, the men said that they had found the drums of paint on board ship and were taking them home for safety: they intended to return them the next day. Not surprisingly, this story failed to convince either the police or the magistrate.[2]

These cases are typical of dozens reported annually in local newspapers in the Liverpool area during the course of the war; some, like the trial of the five dockers, made the front page; others merited no more than a couple of lines on an inside page. It is in this context that the thefts from the Carley floats must be understood: every movable object in a dockyard risked being stolen. In 1940 the superintendent of one shipping company put the rate of loss through pilfering at £800 a month, while another firm, one year later, calculated that theft of its goods amounted to £1,850 worth a month.[3] The Chief Constable of Birkenhead summed up: 'Much of the thieving is ... carefully thought out and varied and ingenious methods of concealment lead me to believe that a great number of offences will remain undiscovered.'[4] This was particularly the case with the export trade: thefts were not discovered till the ships reached their destination and by then it was usually too late for anything to be done.

Dockyard pilfering fell into two broad categories. First, a minority of dockers engaged in what amounted to professional crime. For instance a 58-year-old docker was sentenced to twelve months in prison in July 1942. When the police raided his home (acting on 'certain information') they found

250 stolen articles, comprising 51 different categories, and
varying from a cooking stove and tools (value £8) to cans of oil,
clocks, and dog collars (the canine variety). He argued that he
had bought most of these things from people he met in pubs,
none of whom he knew or could identify.[5] A younger pilferer, a Wallasey dock labourer, was charged with stealing
24,000 cigarettes, seven bottles of gin, and twenty-four bottles
of peroxide (total value £139 10s). He claimed he had only
recently begun stealing, and then only because security in the
docks was so poor,[6] but he certainly knew what to take: alcohol
and cigarettes were in short supply in 1944, while peroxide
was virtually unobtainable.

Such goods were sold to the public through a network of
receivers and 'go-betweens'. A case in Bootle in 1944 involved
a 55-year-old docker who had stolen cloth and razor blades.
He sold them to a 'go-between' who distributed them to
receivers. One of these, a woman, in turn passed them on to a
friend in the National Fire Service (whom the prosecution
described as her 'agent'), where the goods reached their final
destination: girls working in the NFS. Thirteen of them were
brought to court and fined for buying rationed cloth without
surrendering coupons.[7] 'Professional' pilfering, of course,
had a long history in the dockyards, but the war and the black
market were stimulating it as goods ran into short supply and
prices rose.

The second category of pilfering was small-scale and casual,
carried out by dockers for their own use. Sometimes they
removed goods from the dockyards and took them home; on
other occasions they broke into cartons containing food and
drink and consumed what they found as they worked. From
time to time, drunken brawls broke out and the police intervened.[8] When this happened the dockers frequently turned
on the police and minor riots ensued.[9]

Pilfering in Birkenhead docks has to be seen as part of the
conflict between employer and employee in which the police,
stationed in the docks to stop pilfering, sided with the employer. The war appears to have added a number of twists to
this situation. Although magistrates imposed prison sentences
for repeated offences and where signs of organised crime
emerged, they usually preferred to fine offenders. When this
happened, the workmates of the penalised docker made a

collection to raise the fine money – a form of insurance
after the event. Information about such proceedings was
eventually brought to the attention of the magistrates who
endeavoured to counter them by giving defendants only
twenty-four hours to pay, with prison as the alternative if they
failed. This expedient was first tried in December 1940[10] but it
does not seem to have been effective (defendants were able to
secure another job immediately and obtain a 'sub' to pay the
fine) so in June 1941 a new system was proposed. Pilferers
were fined and their cards withheld so that they would be
unable to obtain another job.[11] But this scheme was defeated
by the wartime emergency itself: it obviously went against the
national interest to render fit men unemployed at such a time.

Thus pilfering in Birkenhead docks was bound up with the
system of labour relations in this industry. It represented a
method whereby the dockers supplemented the low wages the
industry had traditionally paid as well as offering them a
weapon with which to score off the employer. A similar situation appears to have existed on the railways: pilfering during
the Second World War seems to have affected nearly every
station and goods yard in the country at one time or another.
The companies were especially vulnerable at two points in
their organisation: in the yards where goods for transit were
stored and in their *road* distribution network. In 1944 an LMS
lorry driver was instructed to take cartons from Cannon
Street to King's Cross but instead of driving there directly he
was seen (by two plain clothes policemen watching the place)
to call at a café in Southwark. Both the driver and his mate
carried parcels into the café and were caught red-handed by
the police. Various items stolen from the LMS were found on
the premises and the receiver seems actually to have been
ahead of the market in the goods he could supply, for the
police discovered a consignment of tins of ham imported
from America which had not yet been released to the public:
they could therefore only have been stolen. The magistrate
sentenced on the principle 'no receivers, no thieves' and the
café owner went to prison for fifteen months, whereas the
drivers were jailed for nine months apiece.[12]

'Mass' pilfering sometimes occurred, as when the entire
staff of five at Cremer Street LMS goods depot in Shoreditch
in 1942 became involved and were prosecuted. They stole

such items as milk powder, ladies' stockings, and oranges, which during the war had almost vanished from the market. Management called in the police when the value of the goods stolen rose to £60.[13] The point at which action was taken varied from one company to another: the railway companies had a comparatively low 'threshold of pilfering tolerance'. A similar prosecution at Daventry a year later revealed that eight railwaymen had been stealing from LNER wagons.[14] They too took items in short supply, mainly cigarettes, whisky and shirts, and their activities eventually required the attention of five railway policemen. The magistrates dealt with the men harshly compared with the sentences imposed on the Cremer Street staff, although the scale of the thefts in both cases looks similar. Only two escaped prison; a carriage and wagon examiner who was the local representative of the NUR received the heaviest sentence (six months); five others were jailed for three months. Of the Londoners only the foreman was jailed; three were fined and one discharged.

How pervasive were these offences? The answer will never be known because the 'dark figure' for pilfering is so large: as prosecutors repeatedly stressed, only a minority (often the most 'brazen' or 'careless') were ever arrested. One London magistrate described succinctly what often happened: 'Somebody gives the tip, "Here is something that looks good." He damages it [usually a carton] and takes something, and then others have a dip, in the hope that they will get away with it. There is a sort of understanding that if anybody is caught the rest will help to pay the fine.'[15]

In two areas of north and east London the local newspapers gave extensive coverage to these aspects of crime during the war. This was unusual: war news tended to crowd everything else out, but this tendency was less marked in London than elsewhere. The diligence of the *Hackney Gazette* was such that, in 1943, a north London magistrate (Hopkin) congratulated the paper on 'its full and accurate reports . . . which enable them to know exactly what is happening in this district. Just now no good citizen can be anything but profoundly disturbed by the number of cases of larceny from the employer which this court has had to deal with.'[16]

In these districts pilfering was endemic, involving all levels of staff (from management to the shop floor) and a wide range of goods and services. In the Hackney area the pilfered included the ARP; the borough councils; Ever Ready; the Ardath, Strathmore and Phillips tobacco companies; several milk depots; London Transport; Shoreditch Sanitary Towels; Bovril; the Post Office; Cossor's Radio; Berger Paints; the Metropolitan Police canteens; Odeon Theatres; several transport contractors: the London Co-operative Society; and numerous small concerns. The spread in the Romford district was as wide; the employers which were hit most severely were Ford's, Plessey's, Briggs' Motor Bodies, and Romford Council. A number of these concerns usually enjoyed good labour relations and, by early-1940s standards, high pay. Thus, although poor industrial relations and low pay could stimulate the workforce to theft, the reverse did not prevent it.

Perhaps the greatest change in cases of pilfering, in wartime compared to pre-war, was the police raids that were made from time to time on the workforce of large companies. Such raids netted quite sizeable hauls of pilferers. From 1941 the *Hackney Gazette* reported thirteen cases in which five or more workers were prosecuted; in the eighteen months immediately prior to the start of the war, however, the highest number charged in a single prosecution was three.

Police were called in when thieving passed the tolerance level: at Cossor's action was taken when the figure had reached £500 a week.[16] Radios and components stolen from this company in Islington found 'a very ready market . . . components were practically unobtainable in the open market'. The danger of pilfering from the management's point of view was that it could spread right across the shop floor and become uncontrollable. In large firms it was impossible to check every worker as he left the factory. The police said 'it was impossible to stop one in less than 60, as 7,000 workpeople rushed through the gates on leaving their employment. There were means and ways of getting property from the works other than by concealing it under coats in the way described by some of the accused.'[16]

At Ever Ready in Stoke Newington, in five weeks of 1941 13,000 batteries were stolen and many must have found their way to the black market where they could 'be sold at any price . . . without any Governmental control'.[17] At Berger Paints, in 1943, 'paint had been taken by loaders and packers working

under the direction of a foreman and passed over to drivers
. . . who disposed of it. The proper price of the paint was 30s a
gallon. The people inside got 4s a gallon, which was split
between two, and the drivers received 15s – exactly half the
price – from the people who purchased it.' Eventually the
situation at this company became 'so bad . . . the managing
director spoke to the assembled employees and announced
that [it] had to stop, otherwise anyone caught would be prosecuted. A résumé of what he said was also put in the pay
envelopes.'[18]

Where a search of the workforce at finishing time was not
possible, the police were obliged to conduct their inquiries in a
more laborious fashion: the inquiry at Berger's took three
months to complete (and resulted in eleven arrests); that at a
transport contractors in north London continued for nearly
two years before the pilferers, 'a group of employees about six
in number known as "The Silver Ring" ', were traced. Between them they had been responsible for the 'systematic thieving of about £40 worth of goods a week'.[19] At the Express
Dairy in 1942 'the employees . . . were asked to sign an authority to the firm to search them on any occasion [because] the
losses at the depot were so disturbing',[20] while at Shoreditch
Sanitary Towels in the same year police arrived at the premises one evening and 'the whole of a shift of girls was stopped
at the exit . . . and . . . their bags . . . searched'.[21] Clearly, the
amount of police resources that could be devoted to such
investigations was strictly limited (especially in wartime); the
impression emerges that pilferers who got caught at the
workplace were unlucky.

Second (and hardly surprisingly), food, alcohol and tobacco
were particularly vulnerable to pilfering, and by all levels of
employee up to and including management. In 1942, two
directors and the manager of a dressing-gown company were
prosecuted for taking home food from the works canteen.
'You fellows', the magistrate said, when fining them a total of
£212, 'were running this canteen for your employees and
using that fact to get more than your fair share of meat, doing
it quite deliberately, and doing it again and again.' He wondered whether to send them to prison but decided against this
because they were 'men of good character so far'.[22] At the
wholesale depot set up in Shoreditch to supply meat to the

Metropolitan Police canteens 'the stores of food had been consistently pilfered, and there had Been very large food shortages'. The chief butcher was 'most' responsible for the thefts, but the assistant manager also helped himself and the magistrate commented on these 'presumably respectable people deliberately and systematically robbing the country'.[23] At the Express Dairy, when careful checks for pilfering were started, stolen goods were found on a security officer, while in the same month a railway detective with twenty-seven years' service was found guilty of stealing £10 of goods from the LMS.[24]

Alcohol and tobacco became almost forms of currency during the war. In 1942 a single tobacco company in the Hackney area was losing cigarettes at an annual rate of two million (value £8,000).[25] People pilfered for their own and their families' use, like the shop steward who was found to have slipped cigarettes inside his socks and who had protested at previous prosecutions of workers, asserting 'that members of his union would not do things like that'.[26]

The police alleged that receivers employed 'agents' like the Hoxton lady who was spotted by police officers outside a cigarette factory one Thursday afternoon in July 1943. 'As she passed the factory she whistled and a shopping bag containing cigarettes came down from a window.' The police managed to trace her contact in the factory: he was a foreman. But even the threat of prison did not persuade either of them to disclose the name of the receiver.[27]

Theft from the workplace was one of a number of points in wartime at which legitimate business touched professional crime. There was always the possibility that businessmen in the vicinity of a large factory would buy stolen products or components, whether wittingly or not. A number of such cases occurred affecting the Ford factories in Dagenham. For example, in September 1944, the director of 'a big concern' in Romford was prosecuted for receiving. When CID men visited his premises, spending 'several hours in the search . . . they found numerous Ford spare parts . . . 150 car springs, 49 rear view mirrors', etc., etc. A Ford foreman identified the parts as company property and noted that they lacked certain inspection marks which indicated that they must have been stolen. The director was unable to produce either invoices or

receipts for these goods and pleaded the size of his business
(annual turnover £45,000) in his defence: it meant that it was
'almost impossible' to trace the exact source of any article or
the date his firm had acquired it. The jury did not believe him
and he was jailed for six months.[28] What security officers in
the factories had to cope with – and businessmen hard pressed
for essential components also – is illustrated by the Ford
worker who, when searched, was found to be carrying two
timing wheels and five axle bearings (in his coat), four cam
shaft gears (in his waistcoat), a gear shaft (in his trousers),
three more timing wheels (in his tin helmet), and two car-
burettors (in his gas-mask case).[29] It is indeed astonishing what
some workers were able to get out of the factories: six employees of Briggs Motor Bodies, also in Dagenham, removed
American machine tools which were so essential to production
that they could not all be spared from the works to be taken to
court as evidence.[30]* Courts tended to blame receivers for
such crime, accepting the argument frequently put forward
by defence counsel that they 'tempted' workers to pilfer, but
evidence presented during cases suggests that employees
themselves often stole goods and then went in search of a
buyer. Indeed, many pilferers were caught because of the
public method they chose of trying to sell the goods. Four
Romford soldiers were arrested selling items of Army equipment around air-raid shelters;[31] pilferers of torch batteries
tried to sell them at a Sunday morning street market;[32] some
thieves offered goods to shopkeepers who informed on them;
others allowed the fact that they sold pilfered goods around
the neighbourhood to become too widely known – and word
reached the police.

The weakest point in the organisation of many firms was
the distribution network. Some van drivers discovered that
excess supplies had been placed in the van by accident and
'retained' them for their own use; others were members of
groups of employees who systematically overloaded lorries in
order to sell the surplus to receivers. Milk was stolen from the
Express Dairy in this way, as was coal from the London Co-
operative Society. The LCS's system for preventing thefts at

---

* Or so the prosecution alleged: the impact pilfering was having on the 'war effort'
could hardly fail to produce an adverse impression in court, and also secured press
interest in the event of a conviction.

one depot failed because the weighkeeper was a member of the pilfering group.[33] A case in Islington in 1942 illustrates a number of significant points about well organised theft from the workplace: its scale, the amount of money that could be made from it, and its connection with legitimate tradesmen and the black market.[34] Five motor drivers were prosecuted for stealing meat from their employer and selling it to two retailers. Once again vans were overloaded at the docks and the 'surplus' delivered to butchers' shops. On one occasion the first butcher the men visited took four sackfuls and ninety-three tins, the second seven sack loads, and they paid £36 between them. The pilferers split this, with £18 going to the 'leader' of the 'team', and smaller sums of between £2 and £10 to the other members. And this was for one morning's thefts.

In a case in Romford, involving corsets, the thefts came to light when a man was questioned about selling clothes to workers in a factory. The police traced each member of the gang through the others till finally they arrived at an LNER van driver with thirty years' service. At his house the police found a bag containing £735 in notes. He admitted that he 'usually' gave a friend a parcel 'in the morning' for him to sell, collecting the money in the afternoon. He conceded that £500 of the money found in the bag was the proceeds of selling stolen goods, but insisted that he had only been pilfering for six months. If these figures are true they indicate that a single individual had been pilfering at an annual rate of profit to himself of £1,000 (in 1941).[35]

To sum up, it appears that, as in dockyards, virtually everything movable was in danger of being stolen. Shoes, handbags and nylons (inevitably); but also 'grosses of sanitary towels'; sacks of sugar; bags of meat; 66,000 knives, forks and spoons from the canteens run by the London Passenger Transport Board (they cost £8,000 to replace);[36] electric fires; dolls; 'miscellaneous rubber goods'; radio sets (two workers stole four a day); soap (one employee was found with seventy-two 'best quality' tablets concealed about his person); 3,000 baking trays from a bakery[37] – and all of this in the Hackney and Romford districts only.

Equally noticeable is the accidental nature of many arrests. Planned police raids of the type launched at Cossor and Berger were exceptional, carried out in response to a very high level of theft. Many arrests, involving only one person or perhaps a couple, were the result of an accident or of carelessness on the part of the thief. Even large-scale thefts were sometimes exposed only by chance. For instance, the 1942 Islington meat racket had broken because a corporal in the RAF happened to be passing when the drivers were unloading the meat and their 'suspicious' behaviour caused him to report what he had seen to the police. The theft of sacks of sugar in Hackney was spotted in almost identical circumstances: a police officer cycling past the thief's van became suspicious and 'hoping he had not been observed, rode round a block of buildings . . . approached [the van] from the other end' and arrested the thief.[38] A railwayman (with twenty-one years' service) walking along the St Pancras Road looked suspiciously bulky to a passing policeman, who searched him and found 'wrapped round his body and underneath his clothing . . . 10 Admiralty shirts'.[39] Similarly, receivers who were arrested seem often to have been careless or over-confident. One in Romford made such errors as keeping the cartons in which the pilfered goods arrived, even though they had other addresses than his own on them, and failing to remove identifying tabs from stolen clothes.[40]

When magistrates sentenced in such cases they tended to identify the receivers as the culprits ('no receivers, no thieves'). There were certainly receivers like the Romford motor car engineer who provided a Ford worker with 'a list of the goods he needed',[41] and the Leytonstone 'middleman' who encouraged a worker at Plessey's to repay money he owed him in stolen articles.[42] But many thieves operated in a similar way to those in the Islington meat case: they played an equal part with the receivers, and neither could have functioned without the other. Yet the magistrate (Blake Odgers) distinguished clearly between them: the drivers went to jail for various periods of between twenty-eight days and two months whereas the receivers got six months and three months respectively and were in addition fined £200 and £100. The magistrate summed up thus: 'The five [drivers] were . . . decent and respectable men who had been tempted by easy money offered by blackguards' (the butchers) who were involved in 'black market activities'.[43]

Magistrates seem to have been extremely reluctant to accept

the implication that ordinary workers, 'the average Englishman and woman', should steal so readily from their employers. Hence their comments that they were disposed to treat
pilfering as 'a sudden lapse'. When two railway employees
were charged in December 1942, the magistrate (Brodrick)
commented: 'It is one of those ghastly cases where people of
good character destroy their reputations for things worth
only a few shillings', and the London accountant of the railway
company told him that "he had known both men for many
years and could give both of them excellent characters. He
could not understand why they had done this.'[44] Six weeks
earlier the same magistrate had remarked of another railway
employee, also found guilty of pilfering: 'It was a most disap-
pointing fact that day after day railway employees were suc-
cumbing to this sort of thing. They were people of the most
admirable characters, except so far as their employers were
concerned.'[45] Other magistrates echoed these sentiments.[46]

At the same time magistrates noted another significant
feature of these cases – the poor security of many firms ('the
risk was non-existent'; 'nothing at all'; or 'almost a tempta-
tion').[47] Associated with this was an attitude on the part of
some managements – though by no means all: the railways
provided a notable exception, as did firms like Ever Ready
and Cossor – which almost seemed to encourage thieving,
certainly up to 1941 or 1942, when there appears to have been
a sharp change. Employers spoke up for workmen who had
been caught stealing and occasionally even offered to take
them back into their employment. For example, the owner of
a Hackney firm, which manufactured nickel products, discovered that a 21-year-old lathe operator had made a cigarette
lighter for another employee using the company's raw materials, machines and time (the lighter took five hours to complete). The owner told the court that the accused was a good
workman and would be retained. But 'the making of lighters
had become rather prevalent, although he had issued a previous warning, and he had brought the charge in the hope that
it would have a little more effect'. The lathe operator was
fined £3.[48] The apologetic tone of the owner's remarks is
striking and raises the question: Did the war affect patterns of
pilfering and influence the attitude of employers and magistrates?

Unfortunately there can only be partial answers to these questions. Isolated scraps of evidence, given in court when prosecutors were trying to persuade magistrates of the seriousness of pilfering, do indicate rapidly rising levels of theft at work. For example, the railway companies estimated that they lost goods valued at £360,000 in 1941 because of pilfering; during the next year the total nearly doubled to £700,000.[49] At Birkenhead docks the number of offences rose from 130 in 1939 to 347 in 1940 and 417 in 1942[50] – but there is evidence that prosecutions there were carefully orchestrated, falling away when the authorities sought the co-operation of the dockers. When a campaign was in progress in 1941 to persuade them to register under a new scheme, the *Birkenhead Advertiser* did not report a single prosecution for pilfering, but, once the campaign was over and only six dockers had failed to register,[51] the prosecutions resumed. At other times – notably the crisis summer and autumn of 1940 – the number rose considerably.

In the area of north London covered by the *Hackney Gazette* there was certainly an increase in the number of prosecutions for pilfering. In twenty-three cases between January 1938 and August 1939, thirty-three employees had been prosecuted. They stole such items as 36 yards of twine (value 1s 9d), three gross of razor blades (value £3 12s), three wireless sets (value £6 15s), and 'a quantity of sweets'. The highest number of persons prosecuted in a single case was three and there were three such cases. For the shorter period from November 1942 to August 1943 there are details of forty-six persons prosecuted for pilfering and, although some had taken only trivial items (a tin of soup, eighty cigarettes, or nine sacks), others had tried to steal sizeable quantities: wireless sets and valves (value £177), forty handbags (£25), or 7,950 cigarettes (£31). Managements talked of 'very serious losses', losses running at £500 a week, 'losses so disturbing . . . running into several hundreds of pounds';[52] or they pointed out how many cases they had suffered during the year (for example, at a cigarette firm the pilferer 'was the third case this week and twentieth case this year').[53] Most striking was the increase of 'team stealing'. In two cases thirteen employees were taken to court.

A second change was a stiffening in the attitude of magistrates. In 1942–3 fifteen defendants were jailed (two for six

months, the rest for terms of between twenty-eight days and
two months); eight were fined (the heaviest fine was £30); and
twelve put on probation. Magistrates, when imposing tougher
sentences, often referred to the war ('this question of stealing
from railways . . . has got to be stopped. It is not only a crime
against the companies concerned, but a crime against the
nation'. By contrast, in 1938–9 only three were jailed (two
were railwaymen); six were fined (the heaviest £5); while
eighteen were either bound over or placed on probation, even
when they had stolen quite substantial amounts. The thieves
who took the fountain pens, shoes and crepe were all put on
probation.* For twelve of them the employer spoke up in
court. Some seemed almost to apologise for having brought
the case at all ('the firm did not wish to appear vindictive, but
they had been losing quite a lot of stuff lately'); others assured
the court of their high opinion of the defendant (he 'was a
good workman'; 'an excellent employee in every way'; 'they
had good characters, and he could hardly believe they had
stolen the things').[54] Still others, while lamenting their losses,
were nonetheless prepared to take the defendants back into
their employment. Six employees were indeed told in court
they could have their jobs back – and this was during a period
of mass unemployment.

Here also the war saw a sharp change in attitudes. In
1942–3 only three employers took the trouble to inform the
court that they would re-employ the defendant. One was the
employer of the lathe operator; the second, a manager at
Bovril, one of whose van guards with thirty years' service had
stolen twenty-four jars of Bovril; and the third, the proprietor
of a handbag-manufacturing company, three of whose employees had stolen forty handbags. The workers in the first and
third cases were highly skilled and probably irreplaceable in
wartime.[55] This alteration in employers' attitudes underlines
how the dimensions of the problem of pilfering had swollen
out of control. Despite the shortage of labour and the virtual
impossibility in semi-luxury or poorly paid industries of secur-
ing replacements, the employers were no longer prepared to
speak up for their wayward employees.

Before the war employers had been prepared to tolerate a

* I have not been able to trace the sentences imposed on the rest.

certain amount of theft provided it remained on a small scale:
it may indeed have represented an unofficial form of reward
at a time when wages were low. Employers may also have
hoped that keeping on employees who were caught would put
them under a sense of obligation. The war changed this.
Much pilfering moved out of the range of what could be
tolerated, while employers themselves were now obliged to
account closely to the various ministries for the raw materials
they obtained or foods they supplied. As a dairy company
noted in 1942 when prosecuting three of its employees, 'Milk
was now a rationed food, and if at the end of the day the firm
found themselves short and some of the registered customers
had to go without milk the Ministry of Food took the matter
up with the company.'[56] Some workers stole what they could
not obtain legitimately, either for their own use or for barter;
others, like the employees at Ever Ready, Cossor, Berger,
Ford or Ardath, stole goods systematically and deliberately in
order to sell on the black market.

And this conclusion is inescapable: the black market was
exercising a transforming influence on patterns of theft, not
only at work but also amongst professional thieves.

CHAPTER THREE

Theft:
Mainly Professional

The origins of the changes which occurred during the war in the patterns of theft in England, and most seriously in the patterns of professional theft, can be detected in developments in the 1930s. The six years of hostilities, however, not only speeded up the process but also produced a dramatic shift in scale.

In the economy as a whole, the war helped to modernise British industry, tilting it 'away from the nineteenth and towards the twentieth century'[1] not only in the types of goods produced and the modes of production but in attitudes as well. In a similar way, a pattern of professional theft, in which craft and technique developed during the late Victorian era were still employed in the 1930s to raid the homes of the rich and those tradesmen who supplied them with luxury goods, was largely replaced by a new 'technology' of crime. Business became the principal target of the professional criminal, and especially at three points: the factory, the warehouse, and the distributive network. The object was to supply the black market. This change in the pattern of professional crime proved, if anything, to be more securely established than that taking place in the big sphere of the national economy.

Consequently changes in the value of property stolen were as anxiously studied during the war as the fluctuations in the number of thefts carried out. In the last years of peace the position in the two largest cities was as follows:[2]

	Metropolitan Police District		Birmingham	
	Value of property stolen	Value of property recovered	Value of property stolen	Value of property recovered
	£	£	£	£
1936	994,000	156,100	19,675	12,387
1937	1,777,200	265,000	24,850	11,118
1938	1,297,400	209,900	17,906	6,191

Though they are the best available measures of the value of theft, such figures must be approached with caution. Many thefts were never reported to the police; in others, the owners exaggerated the worth of what they had lost, often for the sake of insurance claims. The police were well aware of the discrepancy. One wartime survey they conducted put the gap between the two at very nearly double: £13 being the value of the property recovered; £24 the average estimate placed on their loss by the owners.[3] However, it seems unlikely that the amount of exaggeration (or plain lying) varied greatly over time, so that, although the totals of property stolen may be swollen, the movements from year to year are probably broadly accurate.

The figures demonstrate most noticeably the much greater scale of robbery in the capital. Birmingham, with one-eighth of the population of London, averaged only one-sixtieth of the reported theft by value between 1936 and 1938. This criminal pre-eminence of London was to be greatly emphasised by the war. At the same time England's second city had a very much higher rate of recovery. Even in a poor recovery year like 1938 the police recovered one-third of the stolen property, whereas in London the proportion was only one-sixth.

The small scale of provincial theft in the late 1930s, even in important and wealthy cities, is well illustrated by Manchester. In 1939 the value of property stolen there jumped to £56,367, a rise of almost £30,000 on the previous year. But, of this apparently alarming increase, nearly £17,000 was accounted for by two criminals. A confidence trickster secured £13,300 in cash from one of his victims, while a second criminal obtained £3,500 by fraudulent conversion. Arrests were made in both cases, but none of the money was recovered.[4]

In neither the Metropolitan Police District (MPD) nor Birmingham did the figures show the kind of upward trend in theft levels that would have been consistent with increasing skill and ambition on the part of criminals, or declining efficiency on the part of the police, or both. The impression is that, as in nearly all areas of crime in the 1930s, the police remained firmly in control.

Indeed, the figures show that most thefts were small-scale and anything but professionally organised. Less than one in fifty in the Metropolitan Police District in 1936 involved more than £100 worth of goods; in nearly one-third the thief did not manage to steal so much as one pound's worth.[5] In Birmingham a year later there were only twenty-five cases of robberies over £100, and this in a city of one million population.[6] Unfortunately the police did not indicate the recovery rate for high-value thefts in either city, even though it was at the 'top-end' of the scale that particularly significant changes were occurring. During the late 1930s, consumer durables, especially motor cars, were becoming increasingly vulnerable to theft, but the elite of thieves remained firmly traditional in the types of goods they sought, and in the methods they used.

That consumer durables were proving more and more tempting is scarcely surprising: these were years of economic growth in the Midlands and south-east, and increasingly the affluent white-collar and skilled worker in towns such as Coventry, Luton, Croydon and Slough was seeking to enjoy the products of consumer society:

Ownership	1922	1930	1937
Private motor cars	314,769	1,042,258	1,834,248
Motor cycles	377,943	698,878	NA
Licensed radio sets	36,000	4,300,000	8,900,000 (1939)
Vacuum cleaners (annual sales)	NA	200,000	400,000

This list could be extended almost indefinitely: electrical goods in particular were entering mass production during these decades. Such devices were either hard to distinguish or could have their identification marks easily removed, whilst a ready market existed for them, especially at the knock-down prices thieves could offer. At the same time, some of these items were expensive, so skilfully organised theft could be highly profitable. Motor cars for instance:

Number stolen and percentage recovered 1935–9[7]

| | Metropolitan Police District | | Birmingham | |
	Number	Percentage recovered	Number	Number not recovered
1935	3,835	NA	348	NA
1936	5,040	98·5	637	1
1937	7,203	98·5	611	3
1938	9,735	98·4	681	5
1939	10,121	98·6	876	9

Car thefts thus rose by 164 per cent in the Metropolitan Police District and by 150 per cent in Birmingham within four years, figures which demonstrate how consumer society transforms opportunities for stealing. Equally striking is the high rate of recovery in both cities. The police noted that 'amateurs' were responsible for most of the thefts, with juveniles and joyriders prominent.[8] But professional gangs were also busy: one that the Metropolitan Police broke in the mid-1930s foreshadowed in its sophisticated methods the much larger-scale operations of the post-war years.

The men involved (none of them previously 'known' to the police) were legitimately established in the motor trade with a garage near The Oval, before they turned to crime. They stole new models in popular makes – Austin 7s and 10s and Ford 8s, for example – adapting routine garage equipment to dismantle and alter cars, manufacture fresh licence plates, and change engine and chassis numbers (though scientific tests would reveal the originals). The gang solved the problem of registering the cars either by buying vehicles wrecked in crashes and using their numbers and particulars for the stolen vehicles or by producing genuine receipts for new cars of similar make to the stolen ones. These they obtained by virtue of the fact that they traded legitimately as car salesmen. Registration was nevertheless a moment of great risk for them yet the officials concerned never noticed that the same receipt had been used repeatedly (whether their blindness at this time was the result of bribery is not clear). Stolen cars were then 'recycled' through an honest dealer in Penzance who believed the models were new, or were exhibited for sale in a showroom the gang owned.[9]

The system The Oval gang developed combined skilfully legitimate business with crime, anticipating wartime developments. Gang members were not 'underworld types', they were outsiders with – for the time – an unusual capacity for coldly calculating the criminal possibilities of business, and the business possibilities of crime.

However, most professional thieves in the 1930s continued to practise traditional modes of robbery. In forty-one thefts reported in the London press during 1938 at least £1,000 worth of goods were taken. These show that the elite of thieves preferred to keep to tried and tested methods and they proved as 'conservative' in their approach, as reluctant to innovate, as businessmen in Britain's many 'Victorian' industries. Hence, 33 of the 41 involved thefts of furs, jewels, or paintings, and 22 were raids on private homes, often of people 'in the news'. The two biggest (in terms of value) were thefts of 'old masters' from country houses, archetypally Victorian crimes.

In 1930 a retired art thief published his memoirs under the pseudonym 'George Ingram'. In them he described[10] the system he used to burgle country houses of valuable works of art. He carried out research into the whereabouts of the items he was interested in, and into the movements of their owners, in such sources as *The Times* and the *Landed Gentry*. He planned the burglary well in advance, going down to the house if it was open to the public and joining a visiting party. If the house was not open, he endeavoured to suborn a member of the staff or tried to infiltrate an associate into the household. The robbery at Chilham Castle in 1938 was thus a copybook affair: the newpaper account stated that 'the thieves were obviously experts. They lowered the pictures onto cushions and cut them from their frames . . . when the robbery was discovered, it was recalled that a year ago, when the mansion was thrown open to the public for charity, a man was observed to be taking undue interest in the pictures. He was watched, and it is understood that the number of his car was taken.'[11] Two paintings by Gainsborough and one each by Rembrandt, Reynolds and Van Dyck duly disappeared, stolen by a gang the police estimated to number six, and so skilfully that none of the twenty people asleep in the house on the night in question heard any noise and none of the four dogs there barked.

Paintings by Reynolds were in demand in 1938: in August

one was stolen from the Sussex home of Lord Winterton.[12] Crime of this type required ample resources of time, money and expertise, plus first-class receivers with contacts in the art world. The disadvantage of following so well worn a criminal path was that the police also knew where it led and in the Chilham Castle case quickly arrested a Kennington dealer with two of the paintings in his possession.[13] A high degree of skill in lifting the paintings from the castle was nullified because the market for them was so small, specialised and identifiable – unlike the market for stolen cars.

The next largest group of thefts in 1938 was raids on safes: nine of them. Safe-cracking was also a traditional criminal craft, in which the thieves fought a private war with the manufacturers, each side seeking a way to circumvent the latest improvement in technique introduced by the other. By the late 1930s the manufacturers had gone well ahead and safe-cracking was becoming a very risky business. On a single night in January there were three unsuccessful attempts to break into post-office safes in the Chertsey district.[14] A raid on a jeweller's in Regent Street failed to smash a safe containing £50,000 worth of jewels, though when the gang moved next door to the New Gallery cinema they removed £1,000 from its safe.[15] Elsewhere thieves *jammed* a safe in a post office in Paddington, and failed to break the safe at Tottenham Hotspur FC (they consoled themselves by raiding the directors' drinks cabinet).[16] Safe-crackers thus needed either to alter their methods drastically or to move into some other criminal line. Some gangs (like Billy Hill's) used a van to remove recalcitrant safes to a hideout where they could work on them at their leisure.[17] Another gang, which also shifted safes by lorry (and carried heavy safes from the burgled building on a specially constructed truck), included a member who dressed as a policeman. His function was to patrol the road where the van was parked and by his presence reassure neighbours alarmed by the noise and activity the gang's operations caused.[18]

A significant development in the 1930s was the smash-and-grab raid: five of these netted at least £1,000 in furs or jewellery in 1938. The technology of this crime was becoming increasingly complex. Initially only one car had been used, but by the late 1930s the three-car (and even four-car) raid

had been developed. According to one police memoir Claude
Brauch, 'one of the greatest receivers in history',[19] drove the
first car into the jeweller's doorway, used the second for the
actual raid, the third for the getaway, and the fourth to ob-
struct the police. Billy Hill relates the emergence of smash-
and-grab to the technological inefficiency of the Flying
Squad, which suffered from the hostility of the uniformed
branch and was starved of resources. In particular, cars lacked
a two-way system of radio communication, while the inade-
quacies of the telephone service meant that a person reporting a raid had to wait anything from two to nine minutes to
reach the Yard.[20] To make arrests the police had to rely on
informers, but these were a highly erratic source. In 1938
police were on the spot for only one of the five raids.

The elements of military organisation and efficiency in the
successful smash-and-grab raid are obvious, with its emphasis
on split-second timing, initiative, quick thinking and leader-
ship. Here the war consolidated peacetime experience.

Smash-and-grab was, however, an activity followed by a
minority of professional criminals for whom an opportunity
to display bravado and daring was almost as important as the
rewards that could be obtained. Other thieves preferred to
take quiet advantage of an important social development of
the inter-war period: suburbanisation. The industrial cities
were surrounded by an ever-widening band of estates of
detached and semi-detached houses, each with its own little
garden. For once thieves were not slow to grasp the significance of a new social development. They could now 'work' in
the areas far from home, where they were not known, travelling by public transport or in their own car. The carefully
cultivated gardens provided an excellent place in which the
thief could conceal himself from the view of the road, while
the large windows of the house offered numerous easy points
of entry. The police beat in these districts was long and remote
from the station, compared with that in the city centre. And
once inside the house the burglar or housebreaker found
himself among the numerous possessions of the increasingly
affluent middle-income earner. In 1937 the Metropolitan
Police calculated that 56 per cent of housebreaking crimes
occurred in only six of its twenty-two divisions, but all six were
suburban and contained new housing estates.[21] Criminals

became increasingly mobile over wider areas: in Birmingham in the same year only 9 per cent of crimes were committed by non-residents, but they accounted for 42 per cent of the burglaries and 90 per cent of the frauds.[22]

On the eve of hostilities, therefore, three important developments in patterns of theft were manifesting themselves. Thieves were more mobile: by 1945, not merely the south-east, but the whole of England had become the 'backyard' of the London criminal. They were turning their attention (albeit slowly) to criminal opportunities that arose in the process of social change – and here too the shake-up provided by the war and military training proved crucial. Finally, they increasingly exploited the criminal possibilities of business, and vice versa. The role of rationing and the black market as catalysts in all three was decisive.

However, it took time for these trends to become established. The initial impact of the war was to disrupt the criminal population as it did everyone else in the community. The amount of recorded crime in the Metropolitan Police District fell by 10 per cent in the last four months of 1939, whereas in the first eight it had risen by 5 per cent compared with the previous year.[23] As young men were conscripted, crime in the cities declined, but within a few months previously tranquil areas around Army camps found themselves suffering a crime wave. As the Chief Constable of Essex reported in 1941: 'For the first time in several years the number of offences shows a decrease . . . in the parts of the county nearest London, and is probably due to the fact that a large number of youthful offenders, who previously operated from the East End . . . are now serving with H.M. Forces. The reduction is to some extent offset by an increase in other districts where a considerable number of houses . . . have been broken into . . . by military personnel.'[24]

The effects were also felt in France when the BEF landed there in 1939. Professional criminals in the Army quickly made contact with French receivers and the two arranged to plunder the British supply system, feeding goods into the French black market. Army vehicles arriving from England were literally cleaned out – accessories, spare parts, and tools being stolen within hours of the vehicle landing. Cigarettes, clothing, cutlery, and razor blades also vanished by the lorry-load. The dimensions of the problem may be illustrated by the size of the force required to deal with it: the authorities assembled a body of 500 men with police experience and shipped them to France within a week.[25]

Within ten months the bulk of the British Army was of course at home again, where most of it remained until the invasion of the Continent in the summer of 1944. The precise significance of military training for the criminal potential of the troops was a subject to which much expert attention was given; however, there was a minority of alert young men with marginal criminal experience – or none at all – for whom army service provided unforeseen opportunities. Two cases are typical.[26]

'Stevens' had grown up among the gangs of Glasgow. His first conviction occurred at the age of twelve and had been followed by another eight convictions, plus borstal and prison sentences, by the time he was called up. The Army was quite unable to hold him: he deserted frequently and escaped from four different detention barracks. When he reached the Continent in 1944 he joined a party of US deserters who supplied receivers in the Paris underworld with goods for the black market stolen from the US Army. The theft of petrol was his speciality although he also, on at least one occasion, stole a truck-load of goods from a British canteen. His adaptability was particulary impressive: he was able to pass as a Frenchman, using a forged French identity card and documents, and married a French girl. When his Continental criminal career came to an end with his arrest and repatriation he was precisely twenty-one years of age.[27]

In the second case, 'Turner' had first been arrested at seventeen for stealing a bicycle. He too deserted from the Army on the Continent and engaged in the black market in Brussels and Paris. He joined a small gang in the French capital which specialised in the theft of Army vehicles, for which there was enormous demand from French dealers. He stayed on the run from the Army for twelve months, during which time he broke the law in places as far apart as Rotterdam and Toulouse, Graz and Calais. Eventually, in the style of a US racketeer, 'Turner' became involved in both legal and illegal activities, running a successful night club in Cannes with an ex-NAAFI canteen manager, and participating in illegal currency transactions with a 'criminal of international reputation'. His military experience is summed up by John C. Spencer: 'It is difficult to conceive that a lad of seventeen appearing in the Police Court for his first offence for theft of a cycle could have become such an experienced criminal without the opportunities available to him during his year of desertion on the Continent.'[28]

Others were influenced by Army training itself. Defence counsel for men arrested in burglaries after the war would often stress the excellence of their war records, describe the campaigns they had fought in and the medals they had been awarded, and plead that 'after their adventures' they were finding it very difficult 'to settle down to steady employment'.[29] What is often equally noticeable from the descriptions of how robberies were carried out was the military style in which they were conducted.[30]

For the established criminal, on the other hand, the problem was to avoid being called up in the first place. Many, of course, failed, although others managed to join organisations like the ARP, or became fire watchers, which enabled them to stay at home. Members of both these services tended to appear in court rather frequently, charged with looting and other theft offences. Of 228 cases of looting, 42 per cent were committed by men in official positions, or positions of trust, such as ARP wardens, police, and auxiliary firemen.[31] A special anti-looting squad of detectives was formed at Scotland Yard, while Birmingham Police in 1941 felt compelled to warn the public that firewatchers had been responsible for a substantial proportion of the increase in cases of larceny.[32]

Those who did manage to find a way round the call-up (and the numbers may have been considerable) included both criminals and 'ordinary' civilians. Charles Raven claimed to know a crook with a game leg who charged his friends £150 a time to impersonate them before medical boards.[33] This figure seems to have been about the going rate. When a salesman from Brick Lane in the East End was called up in November 1939 the Medical Board found he was suffering from an advanced form of heart disease and gave him an exemption certificate. He decided to turn this to his advantage and by the time the authorities caught up with him he had successfully impersonated nine men – relatives, friends and workmates, most of them involved in the East End rag trade. Some paid him as much as £200, but he then lost all the money gambling. His co-defendants were jailed for two years, but the salesman, who was only twenty, was sent to borstal. The police stated in court that they were investigating three similar cases.[34]

For businessmen the price could be very much higher. Contact men who claimed to be able to arrange a deferment were charging £300, and for an exemption £1,500, in 1943.[35]

In some instances officials were the initiators. It is of course impossible to say how prevalent call-up evasion was – those successful were not caught – but those who did fall foul of the law were particularly crude and inept in their methods, as in two cases tried in Islington in 1943.[36]

A temporary civil servant at the Manpower Board in Leytonstone used to handle claims for deferment of military service. The Ministry of Labour's bureaucratic procedure in the event of a man's call-up papers being mislaid was to regard that man as literally ceasing to exist, and of course in that event he could not be conscripted. Here was a rule that an unscrupulous official could turn to financial advantage – provided he knew the right (or wrong) people. The temporary civil servant, however, concentrated his attention on businessmen for whom the call-up would prove highly inconvenient. He 'mislaid' five sets of papers and managed to collect £20 from one of the men they related to, but two others refused to pay anything. There was not much he could do about this since informing on them would reveal his own complicity. The end came when he approached the managing director of a grocery chain. This man went to the police with the story and the official was arrested in the act of taking a bribe of £200 at King's Cross Station.

The second Islington case was similar insomuch as the official concerned (a temporary clerk at the Ministry of Labour) also lacked underworld connections and so was obliged to tout for customers. He offered to destroy the papers of people likely to be called up so that it would be impossible to trace them and in fact 'obtained sums of money from a number of men'. He came to the notice of the police after making a particularly crude approach to a plumber, offering to get him 'out of the Home Guard for fifty bob'. These two cases, incidentally, heard on the same day at the same police court, resulted in quite different sentences. The defendant in the first was jailed for six months; in the second the sentence was twelve months.

Once actually in the armed forces there was not a great deal a man could do to get out again, save desert. This was nonetheless an option chosen by a considerable number. How many is impossible to say precisely: as the war drew on, British deserters were joined by Canadians and Americans; by 1947, the British alone were estimated by the government to number at least 20,000 men.[37] How many took to crime is similarly problematic, though the police believed that deserters were a factor of very considerable importance because 'being without ration books and other proper papers' they 'had every inducement to prey on the public in order to live'.[38]

By the later stages of the war theft rates were rising fast. The value of property stolen in Birmingham more than trebled in only three years, from £18,831 in 1940 to £71,377 in 1943.[39] This was a very much faster increase than the rise in the rate of inflation, which moved from 100 in 1938 to 189·1 in 1947.* In real terms the value of the average theft probably rose by 50 per cent.[40] And recovery rates were deteriorating. In Birmingham the value of property recovered was less in 1945 than it had been in 1942 or 1943.

Police in the cities attributed the growth in theft to the scarcity of goods ('the enhanced value attaching to articles which before the war were only of nominal value'); the unsettlement due to long-continued war conditions; the presence in England of large numbers of troops, especially in the capital; and, behind the major thefts especially, the requirements of the black market.[41] By 1944 this last can be seen strongly influencing the pattern of professionally organised theft. In that year 53 thefts were reported in the London press in which the value of the goods taken was put at £1,000, compared with 41 in 1938. Of these 41, 33 involved jewellery, furs and paintings, compared with only 22 in 1944. Of the remaining 31 thefts, 9 were thefts of money, pay packets, stamps or coupons; 8 were of clothing, rolls of cloth or carpets; 7 were of cigarettes; 4 of alcohol; 2 of food and 1 of electrical goods. In 1938 only one theft involved cloth, one cigarettes, and none at all food or alcohol.

* The index of wholesale prices.

Furthermore, in 1938, approximately half the big thefts had taken place in private homes; by 1944 the proportion had fallen to under a quarter (12). There were instead 5 raids on warehouses (none in 1938) and 13 thefts of lorries and vans (1 in 1938). Theft of goods had several advantages over the theft of jewellery and paintings, which were easily identifiable and correspondingly difficult to dispose of. Receivers were able to extract particularly hard bargains on them. Cigarettes, bottles of alcohol, and items of clothing, however, were 'anonymous' and nearly impossible to identify: given the shortage of such commodities in 1944 they could be easily and profitably sold. And lorry-loads of goods matched in value the most successful art and jewel thefts. In 1938 the two biggest thefts were the art thefts, both in the £10,000 class, while four more (all of jewels) were valued at £5,000 and over. The shift in 1944 is striking: eleven thefts netted over £5,000 worth of goods, but only three involved jewellery and none paintings. The two largest (£17,000 and £12,000) were lorry-loads of cigarettes – in one hijacking, 1,366,000 of them[42] – rather simpler to dispose of than a Reynolds painting. The remaining six were cloth, cigarettes, spirits and money. The police noted that some of the robberies at private houses were the work of amateurs who did not know very much about the technique of theft ('we think the burglar may be a deserter. Judging by the slap-dash job he made of the burglary he is no expert.')[43] But when they contemplated the van and lorry hijackings they had no doubt that most of these were the 'carefully-planned, cunningly carried out and audacious' work of professional criminals.[44]

Some of the men who participated in these thefts were almost certainly directly involved in the black market. Where arrests were made in 1944 (15 cases) and details published about the men concerned, seven described themselves as tradesmen and shopkeepers. Eight were lorry drivers and five soldiers. In 1938, out of ten men arrested, only one was a tradesman; most (six) described themselves as 'unemployed'. Also noticeable in 1944 is the increase in the number of gangs carrying out robberies. The great majority in 1938 were the work of one or two men; only the theft of paintings from Chilham Castle involved more than three. In 1944, however, gangs of from three to six operated frequently and indeed lorry and warehouse theft required the organisation of what one CID man called 'cunning, ruthless and well-informed criminals'. Many had served in the armed forces, some with distinction. 'They were younger, fitter, harder, more resourceful and more energetic than the pre-war criminal . . . all Britain was [their province] . . . Time, money and distance were no object if the pickings were good.'[45] Many had links with black marketeers (who were the organising force behind some robberies) and where possible they tried to suborn lorry drivers and warehouse staff. One system employed often enough to attract police comment involved road haulage operators who hired out their lorries to gangs which were sufficiently successful to want to move stolen property in bulk. Nightwatchmen were bribed to leave factory or warehouse gates open so that lorries could be driven directly into the yards. Once there, thieves had enough time to pick the best goods according to the requirements of the black marketeer. Such thefts were often difficult to detect because the gang left no sign that they had called. Some were not discovered for weeks and by then the team had been disbanded and the goods long since disposed of.[46]

Breaking and entering also flourished during the later stages of the war, but the precise way it did so surprised the authorities. They had expected the blackout to encourage this type of theft but it did not do so, and neither did the blitz of 1940–1.

Index of thefts known to the police[47]

	1938	1939–41 (av.)	1942–3 (av.)	1944	1945
Breaking and entering	100	101	116	150	220
All forms of theft	100	116	131	149	173

The bulk of the rise in breaking and entering, therefore, was concentrated in the last two years of the war. The very small rise between 1938 and 1941 provided the authorities with a lesson which they missed. The authorities had expected thieves to take advantage of the chaos and destruction caused by air-raid attacks to loot property in damaged buildings. Consequently, scarce resources of police were stationed outside damaged buildings to warn off potential looters, leaving untouched districts exposed.[48] When thieves moved to breaking and entering in a big way – as the police suspected they would – they tended to avoid city centres and bombed areas. The rise that occurred in 1944–5 was concentrated in the suburbs. Many thieves did of course steal from bombed property – but such people were very often 'amateurs', tempted by conspicuously available goods, who stole on the spur of the moment. Breaking and entering, however, requires a degree of planning and the novice professional thieves who dominated this area of crime were observant enough to continue to concentrate on bomb-free districts where the blackout added to what were already considerable advantages. In 1945, the Metropolitan Police noted that in the previous year the rise in larcenies had been greatest in areas that suffered least from bombing, and that the outer districts of the Metropolitan Police District saw the steepest rises of all.[49]

The first years of peace saw these trends develop more fully. Theft rates soared and for some time the police seemed unable to control what was happening. Firstly, petty larceny increased, and in terms of *numbers*, this was the overwhelming bulk of crime. The Metropolitan Police noted that larcenies in the house to the value of £5, which had remained 'fairly steady' until 1941 at an annual total of 5,000, expanded rapidly thereafter until, by 1945, the monthly figure was running at over 1,000 and the total for the year came to more than 13,000. The police had a particularly poor record of recovery in such cases – in 1946, out of £889,000 worth of property stolen in houses, only 3 per cent was recovered; the following year the proportion was 5·1 per cent of a total of £731,900.[50]

Secondly, shops became an increasingly frequent target. In the Metropolitan Police District 5,542 shopbreakings had occurred in 1938, but in 1945 the total was 13,276, and this, it must be remembered, was against the background of a sharply reduced population. The civilian inhabitants of Greater London numbered nearly two million *less* at the end of the war than they had at the beginning. In Manchester there were 880 shop and warehouse break-ins in 1939, but 2,981 in 1946. Police in the northern city also faced a dramatic rise in larceny from unattended vehicles: 735 cases in 1944; 1,937 in 1946.[51]

Thirdly, at the higher end of the scale of thefts, the percentage of burglary and shopbreaking cases in the Metropolitan Police District where property stolen was valued at £100 and

above reached 17·8 per cent in 1945; in 1938 it had been only
1·6 per cent. In terms of the total value of property stolen, the
following changes occurred:[52]

	Metropolitan Police District		Birmingham	
	Value of property stolen	Value of property recovered	Value of property stolen	Value of property recovered
	£	£	£	£
1938	1,297,400	209,900	17,906	6,191
1946	4,360,400	777,800	103,204	43,573
1947	4,632,000	787,500	111,435	43,618

Thus, in Birmingham, there was a sixfold rise in the value
of property taken, and nearly a fourfold rise in the Metropolitan Police District. The proportion recovered remained
approximately the same in London, though it improved in
Birmingham. In some other provincial cities even more
dramatic changes took place. In Manchester there was a *ten-
fold* rise in the value of property stolen between 1938 and
1946, while the proportion recovered declined from over a
half in 1938 to under a third in 1946:

	Manchester[53]	
	Value stolen	Value recovered
	£	£
1938	26,375	13,852
1945	256,675	89,386
1946	262,432	76,985

How much of the increase was the result of the activities of
professional criminals? Only a very rough approximation can
be given, based on a statistic provided by Scotland Yard. In the
first seventeen days of 1947, the value of thefts in London,
most of them carried out by 'well organised gangs', amounted
to £72,000; *if* the gangs maintained that level of activity
throughout the year the total value of their depredations
would amount to approximately £1·5 million – a third of the
total.[54] The police noted that 'clothing and material are
favoured because gangs get a high price from receivers who
can sell at greatly inflated prices without coupons'. Jewellery,
however, was more difficult to dispose of and returned a
smaller profit. Other targets remained, of course, alcohol and
cigarettes.[55] In April eight million cigarettes were stolen in

raids at Redhill (the NAAFI stores) and at Grays (the Co-operative), totalling in value £20,000. In Redhill a gang of six was responsible.[56]

In the seven months of 1947 between February and August, there were twenty-five thefts in the London area, in which at least £2,500 worth of goods were stolen.* Thirteen of them netted over £5,000 worth of goods. Only six of the twenty-five involved jewellery or furs (although the biggest robbery of all was of jewels – £50,000 worth – a carefully planned business in which the keys to the shop were first stolen from one of the firm's employees).[57] Seven involved cigarettes, five carpets or cloth. The remaining seven included consignments of eggs, cameras ('photographic experts, it is believed, were respons-ible . . . they picked their loot from the large stock of cameras in the shop, and escaped with only the best'), and spirits ('they took only the best brands').[58]

The tendency for tradesmen, shopkeepers, and lorry driv-ers to predominate among professional robbers is again noticeable from the details of twenty-five cases in London during 1946 and 1947 in which arrests were made for the theft of property valued at £1,000 and over. Sixty-four men were arrested, twenty-one of whom described themselves as tradesmen of one sort or another (including street traders, merchants and dealers). Eleven were lorry drivers and eight servicemen. They came very largely from the age groups which had served in the war. Only four were aged over fifty and eleven under twenty. The largest number, twenty-six, were in the age group 25–34, while another eight were aged 35–49. There were also eight aged 20–24.† This age pattern was in marked contrast to those for breaking and entering and housebreaking, where young criminals predominated. One Metropolitan Police survey of housebreakers at bomb-damaged property in 1944 revealed that nearly 50 per cent of those arrested were aged under eighteen.[59]

The alarm the police felt emerges strongly in their reports. In Birmingham in 1947 indictable crime reached its highest recorded level, as it did also in Manchester and Leeds, 'a fact which must not be in any way subordinated or sidetracked'.[60] A London CID officer recalled how, in 1945, 'the soaring

* The higher value has been used to take account of inflation since 1938.

† I have not been able to trace the ages of the rest.

black lines on the crime graphs in the map room at New
Scotland Yard showed unmistakeably that the police were
losing the struggle'.[61] Police reports hoped, somewhat
optimistically, that with the restoration of 'normal peace-time
conditions' the crime wave would subside, but they were reck-
oning without austerity and its by-product, the black market.

CHAPTER FOUR

The Black Market

Although Lord Woolton, wartime Minister of Food, devotes only a page and a half of his memoirs to the black market, he is clear about his policy: he had instructed his officials to be 'ever on the look-out for organised attempts at dealings in the black market. The small petty offences that occurred from time to time were of little importance. What mattered was to be sure that there could not be a "market". Now and again a combination of people – very often people who had hailed from other countries and not got accustomed to the British way of life – made such efforts . . . The penalties for infringement of the food regulations were literally ruinous . . . and the consequence was that [black marketeering] became so perilous an occupation that few indeed dared embark on it.' He concludes that 'in spite of all scarcity of supplies and the rigidity of rationing, there was little or no black market in Britain' and he attributes this to 'the British character . . . the British public disapproves of black markets'.[1]

Historians have been cautious about these claims; as Angus Calder points out: 'It was in the nature of a successful black market transaction that it was left out of offical statistics and evaded the courts of law.'[2]

The police were also rather less optimistic than Lord Woolton: in his report for 1944 the Commissioner of the Metropolitan Police felt he was not able 'to substantiate by *any reliable evidence** the somewhat lurid descriptions published in some newspapers of super criminals controlling a vast organisation with widespread tentacles. This may nevertheless be a

* Author's italics.

true picture . . . and if it is we should be extremely grateful for any evidence on which we could take action to deal with it. But in any case there is undoubtedly a large number of individual transactions in the Black Market which in the aggregate must represent a high turnover . : . Experience shows how quickly the contents of a stolen lorry can be disposed of . . . It is significant that cases of receiving in 1944 were three and a half times as many as in 1938 . . .'[3]

If 'a market' is seen in terms of the US black market (which took on 'immense proportions' and 'engulfed [the] country in a relatively short period of time')[4] then there was indeed no equivalent in wartime Britain. But how great was the aggregate seriousness of the numerous individual transactions which Woolton dismisses as 'of little importance' but which the Commissioner suggests represented *in toto* 'a high turnover'? Maybe the answer lies in the extent of the black market the authorities were prepared to tolerate – or turn a blind eye to – for whereas some cases were treated seriously by the courts, others were not, and some officials were less than energetic in chasing up reports of black-marketeering. A certain level of black-market trading may have been seen as a useful safety valve; the danger was that, once established, it would become uncontrollable.

By 1941–2 serious strain had begun to develop in the country's distributive system. Black markets were emerging at the traditional markets in the great cities (for example Leeds market and Petticoat Lane in East London). Furthermore, market towns located in agricultural districts but within easy travelling distance of a conurbation (Romford, Chelmsford or Watford, for instance) were vulnerable to the activities of black-marketeers, as was the trade in consumer goods in short supply (clothing, cloth, razor blades, soap and electrical products). Where a major producing base existed but remained the preserve of numerous small-scale (often one- or two-man) businesses (for example the clothing trade in the East End) black markets developed very rapidly indeed. Nor were industries dominated by large companies immune, for pilferers supplied the black market. Finally, certain goods proved particularly difficult to control everywhere, most notably poultry and eggs, meat, fruit and vegetables.

Sometimes, most of these features coincided. To the east of

London, a number of trading lines crossed at Romford. The town had traditionally been a focus for traders from the East End who brought manufactured goods for sale at the market. Similarly East Anglian farmers brought agricultural produce to the town and the two groups knew one another well before the war started. Once shortages began to make themselves felt, lines of distribution were readily available to carry food to the markets of London on the one hand and, on the other, clothing and manufactured goods to the towns and villages of Essex and East Anglia. Around this nexus other rackets developed. Arrangements were made at the town for black-market trading in stolen products. Hoteliers and restaurateurs from the West End turned up, anxious to acquire food in bulk, and not too scrupulous about where they obtained it. They became notorious for their 'blatant buying'. It was not long before 'word' of what was going on at Romford got around, and traders and customers from all over north and east London converged on the market. Finally the 'underworld' itself was attracted by news of the pickings to be obtained. Pickpockets and thieves worked the stalls, while gaming entrepreneurs and their touts made arrangements for those traders who had a taste for gambling to indulge it. Romford was by no means unusual in this; some at least of these features were present at other markets such as Chelmsford, Watford, Braintree and possibly Maidstone; and there were certainly others.

This state of affairs flourished for a surprisingly long time. The first signs of public anxiety appeared with letters to local newspapers, a press campaign, and questions asked in the council chamber. In March 1942 the Town Clerk of Romford wrote, on the instructions of the Council, to all stall-holders in the market warning them that if they were convicted of a black-market offence they would be deprived of the use of their stall 'immediately' and would not be allowed back 'at any future time'.[5] The Romford *Recorder* decided to test the impact of this letter by sending a reporter to the market on the day it was distributed. He 'found no change in the usual state of affairs. At least four stalls were doing a roaring trade in dress materials, but none were taking coupons. I approached one stall which was surrounded by a large crowd of women. In a few minutes the stall-holder was piously saying "coupons, please, madam", and not long afterwards the crowd had disappeared. I had been recognised, and until I left the stall the stall-holder asked for coupons. It is known that he did a roaring trade in couponless clothing both before and after my visit. The black-marketeers are contemptuous of the plain-clothes police . . . and continue calmly to make illegal sales under their noses. They know that the police don't prosecute in these cases; it is the prerogative of the Board of Trade.'[6]

Despite the Town Clerk's letter and the reports in the newspaper, prosecutions were not initiated till more than two months had passed. In the interim a campaign was launched by the Romford Stall-holders Association to persuade the press, Council and public that the culprits were outsiders, from London and by implication Jews.[7] In this situation the inspectors of the ministries responsible (Food and the Board of Trade) had to take some action. A decision was taken to raid the market on a certain day but the traders anticipated what was coming. Only two were arrested: both had made only technical infringements of the law and were able to provide plausible explanations. One was deaf; the second made an error of only one in the number of coupons she collected. Her case was dismissed; the defendant in the other was fined £45 (he took four coupons instead of the correct number, which was eight).[8] Intermittent prosecutions occurred during the next twelve months, but the conviction rate was poor. Some defendants got off on technicalities (stall-holders were doing well enough to be able to afford good solicitors); in others the magistrates convicted but imposed fines that were too small to be a deterrent.[9]

As well as the black market in clothes, Romford, like Chelmsford and Braintree, was a centre for the black market in food. A racket which seems to have been universal was the sale of poultry, officially for breeding purposes, but in fact for slaughter and sale. Here hoteliers and owners of restaurants were very active and many of the birds sold for breeding 'inevitably' found 'their way into the restaurants . . . of the Metropolis'. What happened was described by a journalist with the *Essex Chronicle*,[10] who visited Braintree poultry market and 'had a look round the "stock" pens. It was obvious', he wrote, 'that these birds could not, by any stretch of the imagination, be called stock birds. Some were blind. Others could hardly stand. Some were obviously aged and useless as stock. Yet they were sold as such. They were, of course, killed later and sold for food. As much as 3/6 a lb was paid.' This represented an excess price of nearly 100 per cent as the controlled price per pound in the shops was 1s 10d. 'It is small wonder', he concluded, 'that there are no chickens in the shops'.

The authorities took a serious view of this trade. A butcher from Forest Gate, who forged the name of a dead man when signing for birds, was jailed for three months in 1943, while two weeks later a Chelmsford butcher was sent down for six months and fined £120.[11] A Miss Goldspink had visited his shop and bought a small quantity of meat. When she offered coupons he told her that 'it doesn't matter'. He had made a good customer by this gesture and Miss Goldspink returned in time to catch him carrying a tray of cakes into his shop. He had no licence to trade in cakes or groceries but when she asked for a cake he sold her one. She also bought a rabbit for 12s 6d (the controlled price was 5s 6d).

The butcher now became confidential and told Miss Goldspink, 'I can get rid of as many eggs as I like to East End Jews at 7s a dozen. I don't sell them to locals. The Jews sell them again after that.' Miss Goldspink agreed that it was a high price but she persuaded him to sell her half a dozen. 'I can spare what you like', he said, 'but you won't have to tell anybody.' He was now inclined to do Miss G. a big favour and offered to show her his 'back room'. There a woman associate of his was selling clothes and she let Miss Goldspink have two pairs of stockings and a coat for £5 10s without surrendering any coupons. Unfortunately for the trader, Miss Goldspink was a Ministry of Food inspector, and when the police raided this Aladdin's cave they found over sixty items of clothing, including dresses, coats and costumes.[12]

As this case shows, some officials could be very diligent indeed in their pursuit of black-marketeers. Magistrates could usually be relied upon to give strong support to the police and public officials but, when some of the measures that were taken to trap black-marketeers were described in court, they often felt unhappy (after all, many of them were traders, businessmen and shopkeepers). For instance, a Brick Lane poultry dealer who had been buying black-market poultry and eggs in Essex was prosecuted. Word had eventually reached the Ministry about his activities so an inspector, using the name of Joyce and giving an address in Braintree, entered into correspondence with him. The inspector pretended to have quantities of hens and eggs for sale and named an address where they could be picked up. Of course, when the dealer called for his poultry he found birds of a very different sort waiting for him.

The magistrate asked if it was 'absolutely necessary' to set a trap? The inspector replied: 'Yes. There were complaints at Christmas time of people coming into the Braintree area and buying poultry at above the controlled price, and it was found that the records could not be relied upon, so a trap was necessary.'

The sharpness of this reply satisfied – or silenced – the doubts of the magistrate about the 'theatricals' at the house in Braintree. The hens were actually available in the house, while one of the lady inspectors dressed up 'like a farm woman' and wandered around 'carrying a pail'. But the proceedings were effective: the Brick Lane dealer revealed that he had connections who could supply other black-market products. After buying hens at 3s a pound (and giving a receipt saying he had paid 1s 6d) he asked 'Mrs Joyce' if she would like some sugar. 'Mrs Joyce' said: 'I never say no to sugar.' So the two arranged to barter sugar for poultry. 'If you look after me,' the dealer concluded, 'I will look after you.' 'Mr and Mrs Joyce' duly obliged and the dealer found himself in court paying a £200 fine.[13]

The black market in eggs seems to have been general. Eggs did not come under control if a declaration was signed that they were being sold for hatching purposes. Here was a loophole that numerous dealers and customers endeavoured to slip through. Before the war eggs were seldom sold for hatching at auctions, but during the six months ending 31 January 1944, 1·6 million were sold for this purpose at eighteen markets (including Maidstone and Chelmsford), and the trade was rapidly expanding. At Maidstone, 12,000 were sold in January 1943; 79,000 in January 1944.[14] In the spring of that year investigating officers carried out a series of raids and seized the records of dealers. These showed the contempt that

both buyers and sellers felt for the regulations. They signed
themselves 'Neville Chamberlain' and 'Winston Churchill'
and no one objected. Four dealers brought to court received
jail sentences of from two to four months; the magistrate
observed that the books they produced were 'of no or very
little value'.[15] Fiddling the books was clearly widespread.
Transactions were either not recorded at all or were 'fictitious', and some substantial and supposedly 'respectable'
tradesmen were brought to court.

Within a fortnight of the jailing of the four dealers, the
proprietor of four shops in north London was imprisoned for
three months. He had sold 83,000 eggs for hatching purposes
inside seven months, but the magistrate decided that 'in a
purely urban area [this] was not possible'. Witnesses testified
in court that they paid him as much as 15s for a dozen eggs.*[16]

A standard defence offered by retailers in cases of overcharging was that they themselves had been overcharged by
the wholesaler. However much truth there may have been in
such allegations, the problem was how to prove them. If
retailers did not comply with the requirements of the
wholesaler they would not be given supplies, while if they
informed on him then once again their source of supply
would dry up. In order to stay in business they were obliged to
do what the wholesaler wanted. Therefore, when the inspectors of the Ministry came across such cases they instructed
their solicitors to press for the maximum sentence. A Middlesbrough wholesale fruiterer was sent to six months hard
labour and fined £600 for offences concerning the sale of
apples. The amount of money involved in the transaction for
which he was prosecuted was not large (he had sold 135 crates
of apples at approximately 4s a crate above the controlled
price – his second offence); the inference in the case against
him was that it represented only the tip of an iceberg.[17]

In another case in north London, the prosecution stressed
the interest the Minister was taking in the proceedings: Lord
Woolton, counsel said, 'wants me to point out that he places
great importance on this matter, for it corroborates what
shopkeepers have said in various courts – that they sell at
excess prices because they have to pay excess prices to the
wholesaler'.

* The maximum selling price was 3¾d per egg.

A wholesaler from Stepney was reported by a grocer, and the Ministry of Food sent round an enforcement officer and an assistant. They 'hid behind a door leading from the shop' and heard a traveller employed by the wholesaler say to the grocer, referring to eggs, that 'the specials cost 40s and will be all right for you to sell at 4½d'. The maximum price to the man in the street was 3¾d. The officials also heard the traveller collect 15s in cash from the grocer. When his order book was examined by the officials they found that the deal had been entered at the correct price of 35s. He immediately put the blame on his employer, the wholesaler: 'I am instructed by my firm to collect 15s on every box of home-produced eggs, as they cost more.' The wholesaler, however, blamed him: 'I have not authorised him to make any such charge. I can't get anyone in his place.' Meanwhile the grocer (who 'could not get English eggs unless he paid the extra') and the customer were obliged to foot the bill. The prosecution repeated the interest of the Minister in the matter (he 'regarded it as a very gross case') and the magistrate did indeed find the wholesaler guilty. But the fine imposed, which was £100, hardly seems 'ruinous', despite the sudden and rather sinister courtroom alliance of the wholesaler and traveller when they united to blacken the character of the grocer, accusing him of having asked for 'favours' and in particular to 'let him have more eggs for a little consideration'.[18]

Another wholesaler had a son who was overheard by officials in a particularly revealing conversation with a retailer. The son told her to charge above the controlled price for eggs. When she asked how she was 'to get on' if she was caught the son replied: 'You must take a chance, as I do, and treat it as an ordinary business risk, only selling to your own customers. Don't serve strangers . . . Anyone who wants eggs nowadays must pay for them, and it is really a form of blackmail. Everyone must pay more or go without.'[19]

By the middle of the war the quality of some of the meat coming onto the market was low. In 1942 an Enfield butcher was prosecuted for selling horseflesh as stewing steak to a British restaurant in Tottenham (he made a profit of 195 per cent on the transaction). The magistrate sentenced him to six months jail.[20]

The deterioration in the quality of meat was particularly

pronounced in that supplied to the black market. Unscrupulous farmers were slaughtering aged or sick cattle and selling the meat illicitly.[21] Arrests were sometimes fortuitous. When a food inspector happened to visit one of the four shops of a north London butcher to examine a refrigeration plant he noticed a piece of meat which 'though beautifully trimmed' showed signs of having been dyed green as unfit for human consumption. This led the inspector to examine the butcher's books and there, almost unbelievably, the man had carefully recorded all his black-market transactions! He refused to disclose his source of supply but he had bought 708 stone of meat in the previous five months for the manufacture of sausages alone.[22]

Earlier that year there were three almost identical cases in Hackney and Islington; in two instances the butchers had bought meat from a concern named 'Fido's Food Stores'. In one shop, inspectors 'acting on information' caught the butcher's assistants loading tuberculous meat into a sausage machine; in another four sacks were discovered, 'three of which were filled with boneless cow beef. Some of it was dropsical; in some the glands were affected, and other pieces had areas of inflammation.'[23]

Such cases occurred in every town and some transgressors were taken to court as many as fifteen times.[24] Furthermore, the situation worsened as the war lengthened, and major rackets emerged between late 1944 and 1946.

Certain urban markets, where a proportion of the traders possessed good connections with the underworld, soon acquired a reputation for black-marketeering. Professional thieves and receivers supplied such traders with illicit goods, supplies being transferred 'from one car to another in a London street for a cash transaction'.[25] In some cases receivers themselves hired a market stall. One railway company noted how, as soon as goods became rationed, the market for stolen property strengthened and theft of the goods started.[26] Black-market prices paid by receivers sometimes came within two-thirds of the official selling price of the material. For instance, eighty cartons of Vim reached a stall-holder in Romford market in 1941, having been stolen by a couple of van drivers from the LNER. They were paid £2 10s each by a receiver for a consignment valued at £89. He sold the Vim to a second receiver for £27 who in turn sold for £65 10s. The closeness of the second receiver's selling price to the actual value of the Vim indicates the strength of the demand for such products in the market.[27]

When inspectors raided Chelmsford market in December 1944 they found: hair grips being sold at a profit of 450 per cent (the stall-holder pleaded guilty and was fined £5); overcharging of cotton elastic, snap fasteners and hairgrips (fined £16); elastic sold at four times and hairgrips at eight times the controlled price (fined £15).[28] Such fines were wholly inadequate either in terms of deterrence or to recoup the excess profits the traders had been making, yet they are typical.

Throughout the war, traders would often refuse to sell an article the customer wanted unless he also bought something he did not want. Imposing such a condition of sale was illegal but hardly a week passed in most towns without at least one shopkeeper being prosecuted for it. In some cases the arrogance of shopkeepers and their contempt for the law were equalled only by the derisory fines magistrates imposed. A Wallasey greengrocer was charged in 1944 with selling tomatoes on condition that the customer also bought lettuce. Two women objected to the poor condition of the lettuce and went to find an enforcement officer. When she arrived the greengrocer took her to his office and locked her in for twenty minutes.[29] If he had treated a police officer in this way he would have found himself in serious trouble, but the magistrate fined him only £6.

Nonetheless, if such shopkeepers had been familiar with the conditions prevailing in other markets, they might have considered themselves unlucky to have been prosecuted at all. Reporters from the *West Herts and Watford Observer* visited Watford market on two occasions in December 1944 and discovered that 'exorbitant prices are being charged for quite a number of things . . . the worst ramp of all was . . . cosmetics and toilet preparations . . . razor blades, priced at 1½d in the shops, are . . . sold for . . . 3d in the market . . . in one instance [we were] asked 4s for a well-known brand of hair-tonic – priced in the stores at 1s 10d . . . Those scarce, but essential articles, combs' sold at between 2s and 3s 6d on three stalls, though a 'popular store' in the High Street was selling them for 5½d. Nail files, which had not been seen for two years, could be found in the market ('rusty and of inferior make') for 1s 6d apiece. Excessive prices were also asked for fancy jewellery, hairpins, writing paper and toys. People bought, the reporters concluded, because goods were so scarce; at Christmas especially, virtually any article could command a price as a potential present. The problem was how to prevent the universal overcharging. The council seemed powerless and when the local food committee was pressed for action their spokesman, an alderman, put the responsibility elsewhere. Watford, he said, came within the Cambridge Region, and the officials were based as far away as Cambridge. He offered the hope that the recent publicity 'would awaken them from their deep sleep'.[30]

What frequently happened when individuals complained was illustrated when a woman who had been overcharged for cosmetics wrote to the Price Control Committee: they replied (twice) asking for additional information which she herself had to supply by writing to the manufacturers and the local council. Three months later she had still not been informed what action, if any, would be taken.[31]

Many persons would have given up long before (perhaps that was what the officials hoped: not all inspectors were as energetic as those in East Anglia.) When a prosecution *was* initiated this sometimes relied not on the police or the officials but on the determination of private individuals. People who exposed black-marketeers were exceptional characters: at a time of painful shortages many members of the public who discovered the existence of one must have been tempted to keep the fact a dark secret and pray that he remain at liberty and continue to supply them with otherwise unobtainable goods.

And shrewd black-marketeers only did business with people they knew, or who were introduced to them as 'reliable'. A customer who *was*, however, determined in her pursuit of a black-marketeer was the proprietress of a temperance hotel in Chelmsford: 'I came out of the Post Office . . . and decided I would go across to the market . . . I stood near the entrance, and saw that a stall nearby was selling a lot of things that are hard to get in the shops now.' She walked on and met a plain-clothes detective. 'He said something about keeping an eye open for the black market. "Black market," I said, "there's a lot of that going on here." ' She described how she had seen seven or eight people being served with rationed goods without surrendering coupons. 'We walked back to the stall, and stood quite near it. [The detective] asked me what the packages were which the man was selling. I told him, and he said, "You must have good eyesight" . . . I saw the stall keeper get some grate polish from a box on the ground. You know grate polish is practically unobtainable now; there have been recipes in your paper telling you how to make some; so I thought I would buy some. But you don't go up to a stall where you are not a regular customer and ask immediately for something rare like grate polish, and expect to get it, do you? So I bought a few other things first, and then, after I had put the grate polish into my basket, the man picked up something else and put into my basket, underneath a packet of oats. I said, "What's that?" and he said. "Sh. If you come and see me as late as this every Friday you can have what you want. I get plenty, but I don't let everybody know it." And my change was 7d short of what it should have been.' He had given her tea. The stall-keeper was prosecuted and fined £30. But even the hotel proprietress was uneasy about what she had done and she 'salved' her conscience by paying the fine of a widow who was prosecuted along with the stall-holder for buying black-market soap from him.[32]

Whereas the prosecution of large-scale black-marketeers was often (though by no means always) pressed hard and severe punishments both sought and inflicted, in lesser cases the penalties were equally often almost derisorily light, even though big racketeers would have been unable to function without small ones, who provided them with numerous outlets for the goods they obtained. Policy was thus inconsistent. In part this was because police courts could not be relied on to punish severely: prosecuting counsel might suggest very strongly that the case deserved a harsh sentence but it was impossible to guarantee that the magistrate would agree. Even so, prosecutions were often less than relentless, even when they were initiated. For instance, the Price Regulation Committee of the North-East Region, based in Leeds, received 860 complaints in 1944. The great majority came from the public (705); the rest from inspectors. In only 27 were court proceedings taken; in the 239 where the Committee decided that an offence had indeed occurred, the trader was either warned and obliged to make a refund, or merely warned (which happened in 129 instances). The courts may have been unable to cope with all 239 cases, but even so a proportion prosecuted of only 11 per cent seems small.[33]

There were a number of reasons for this. Firstly, not all officials were as efficient or persistent as East Anglia's 'Mr and Mrs Joyce'. Some were overwhelmed with work while others may have felt that the amount of labour involved in carrying prosecutions through was simply not worth the effort in terms of the penalties that courts imposed. People who came across instances of black-marketeering were urged by politicians, civil servants, the police and the press to report them, yet the time and trouble required must have deterred many. When a Yorkshire woman bought blankets in Castleford market, not only was she overcharged but the utility labels on the corners were removed to suggest they were of better quality than was the case. She complained to the police, who directed her to the Board of Trade. *Twelve months later*, despite 'repeated visits', nothing had happened, even though the Board retained the blankets for use as evidence. Finally a letter arrived from the Price Regulation Committee explaining what had gone wrong. The committee agreed that the Castleford trader had broken the law and decided to prosecute him, so the relevant papers were posted to a solicitor in Wakefield. But the papers never reached him and furthermore the Committee did not learn of this until six months had gone by. And as copies of the documents were *not* made, there the matter ended. The letter concluded: 'In the circumstances stated, this committee have endeavoured at least to secure for you a refund of the amount overcharged. There seems to be a good prospect of this . . . in the meantime I am returning the blankets with apologies and regrets.'[34]

Possibly officials tended to regard a certain level of black-marketeering as inevitable, while if the black market had been completely suppressed, uncontrollable social and economic pressures might have built up. Many persons in positions of authority, as well as among the general public, took advantage of the black market to secure 'more than their fair share'. The journalist J. L. Hodson, after describing two sumptuous meals he enjoyed in May 1942 (including 'a first-rate lunch – as good as you could want in peacetime'), concluded: 'It's clear to me that if you have the brass . . . you can live in London very well in this third year of the war.' An acquaintance told him that he could get a black-market steak as big as two fists at his club at any time.[35] Finally, some policemen also tended to view rather lightly minor instances of trading in the black market. Chief Superintendent Arthur Thorp was in Wales to pursue a murder investigation; one day, at his hotel, he found concealed under his bed 'a fine leg of ham'. When he made inquiries he learnt that it had been left there by a journalist friend who told him he could not think of a safer place to hide it. Thorp adds, 'I went through the motions of inquiring how he had come to be in possession of the meat, but soon discovered I was getting nowhere. And anyway – I was busy.'[36]

The black market was supplied from three major sources: theft and pilfering; illicit sales of agricultural produce by farmers and smallholders; and illicit manufacturing. Warehouse and lorry theft became highly organised as the war proceeded, and receivers with good business connections were able to dispose of considerable quantities of goods. A café proprietor at Colnbrook was caught by the police in 1944 in the act of receiving sixty stolen carcases of meat representing, the prosecution told the court (perhaps with an eye on the journalists present), one week's rations for 1,718 people. The meat had come from Avonmouth docks where a lorry driver and dock worker had systematically overloaded the lorry. On his way to deliver the meat to a depot in London, the driver would call off at the café and leave the surplus there. While they were searching the café the police found, in addition to the meat, a large quantity of stolen furniture. The proprietor was also acting as receiver for an RAF clerk in charge of a centre distributing furniture. He sold a proportion to the proprietor, arranging overloads with two van drivers.[37] In a similar case in London in 1942, which the magistrate declared 'was part of a big meat swindle – a real black market', he attempted to find out the extent of the racket. The defendant, a lorry driver, was told in court that 'if he disclosed names, dates, and methods, and how he got involved he would not go to hard labour: if he did not, he would'. Sentence was delayed to give the man time to think about this offer (perhaps it also gave his associates time to bring pressure to bear on him); at any rate he declined to co-operate. The magistrate punished him with six months hard labour: 'the full sentence which this court can impose'.[38]

To prevent the manufacturing of non-essential goods the government had established elaborate systems of control on both labour and materials,[39] but instances of the illegal manufacture of non-essentials occurred regularly even so – certainly in London and the big provincial cities, and, most strikingly, during the last year of the war. These illicit trades often sprang up close to legitimate centres of production where craft methods of manufacturing remained the rule.[40]

The manufacture of toys was a particularly severe casualty of the war. In Leeds numerous 'private traders' conducted business from their own homes by means of newspaper advertisements and by 1945 the trade had 'reached enormous proportions ... fantastic prices ... being paid for toys of pre-war quality ... rooms in private houses' were 'stacked with these goods'.[41] Even persons working on their own could earn considerable incomes. Toys were made by a public house licensee in Hemel Hempstead who also had a job at an aeroplane factory – in order, it seems, to steal suitable raw materials. Stolen property valued at £766 was found in the pub and he had managed to extract such items as gearboxes (two of them worth £53 each) and a generator worth £30. Although he had been making toys from stolen perspex, which was unobtainable in 1943 to ordinary members of the public, his thefts were only discovered in the course of a routine check at the factory gate.[42]

It is of course impossible to know how prosecutions related to the total amount of illegal manufacturing taking place, but an indication from London shows that in only six months of 1944 there were four such prosecutions in the Willesden area alone. The products made were furniture (7,666 chairs, 4,040 towel horses, 2,952 bread boards, etc.); garments and bags; mechanical lighters; and imitation jewellery (26,146 items). The total value of the products named in the charges was £20,965, but it seems that three of the firms, which were of some size, had also been working on government contracts (so they were able to obtain raw materials) and had already been involved in illicit manufacture.[43] Evidence given in these and similar cases suggests that those who were caught were very much a minority. A retired Hatton Garden jeweller commented: 'I am one of the unlucky ones. Someone must have tipped you off . . .'[44]

As in so many black-market cases defendants protected their contacts. A Clapton man who had been manufacturing jewellery was obliged to admit to two contacts, but would concede no more than that one was an American named Joe and the other a bus conductor in Southend whose name he 'refused to disclose'.[45]

What did the black market amount to in terms of convictions? Almost 114,000 persons were found guilty of offences at police courts during the war, the peak year being 1943 (30,000), but such statistics have very little meaning as an indication of the total amount of unlawful activity in the community. Firstly, assembling evidence that the law had indeed been broken was extremely cumbersome. For instance, when poultry was bought for breeding purposes but in fact was slaughtered, it was necessary to obtain proof that false declarations had been made concerning three points: that the buyer had signed for stock, killed the bird and then sold it as food. Secondly, the statistics do not discriminate between petty offences and large-scale rackets. Nor, from the statistics, would one suspect the existence of that characteristic figure of the immediate post-war years, the spiv, defined in one dictionary as a 'flashy black market hawker'.

Spivs operated in a world grown tired of shortages, austerity and war, and bored by such exhortations as 'export or die'. The last year of the war and the first year of peace were notable (as regards crime) for the way racketeers consolidated their wartime experience, for the amount of money that could be made from involvement in the black market, for the widening circles in the community which were prepared to buy in it, and for the deepening public anxiety about what was happening.

Even 'amateurs' could do very well from the black market. A woman dealer in Rochester had lived until 1943 in Upton Park, where she had become acquainted with a number of traders. After she removed to Rochester she continued to visit them and obtained clothes, which she sold without taking coupons. The demand that built up was such that she recruited three female assistants to help her. She made no attempt at secrecy and eventually 'information' reached the Board of Trade. When her home was raided invoices were found in a vase on the mantelpiece showing a money value of £1,012 and a coupon value of 5,580. These were invoices she had not yet found time to burn, which was her usual practice. Her annual turnover was at least £10,000 (in 1944). The court jailed her and her principal agent for six months each.[46]

Similar cases occurred in most big towns (and many small ones) during 1944 and 1945.[47]

By the last year of the war, much of this black-market money was finding its way into gambling and similar activities, helping to fuel a boom in London's underworld. The police held black-marketeers responsible for the growth of illicit gaming clubs in 1944–5. 'Night after night', reported one senior policeman, 'in so-called social clubs, you can see as much money on the gambling tables as you would normally see in peace-time Cannes, Le Touquet and Monte Carlo'.[48]

The police and the Ministry of Food had become sufficiently worried about the black market by January 1945 to set up a joint committee to co-ordinate prosecutions. They estimated that 'large-scale gangs' comprising 'probably' about fifty men were operating in what they described as the 'L' triangle (London, Liverpool, Leeds).[49] Black-marketeering in Leeds was said to be 'more open' than in any other big city in Britain. Leeds was a centre for the illicit trade in cloth, but there was also a flourishing traffic in cosmetics, silk stockings, shoes, underwear, tea and sugar. Only coupon trafficking was less extensive than in other big cities, the reason being that 'you do not need coupons in Leeds if you are prepared to pay the price'.[50] In 1947, serious allegations were made that some of the police force had become involved in the black market.[51] Racketeers were accustomed to carry considerable amounts of ready money about with them, and an important source of supply was military depots. When three men were prosecuted in 1945 in Liverpool for trying to bribe US soldiers to steal army goods for them, it was revealed that, when arrested, they had £3,683 on them in £1 and £5 notes.[52]

The 'US soldiers' were in fact members of that army's Investigations Department and they set up the meeting which trapped the black-marketeers. But elsewhere members of the US military, like their British counterparts, were actively engaged in supplying the black market. Before June 1944 the principal source was the USA itself, through some supplies also came from the Irish Free State. But after the liberation of the Continent, the flying of scarce and luxury products into Britain became a major endeavour. In one instance US airmen flew 1,000 bottles of champagne (which would have brought £5,000 on the black market) to an air base near Chelmsford. The wine was taken by lorry to (presumably the wrong) 'quiet residential district', where it stood in the rain for five hours till the police spotted it.[53] Inspection procedures of Allied aircraft flying between Britain and France were thereafter said to have been tightened up but the sea trade remained uninterrupted eighteen months later when a range of more expensive goods (including suits and leatherware) were smuggled into England from Germany by army and navy lorries.[54]

Meanwhile, the domestic black market flourished. In 1946 the range of goods affected in the East End had become wide, from poultry to bananas, oranges to oil. The Chairman of Stepney Food Control Committee complained that the position had reached such serious proportions that it gave 'the most serious concern', formulating and imposing restrictions on it proved an impossible task. Some people at the time were prepared to pay 1s an egg, or 2s a pound for apples, and not report what was going on to the authorities.[55] Similar allegations were made in councils and food control committees elsewhere in the capital (for example Poplar and Fulham).[56] In Fulham at the end of the war the black market extended to coal and coke, with the connivance of the drivers of heavy lorries in charge of making deliveries to west London blocks of flats and offices. They failed to 'shoot' the full amount, retaining at the end of each journey a number of sacks which they sold on the black market. Names and addresses of buyers were freely exchanged among the drivers.[57]

The various branches of the distributive trades blamed one another: retailers held that wholesalers were responsible, and vice versa, though the two sides would occasionally unite to criticise the Ministry of Food. Its enforcement officials were 'asleep' and failed to attack the 'real racketeers'.[58]

The shortages of the immediate post-war period, however, put the wholesaler in a strong position. Retailers alleged, for instance, that at Covent Garden only four wholesalers were 'honest' and that if any retailer complained he 'would be promptly blacklisted'. Even to question the prices the wholesaler charged was said often to result in a refusal by him to trade. Food control committees attempted to extract the names of culprits but failed; 'retailers were afraid of losing supplies if they gave such details'.[59] Independent observers (such as a Liberal LCC representative for Bethnal Green) supported these allegations: at Spitalfields and Covent Garden 'for two hours . . . I saw the market salesmen "dictating" to the shopkeepers what they were to buy if they wanted cherries. There was grumbling and discontent everywhere, but I could not find one buyer who thought anything can be done about it – except passing the buck to the housewife.'[60] That, of course, was the wholesaler's defence: he alleged that overcharging, for instance, was imposed by the retailer who then tried to evade responsibility by shifting the blame elsewhere, and so it went on, all sides playing both ends against the middle – the customer.

In this situation those with the most money of course fared best – provided they were not caught. The Criterion Restaurant, Piccadilly, in 1946 was prosecuted on sixty summonses for buying £1,660 worth of poultry at 'almost double' the official price. The magistrate fined the restaurant £900. They had been making use of the services of two dealers who bought poultry from 'unlicensed persons' in Scotland and sold it in West End clubs and restaurants. The charges against them referred to £4,500 worth of poultry which they had bought illegally. The management of the Criterion claimed that no profit had been made on the transaction and that the poultry was needed at any price if the restaurant was to continue to supply its clients with food, but the defence was not accepted.[61]

All the same, it does appear that even some comparatively large concerns would not have been able to stay in business if they had not been prepared to buy on the black market. A similar defence to the Criterion's was offered by the Maldon Co-operative Society, which pleaded guilty to buying over 500 birds in excess of the maximum price. The society was fined £1,050 and the secretary-manager £750. He claimed in court that 'for years they been unable to obtain Christmas poultry for their 5,000 members and arrangements were made . . . so that the society should get the fair share to which they considered they were entitled. The whole of the consignment was distributed on the basis of one per customer and every bird was sold at strictly controlled prices. The result of the transaction was *a loss* of £667 10s 11d by the Society.'*[62] The problem of obtaining supplies and ensuring that customers did not quit in difficult times (they would certainly not return in the good) made many hoteliers, restaurateurs and tradesmen susceptible to the blandishments of black-marketeers. It was only too easy for them to persuade themselves that, if they refused an offer, a competitor would be very glad to accept it. The response of many traders, large and small, was summed up by a Hackney shopkeeper in December 1944. When a stranger 'walked into the shop and said he had a Christmas line he was only too pleased to have it'. The line was balloons – five gross of them – and they had been stolen from Lea Bridge (Rubber) Industries. The circumstances were suspicious but the shopkeeper 'did not obtain a receipt or record' and as he was 'busy with his evening papers at the time . . . he did not think of asking for whom the man was travelling'. He was prosecuted for feloniously receiving the balloons, but the magistrate seems to have been aware of the difficulties of the retail trade at this time: despite the feebleness of the shopkeeper's defence he dismissed the charge against him.[63]

Within five months the war in Europe had ended, and people were released from its immediate tensions. Many no longer felt that sacrifices were required of them. They wished to enjoy the benefits of victory and racketeers had learnt during the war years how to supply them with the material goods they wanted. At the same time, however, the country was nearly bankrupt and the Government believed it was essential to retain the full network of controls, and indeed, to add to them. That an outbreak of crime should occur in such circumstances is hardly surprising: it is perhaps of most interest that it was not more serious and that some chief constables (at least) retained the confidence that given time, more resources, and a return to 'normal' conditions, they could cope with it.

'Normal' conditions meant, however, an end to austerity, shortages and rationing.

* Author's italics.

CHAPTER FIVE

Rationing

By 1942 it was no longer possible to obtain most goods without coupons so people who wanted more than the ration to which they were legally entitled had to find a way of obtaining it which did not mean handing over precious 'points'. Alternatively, they could try to collect extra coupons from an illicit source. Businessmen also (and traders especially) had to support transactions of their own with coupons which had become a form of currency: 'real' money was useless without them where trade in many products was concerned. This was a situation tailor-made for the professional criminal, and above all for thieves, forgers and confidence men. In addition many 'respectable' people, who would not remotely have considered themselves 'criminals', felt they were permitted, because of the rigour of the regulations, to connive at breaches of the law. Why they felt so becomes apparent when it is recalled that, for example, the basic clothing ration from the spring of 1942 only allowed a man to buy an overcoat once every seven years, a pullover every five years, a waistcoat every five years, a pair of trousers and a jacket every two years, a vest and a pair of pants every two years, a shirt every twenty months, a pair of shoes every eight months, and a pair of socks every four months.[1] For most of the working class, of course, this sort of situation had always been the economic rule, but for the better-off it represented an intolerable lowering of standards.

Furthermore, from 1941–2, the working class entered a period of rising real wages, and their expectations rose along with them. Both sides to a shopping transaction had an incentive to avoid the rules, and shop- and stall-keepers knew they could sell anything they could lay their hands on. Buying and selling outside the normal retail network flourished. With the vast demand for coupons in the wartime economy, a market in them also developed, with thieves and forgers anxious to supply it.

The danger of the whole business getting completely out of control is obvious. Movement of goods in the market were carefully monitored and an army of inspectors endeavoured to check what was going on. They varied in efficiency and energy and in any case the authorities tended to distinguish sharply between 'large-scale' and 'small-scale' offences. Yet the 'big man' could not have functioned without numerous 'smaller' ones, such as, for example, the proprietor of a hotel in Clacton.

In the autumn of 1941 he was prosecuted for a number of food offences, including failing to cancel coupons for rationed food he had supplied to his guests. The offences were discovered when four ministry inspectors paid a visit to the hotel, posing as guests, while a dinner dance was in progress. 'Having consumed the repast they disclosed their identity and the names of the people attending the dance were taken.' The prosecuting counsel told the court, however, that the case was not regarded as 'bad or flagrant': the hotelier had conducted his establishment 'in the most exemplary manner, and was doing something for Clacton that was appreciated'. It is almost as though he was apologising for bringing the case: perhaps the solicitor's department was under pressure from the inspectors (who included the indefatigable Miss Goldspink). 'Large numbers relied on him [the hotelier] for entertainment and food, but the fact remained that the regulations had been broken.' After this the defence counsel decided that the best approach was to try to have the case laughed out of court, and he managed to secure some amusement from his cross-examination of the inspectors. In his address to the bench, however, he became serious and accused the inspectors of employing methods 'repellent to the ordinary citizen'. The magistrate, in imposing fines totalling 15s, seemed to agree.[2]

This case illustrates how minor breaches of the law, like motoring offences, 'were not really crime at all', yet the supplies of goods which enabled the offender to break the law frequently derived from the activities of criminals. A more serious offence committed by the hotelier had been to supply his guests with more than the legally permitted number of courses during a meal, for which he obtained supplies on the black market. This aspect of the case, however, was lost behind the exposure by the defence of the seemingly devious behaviour of the inspectors: first they ate the meal, then they prosecuted the person who had supplied it. Yet it was precisely the desire of many members of the public (and in cases like this, the better-off) to obtain more than their fair share that gave black-marketeers, thieves and forgers their opportunity.

Abuse of the rationing regulations in markets in important cities was a daily occurrence. In September 1941 a reporter on the Romford *Recorder* visited the town's market and wrote a shocked article about the 'wholesale evasion . . . of the clothes rationing regulations' he found there. 'Never once was a customer expected to produce coupons . . . a very brisk trade was being done in suitings, over-coatings, underwear and artificial silk stockings. The only reference that was made to coupons was by a stall-holder who was selling [new] ladies' silk stockings when, quite wrongly, of course, he said: "These stockings have a defect in them, so there is no need for coupons" . . . one woman bought three yards of overcoat material at 12s 6d a yard almost under the nose of a Council official. She received the material and handed over the money for it, but there were no coupons accompanying the money.' He proceeded to ask how stall-holders could obtain replacements of stocks if they did not provide coupons in respect of the stocks they had sold? 'Sufficient business was done . . . to have produced many thousands of coupons, but during the whole of the time in which a watch was kept none at all were seen and none of the stall-holders had a receptacle into which they could have put the coupons, even if they had been offered by customers.'[3] The answer lay, of course, with the black market itself, either in clothing, or in coupons. Lord Woolton was particularly firm on this point. He wrote: 'I determined to secure punitive powers of such severity that breaches of the rationing law would involve ruinous penalties.'[4] Ruinous, that is, provided magistrates agreed to sentence appropriately. They did not always do so, even in London.

When the City and Metropolitan Police raided Petticoat

Lane in August 1941 they detected five persons trading in goods without taking coupons. These people were fined an average of £15 which was in no way ruinous, particularly when compared with the fines imposed on their customers (from £2 to £5).[5] Inspectors often faced considerable difficulty in assembling sufficient evidence to show that the law had been broken, and once they obtained that evidence they had to convince the court. In the process they became known, as did reporters and plain-clothes police. Stall-holders devised 'a system to warn each other of the presence of inspectors. Notes were sent round, and they also had some signal of the "tick tack" type to warn their colleagues and thus prevent the detection of offences.'[6] Even when a trader found himself in court, there were a number of defences he could offer, one of which might satisfy a magistrate that only a technical offence had been committed. He could try to persuade the court that the goods were second-hand or defective and therefore did not require points, or that the customer had rushed off before he had had time to ask for the coupons. Three tradesmen who offered such defences in late 1941 were fined an average of £20.[7]

Courts took a more serious line, however, on coupon offences which occurred 'out of the public view'. A secondary economy developed in which goods were sold in secret, moving from thieves or illicit manufacturers to receivers or middlemen. These sold them through agents to customers in factories, workshops, among the clientèle of certain pubs, and to neighbours who would not betray them to the police. Employees in factories, for instance, would more or less systematically pilfer goods and take them to a local receiver. By no means all of these were shopkeepers; some were private persons conducting their business from their own homes. There was no outer sign to indicate what was going on inside the house: entry was by introduction only. Police depended on tip-offs to discover such establishments, or on shadowing.

In 1940 two policemen went to the Finsbury home of a 65-year-old widow; they found the inside of her house 'stocked from top to bottom with every sort of clothing, and with toys, clocks and wireless sets . . . Most of the stuff could not be identified as the labels had been torn off or altered. Everything was brand new . . .'[8]

From these receivers, or middlemen, goods passed to an agent with suitable contacts. When one 56-year-old woman was introduced to a pedlar by her sister she bought sets of underclothing and silk stockings from him. These she resold to workmates at a Stoke Poges factory; naturally no coupons changed hands in the process. The magistrate told her that only her 'physical condition' prevented him sending her to jail.[9]

Sometimes the middleman was a shopkeeper. One, in Tottenham, was fined a total of £1,480 for coupon and associated offences. His distributor in a local factory, who may have been one of several, the rest escaping detection, disposed of £400 worth of couponless goods (equivalent to 3,750 points). They included 600 pairs of stockings. The error the shopkeeper made was to permit girls from the factory to come to his shop to buy couponless goods. The word 'got out', eventually reaching the ears of a 'common informer'. The shopkeeper in his defence tried to put the onus of responsibility on the girls ('he only let the girls have the articles to oblige them. Some of them came into his shop and threatened to tell the police if he did not let them have stockings without coupons') but the girls were only fined from one guinea to £15.[10] Similar cases occurred with great frequency – in early 1943 in Slough, Rochester, Brighton, Romford, Manchester, Leeds, and Portsmouth, among other places.

The second method used by persons who wanted more than their share was to acquire additional coupons from some illegitimate source. Coupons were surrounded by a barrage of regulations, some readily comprehensible (books must not be bought or sold or given away to anyone outside the family), others less so. For example, when customers were shopping over the counter, only the shopkeeper was allowed to cut out or tear out the coupons, never the customer, yet if an individual was sending away for goods by mail order then he *was* permitted to remove the coupons himself. Many people sold coupons they could not use or did not want, to raise some money, and if they were caught they were prosecuted. Two such cases occurred within days of each other at Leicester in 1944.[11] In the first a family 'in poor circumstances' sold their clothing coupons, a neighbour selling them to friends in the locality. Books changed hands at about 10s or 12s 6d. The saleslady pleaded in her defence when she was caught that she was trying to do the family 'a good turn'. They were 'well-nigh starving ... one of [their] five children being seriously ill'. Small fines were imposed. In the second case the landlady of a pub exchanged money and old clothes for clothing coupons with a former employee. Once again the defendant pleaded that she had bought the coupons to assist people 'suffering from poverty' who 'lived in a small four-roomed house which contained 10 people'. The offence was discovered when a Board of Trade official visited the house and asked to see the ration books, which of course the family could not produce. Such prosecutions enabled the authorities simultaneously to demonstrate what the law was and warn people of the consequences if they broke it.

It soon became apparent that officialdom was not able to keep pace with its own rules and regulations, and plug the gaps that existed. The most notorious emerged out of the procedure whereby the retailer exchanged his loose coupons at the post office for a voucher. The GPO refused to take responsibility for checking that all the envelopes contained the correct number of coupons, so vast numbers of envelopes passed over post-office counters with anything but coupons inside them. The vouchers obtained were later sold to retailers who used them to obtain 500 extra points worth of goods. Hence the spectacle of stall-holders in Romford and many other market-places omitting to take coupons: they knew they could obtain more on the black market whenever they needed them.

Some criminals organised rackets in order to obtain these vouchers: gangs numbering up to ten people were involved. They endeavoured to protect themselves by paying boys to hand in the envelopes, giving them perhaps a shilling a time.[12] Some adolescents, however, proved hard bargainers, and, when three Stepney youths (aged fifteen, sixteen and seventeen) were prosecuted, it was revealed that they had been paid as much as £4 'by a bookmaker called "Chopper" ' for each envelope they handed in. One of the boys made £120 in this way and between them they accounted for 130,000 coupons during a period of two months. They used torn up telephone directories taken from kiosks in the East End and got through so many that entire districts were cleaned out. Two were sent to approved school, the third to borstal.[13]

The boys had been used by criminals who do not appear to have been brought to court; however, 'honest' businessmen also carried out coupon frauds in a similar way. A hosier of Maida Vale was fined £1,000 and jailed for six months for a fraud involving some 'thousands of coupons'.[14] These frauds were eventually checked by modifying the regulations to permit traders to pay their coupons into banking accounts, but even so they continued to surrender as few as possible. They were obliged to state on each envelope the number of coupons it contained. Inevitably many traders gambled that the officials concerned would not count the contents of every envelope, or even a large proportion of them. Occasionally the authorities received 'certain information' about an individual. One instance was a Poplar tradesman who was prosecuted for sending in three envelopes containing 602 coupons less than was stated on the covers. His explanation was typical: he blamed a young assistant who had since left and could not be traced at the address he had given. The magistrate fined the tradesman, who had a previous conviction for a black-market offence, the sum of £60.[15]

From time to time the authorities decided to check a proportion of the envelopes coming in from certain districts. One such investigation, in Willesden in January and February 1944, resulted in the prosecution of ten local traders. The quantities short (from 59 to 2,452) varied more than the fines (from £5 to £7), while the excuses some of the defendants offered were little short of contemptuous: 'There has been a mix-up somewhere' (2,452 short); or 'ill at the time . . . got a boy to count them' (487 short). Most blamed either an employee or a relative – in short, anyone but themselves.[16] The authorities must have known that wholesale evasion of the regulations was taking place, but they were not prepared to take sufficiently drastic action to stop it, partly for political reasons, but mainly because of the size of the problem.

They seem to have been more willing to do so when private individuals used fraud to obtain more coupons. During the first year of clothes rationing some 800,000 people claimed to have lost their ration books and applied for replacements. They were compensated with 27,000,000 coupons.[17] The majority were most probably genuine, but many were not.

Comparatively few prosecutions were reported in the press, however, which may indicate that the offence occurred so frequently that editors did not consider it newsworthy. Only when there was an 'unusual angle' did the case get attention.

For instance, a 45-year-old barmaid was jailed for three months for possessing two sets of clothing coupons and two identity cards. The police discovered her one night drunkenly 'clinging' to the railings at Camberwell Green; at the station they learnt that she had been living for five years under two names and each week she drew full sets of rations for both ladies.[18] She was much more harshly treated than a Paddington woman who also possessed two sets of ration books (she was fined £50). She had lived with a number of men, used their names, and acquired the books in the process.[19] Even more fortunate was a Wembley woman who was fined £25 on a similar charge. She may however have had a difficult time with her neighbours because the amount of additional rations she obtained as a result of having two ration books was carefully detailed in court and duly reported in the local paper (10½lb of sugar, 5½lb of margarine, 16 weeks' supply of eggs, etc.).[20]

These persons, and others like them, had been concerned to secure more rations for themselves; others tried to work up a market in the coupons. A significant social development of the war was the way it provided 'meeting-places' for the criminal and business worlds.

The black market was the most serious, but the coupon system also created fresh areas of contact. Such was the nature of the regulations that some businessmen would have been obliged to close down if they had not managed to secure a supply of coupons from an illicit source. One north London clothier anticipated that the war would bring severe shortages so he stocked up with a considerable quantity of goods during the first months of hostilities. As prices rose he gradually and profitably sold off his stock. However, the point eventually arrived when he needed coupons to augment dwindling supplies and he bought 1,000 from an 'unlawful' source for £80. He was prosecuted, pleaded guilty and was fined £300, after 'information' had been 'received'. The authorities were nonetheless unable to persuade him to give any accurate details as to how he acquired the coupons. His story, such as it

was, involved encountering 'an unknown man' on a train
going to Leeds. The meeting was of course accidental: the
clothier was travelling to Leeds to visit his sick wife. They 'got
talking on business' and 'the man offered to sell him coupons
at 3/- each and pulled packets of them from his pocket for . . .
inspection'. As the clothier did not have sufficient funds with
him at the time they arranged to meet at Oxford Circus,
where the transaction was completed.[21]

The authorities found great difficulty in extracting details
in these cases: many purchasers were determined to defend
their source of supply.

A businessman whose source of supply *was* revealed, however, was the manager of a north London millinery company.
As he presented his case in court, he would either have had to
close down and dismiss 100 irreplaceable members of staff, or
find a way of obtaining some coupons to keep his business
going. He began by borrowing points from friends and fellow
merchants but could not amass nearly enough. Salvation
appeared in the form of an assistant at Hackney Food Office,
a man who before the war had been a Conservative councillor
and party agent in that borough. In the course of his work he
visited restaurants in the area and the Italian proprietor of
one of them told him that he had a market for coupons if he
could extract them from his office. He did so and the Italian
was able to sell them at 4s a sheet, double the price he had
anticipated because 'the market was better' than he expected.
They met once a week to exchange coupons and money, and
in seven months the Italian had made £900, of which he gave
£250 to the official. The manager of the millinery company
alone bought 130,000 coupons. Heavy sentences were meted
out in this case, with one interesting exception. The businessman – who had a 'lifelong good character' – was jailed for nine
months and fined £100. His company was fined £7,985. The
food office assistant, whose salary was £250 p.a. plus bonus,
was jailed for five years. The Italian café proprietor, however,
went free. He was the principal witness against the others and
presumably the authorities had agreed not to prosecute him if
he would give evidence, even though by his own admission he
was the initiator of the civil servant's depredations, and also
profited most by them. Presumably he kept the money he had
made.[22]

The official may have turned to theft to supplement a salary that was failing to keep pace with inflation. Another who did so was a clerk at Willesden Food Office (also a local councillor). The law required that at the end of each month surplus coupons be thrown away, but he had been handing some to a local shopkeeper, who paid him with rationed goods. This 'racket' was on a very much smaller scale than the one in Hackney but the magistrate nevertheless declared in sentencing that 'if trusted officials can play ducks and drakes with the rationing system and retailers can obtain more than the quantity of rationed goods to which they are entitled the rationing system comes in danger of collapsing'.[23] After these firm words the sentences imposed (fines of £30) seem somewhat feeble, especially by comparison with the Hackney case, and even allowing for the difference in scale.

The mix of dishonest officials, unscrupulous businessmen and coupons occurred frequently enough to inspire professional criminals to imitative work. Their wartime memoirs contain numerous anecdotes designed to show their skill, daring, and the gullibility of almost everyone else.[24]

One confidence trick imitated closely the process of inspection carried out by Board of Trade officials. A gang was organised by a solicitor who prepared a list of shopkeepers who had already broken the law and been fined for it. Therefore they faced the maximum fine for a second offence. A girl associate of the solicitor would visit the shopkeeper, buy a coat or a dress, and persuade the shopkeeper to accept cash instead of coupons. She would leave the shop and return with a con-man who posed as a (bribable) Board of Trade inspector.[25]

There were several variations on this theme. Whether they were as successful as the authors claim cannot be tested: but those that did reach the courts seem crude and inept by comparison.

The two principal methods of supply of coupons to the market were theft and forgery. Gangs of professional thieves raided offices where coupons were known to be held, and some of these robberies secured considerable quantities. In the early summer of 1944 there were two such thefts. In the first, in Hertfordshire, 14,000 ration books (with a value on the black market of the order of £70,000) were stolen, and the gang responsible required a large lorry to carry away their haul. Two months later, 600,000 supplementary clothing coupons were stolen from the employment exchange in Moorgate.[26] The market apparently had no difficulty in absorbing these quantities: an engineer from Preston who was prosecuted in 1944 for conspiracy to steal clothing coupons from the Board of Trade boasted that he had a market for twenty million coupons.[27]

The thieves responsible for the raid in Hertfordshire do not appear to have been caught but the ration books turned up all over the place. Eleven were found in the possession of a Stepney greengrocer who paid £5 each for them. His explanation as to how he came by them told of a party in the West End at which everyone was 'rather the worse for drink'. There 'he met four men, one of whom asked him if he was interested in ration books'. As to their names, addresses and the details of their appearance, alcohol confused his memory.[28]

Large-scale thefts were supplemented by numerous small ones. Housebreakers and burglars took ration books if they found them in a house – over 2,000 (and 500 identity cards) were stolen in this way in Birmingham in 1947.[29] Petty thieves sustained themselves by selling clothing coupons, in addition to the traditional system of forging entries in a post-office savings book.[30] Others posed as war damage victims; one did so successfully three times and on each occasion received 120 clothing coupons and £12 from the Assistance Board.[31] A thriving trade in clothing coupons grew up in the dockside areas of big ports. Seamen sold coupons to receivers who passed them on to shop salesmen, especially in the clothing trade. Two Stepney salesmen both jailed for twelve months in July 1943 had 2,480 coupons in their shop when the police called.[32]

The coupon distribution system had a number of weak points. Consignments of books were sent through the post. A temporary postman in London stole 'a considerable number' and took them home to his wife, who sold them to a friend for 2s 6d each. The books then passed along a network of buyers and sellers in the East End rag trade, rising sharply in price each time they changed hands. One man bought a book at 30s and sold at 48s. When the police searched the postman's flat they found nearly 50,000 coupons there and almost £1,000 in cash. 'I did this in order to buy my own house,' he pleaded.[33]

Coupons were also vulnerable at the beginning and at the end of their lives: at the printers and at the pulpers. In October 1942 a firewatcher and an ARP man were jailed for stealing and receiving coupons sent to be pulped. When the police searched the firewatcher's house they found over 1,500 cards and a forged rubber stamp used to make the coupons authentic. The ARP man was arrested in the street with £123 in notes on him – presumably from sales he had been making. Both men had records.[34]

Informers and 'information' were important to the police. Because of the very nature of the rationing laws, bound up in the worlds of manufacturing and retail, they were not able to pursue their customary methods of investigation. The necessity of penetrating what are often tightly knit trading circles placed a high value on the informer, on persons with a grudge, and on those who wished to eliminate a rival. 'Information' can have represented a route only to a minority of the offences that were being committed: here again the proportion of lawbreakers who found themselves in court was small. Police often referred, in the larger prosecutions especially, to their suspicions about the involvement of other persons whom they were unable to charge for lack of evidence.[35]

The second main source of supply of coupons was through forgery, a craft which had fallen into decay during the 1920s and 1930s, becoming, according to one authority, 'the Cinderella of the criminal arts'.[36] Between 1900 and 1910 London forgers had cost the banks of Britain over one million pounds,[37] but the development of scientific aids to detection had put an end to the greater part of this crime as the Mint, the banks and the police together gained unassailable advantages over the forgers and distributors of banknotes. The persons who were brought to court in the late 1930s were amateurs painstakingly minting two-shilling pieces and half-crowns, and very often getting caught in the act.[38]

The war, rationing and coupons together managed to revive this trade. Coupons were crudely designed and did not present anything like the technical problems involved in the forgery of banknotes. Even so, persons who were accustomed to handling large numbers of them were able to separate the spurious from the genuine in many cases, but this process of inspection occurred too far from the manufacturing base to do more than permit an estimate to be made of the number of detectable forgeries coming onto the market.

Criminals who wrote their 'war memoirs' produced some very large claims for what proportion of coupons was forged. Billy Hill describes a complex racket concerning logbooks and petrol coupons which was 'one of the most profitable black-market jobs' and which threw 'the whole British petrol rationing scheme . . . completely out of gear'.[39] It is certainly the case, as will be seen, that the police encountered great difficulty in breaking at least one important gang of forgers.

Those that they did manage to trap were often amateurish as regards the forgeries they made (if not in their methods of manufacture), whether they were persons operating on their own or gangs.

Even highly organised rackets came to grief through an error in the design or style of the coupons. A Manchester syndicate had managed to distribute coupons to at least 38 firms in London and Manchester, forging the points on a printing press. In this instance 'information' took the police to a factory in London where they found the owner in the act of handling the coupons. Others involved were traced via a Manchester man who had been giving in coupons at the post office in exchange for vouchers. The police worked methodically from each recipient of the forgeries to his supplier till eventually twenty-two people found themselves in the dock. It seems that word had gone around certain sections of the clothing industry in Manchester that if coupons were required they could be bought at the office of a businessman in Great Ducie Street. Those who were arrested claimed that they had no idea that the coupons were forgeries.

The trial of the twenty-two attracted much publicity. It was regarded by both sides as a test case and most of the accused (some of whom were in a substantial enough way of business to be able to afford good counsel) were ably defended and the charges against several were dismissed on technicalities. In the end only ten were found guilty, including the forger and his principal accomplice. Sentences varied from four years (the forger) to three months. Yet, even in a case like this one, seen as important by the authorities, the forger had failed to ensure that all the details of the coupons were correct. Prosecution witnesses commented in court on the distinctive style of the forged coupons: they were 'cut more regularly than was customary and they were clean looking'; they had a 'smooth and glossy feel'. The forger had made such elementary errors as failing to note that most genuine coupons were torn off the sheet, not cut from it.[40]

The question remains: how many coupons were sufficiently skilfully forged as to be undetectable? That *some* were is clear from statements made by Scotland Yard between 1945 and 1947.

In the initial stages of peace at least two gangs were distributing forged coupons on some scale. By the end of 1946 the police had broken one of them while the other 'expert gang', which had forged 'hundred of thousands' of clothing coupons, had been the subject of police inquiries since the end of the war, and as late as 1947 no arrests had been made.[41] Coupon forgers no doubt remained prosperously in business as long as rationing itself endured.

In many rationing and black-market cases businessmen, traders and shopkeepers were deeply concerned. Also involved, in rationing offences especially, were a number of civil servants and local government officials: typically middle-class 'white-collar' occupations. Such people, 'of intelligence and substance' as one magistrate (Rowland Thomas) described them, had 'done wrong from the very beginning with their eyes open' although 'if it was said they had betrayed their country' they 'would be the first to resent it'.[42] But what, in the words of the *Hackney Gazette* on the same problem, was the extent of 'this weakening of the moral fibre' and how far was it related 'to the strain of the times' and the 'uncertainty of life'[43] during the war?

CHAPTER SIX

White-Collar Crime

In *The Criminal Area*, published twelve years after the end of the war, Terence Morris discusses the relative potential of the wealthier and the poorer classes in society for criminal behaviour. He concludes that 'however reluctant we may be to feel that the poor are less honest or the rich more law-abiding, the facts of the matter are crime and delinquency are almost exclusively a proletarian phenomenon . . . The vast majority of crimes consist of the straightforward stealing of property and their numbers are by no means balanced by elaborately contrived frauds and deceit on the part of businessmen and large corporations'.[1]

In the extremity of the war emergency some businessmen, traders and shopkeepers did not hesitate to find criminal solutions to problems that would otherwise have remained intractable. Two other occupational groups showed a predisposition to white-collar crime: public servants, and employers and managers in the building industry. Since the authorities pursued during the war a policy of prosecuting with vigour wealthy or well-known persons who had broken the law, it was no longer possible for such persons to cover up their misdeeds by bringing pressure to bear in the relevant quarters (and there is evidence that this did happen).[2] Whereas previously the prosecution of a person in the public eye might be thought to cast a poor light on all celebrities, after 1939 punishment of such offenders satisfied a double purpose. It gave the appearance of meeting the wartime demand for greater equality while simultaneously ensuring that the law was brought forcefully to public attention through the press.

In August 1942, the Countess of Mayo was prosecuted for a comparatively trivial rationing offence, and despite the presence on the lady's side of the distinguished counsel Mr Christmas Humphreys, the magistrate fined her £5 plus 10 guineas costs.[3] The point that even minor infringements of the rationing law would be followed up and punished, and that the publicity would be unflattering, was being clearly made.

Cases involving Lord Donegall and Noel Coward also received much press attention. They related to the wartime system of currency regulations. Prosecuting counsel in the first, H. A. K. Morgan, told the court that the case 'was considered serious . . . because of Lord Donegall's rank'. He had failed to register securities worth $20,000 in New York, which meant that the Treasury had been unable to use the dollars or the income from them. Defence counsel pleaded that the offence had occurred because Lord Donegall had not understood the regulations. The magistrate accepted this, but nonetheless fined the peer £180.[4]

Noel Coward appeared before the same magistrate later in 1941 charged with a similar currency offence. He had failed to offer $57,847 to the Treasury and was informed in court that he was liable to a maximum fine of £43,062. Once again the defendant pleaded ignorance of the regulations and took refuge in a declaration of artistic indifference to all such concerns ('he never interested himself in matters of finance or business if he could possibly avoid it'). He stressed the contribution he had made to war work at home and abroad 'for which he received no payment' and which (he did not spell this out) was in such marked contrast to so many British actors, writers, and film directors who had established themselves in the United States and clearly intended to remain there, come what may. The magistrate (McKenna) was sympathetic and said, 'I am very much impressed by the fact – I think it is the dominant one in this case – that he went abroad with the knowledge and approval . . . of the Government', and imposed a fine of £200.[5] There was, however, another charge, relating to shares Coward held in the USA which he had sold without asking permission of the Treasury, which was heard at the Mansion House before the Lord Mayor.

A Bank of England clerk 'during his leisure hours' had been reading Coward's autobiography *Present Indicative* and noted a passage about the actor's American representative 'having already wisely invested a lot of my money in American securities —'. He at once brought the passage to the notice of his superiors who began to make inquiries. Coward in court was once again artistically vague ('perfectly idiotic') on business matters but the Lord Mayor was not impressed. He declared coolly that Coward's 'temperament' as an artist did not release him from his obligations as a citizen and fined him £1,600.[6] The details of the case leave the impression that the Bank of England was looking for an opportunity to bring an exemplary prosecution and was delighted to discover a celebrity who fitted the bill.

These prosecutions occurred during the summer and autumn of 1941. Wavell's offensive in Libya had been smashed in June; shortly thereafter, the Red Army was reeling under the onslaught of the Wehrmacht. Meanwhile the USA was neutral and looked as though she would remain so. The problem of how to pay for a war that seemed unwinnable increasingly exercised the British Government, which tried to ensure that no financial source (and especially US dollars) was lost to it.

In contrast, in late 1944 when the bandleader Victor Silvester was prosecuted on the serious charge of 'deliberately embarking on a smuggling venture and using the services of the US forces for that purpose', he was fined less than a third of the fine imposed on Coward three years earlier. By late 1944 the war appeared on the verge of being won, but, even more important in assuring comparatively lenient treatment for Silvester, US military personnel were involved. The British authorities sought at all costs to avoid antagonising the Americans, yet if an Englishman was punished for an offence while his American collaborator went free the public might lose sight of the lesson the authorities were trying to instil in complaints about discriminatory treatment. Hence the fine for an offence which carried a maximum prison sentence of two years.

The prosecution took place during a significant period. With the invasion of the Continent a new source of goods unobtainable in Britain was opened up, one much closer than North America. Supplies from there had found their way to the British consumer from the moment of the arrival of the first US troops. There was nothing the British could do to stop the Americans bringing in quantities of luxury goods – their protests were ignored – so they tried to tighten up on the British side. It seems that the authorities discovered (probably as a result of 'information') that Silvester was receiving smuggled goods from somewhere, and later an incriminating letter surfaced inviting him to pick up two parcels of goods from an address in Old Quebec Street. The authorities had obtained a copy of this letter, and as it would hardly have been from Silvester, they had presumably been opening his mail at the post office.[7] It seems that the address in Old Quebec Street had been used systematically for the deposit and collection of smuggled goods and that this was a racket of some size. How many other such stores existed will never be known, but the underworld was sufficiently alert to what was going on to base several confidence tricks on it.[8]

The wartime practice of making an example of celebrities who broke the law is most clearly demonstrated in the prosecution of Ivor Novello and a woman clerk for a motoring offence.

Novello had applied for a permit to run a car and had been refused. Miss C., the clerk, who was a devoted fan of the actor, concocted a complex scheme whereby Novello's own car was transferred to the company which employed her. She then applied in the company's name for a permit to run the car on work of national importance, forging the various letters that were required. The idea initially seems to have been that Novello should be given lifts in the car when it was used on company work, but in fact he went much further than that. He used the car often and his own chauffeur always drove it and carried with him a letter signed by Miss C. saying that he was an employee of her company. Miss C.'s idea seems altogether hare-brained but Novello went along with it and rewarded her with a pair of his mother's ear-rings. Miss C. was fined £75 including costs; Novello went to jail for eight weeks. As the actor himself pointed out, the central point of the trial was the example his name would enable to be made: 'Oh!' he cried, when served with the summons, 'the publicity it will mean!'[9]

The wartime shortage of petrol, a matter which touched raw political emotions, meant . that even quite minor infringements of the law were regarded seriously by the courts. This was particularly so during 1941–2 when the

U-boat warfare was at its height and the petrol shortage espe-cially desperate. As most cars were in any case owned by the better off, and those who were permitted to run them had to be 'engaged on work of national importance', infringements of the law were almost entirely committed by the 'white-collar' strata. Using motor cars – and, more important, petrol – for a private purpose was forbidden. Yet car owners continued to take risks and break the law, using petrol on 'unnecessary' journeys, just as some of the poor, lacking the means to buy the goods they wanted, stole them. Courts fined heavily for petrol offences, more heavily than they fined most first-offending pilferers or shoplifters. For instance, the Secretary of South Essex Waterworks made three unnecessary journeys in 1943, the longest of them taking his daughter 90 miles to a farm in Essex, using 5 gallons of petrol in the process. He pleaded that he was 'suffering from overwork' and that he needed to protect his daughter on what he claimed was a dangerous journey. Nevertheless the magistrate fined him £145 and 10 guineas costs.[10] There were numerous similar cases during 1941–2.

Where the petrol was stolen the courts were much harsher. In five cases in the Romford area between November 1941 and April 1942 the receivers of stolen petrol were all jailed for terms of between three and six months. The quantities taken varied from 35 gallons to 500 gallons, and all the receivers were businessmen or employed in higher management.[11] Some petrol thieves were operating on a fairly large scale.[12]

The two occupations most susceptible to white-collar crime in wartime – to judge by the number of prosecutions – were the managerial sector in the building industry and the civil service. The incidence of criminal activity in the civil service seems to have been most high in three areas: among the bureaucracy established to cope with social problems emerg-ing directly out of war damage; within the organisations set up to distribute food; and among officials supervising the placing of contracts with private business.

During the war the government provided various types of grant to assist people whose homes and property had been damaged or destroyed by bombing. Criminal activity developed on both sides of the office counter; members of the public endeavoured to impersonate claimants, while some officials were tempted to arrange frauds of their own. The very procedures laid down by the authorities to prevent abuse proved on occasion to be susceptible to it. For example, the possibility of fraud in the payment of claims for financial assistance for bomb damage was supposed to be prevented by separating the investigations and the payments offices. The first decided whether an award was justified; the second handed over the money. This worked so long as the officials concerned 'did not put their heads together'. In Barking they did precisely that and 'by forgery' and 'falsification of accounts' stole at least £130 in four days (which was nearly half the annual salary of one of them and more than half that of the other). Courts punished such offences severely. Long service, which sometimes persuaded the magistrate to put a pilferer on probation, seems not to have been regarded as a mitigating factor with white-collar criminals, and the defendants in this case were jailed for three years and fifteen months respectively.[13]

This attitude of the courts may indicate, firstly, the difficulty of detecting such offences, and secondly, because of that, the need to make stern examples. For instance a billeting officer turned to his advantage the fact that persons who had evacuees billeted on them were entitled to claim financial help. Hence he issued billeting allowance forms in fictitious names and then presented the forms at post offices for payment. As his work involved travelling he was allowed to use a taxi when necessary and the driver collaborated with him in his frauds. The two shared the money they obtained (it amounted to some £1,100) and the offences were carried out for nearly a year before they were detected.[14]

In peacetime it had been the practice to trust officials in managerial positions to behave honestly; the war added the complication that shortages of staffing meant that even such supervision as there was, decreased. Consequently some white-collar crimes only came to light as a result of coincidence or accident. That involving the temporary chief clerk of the health department of Wembley Council in the spring of 1945 shows how fortuitous the discovery of certain local authority frauds was. He normally handled some £9,000–£10,000 of council money every year and among his duties was the task of collecting fees from the mothers of

children in the council's day nurseries and transferring it to
the Borough Treasurer. However, he did not always pay over
the full amount and on one occasion kept back £75 (out of a
total to be transferred of £130). Simultaneously, the district
auditor made an unexpected visit. The chief clerk panicked
and immediately secured a loan to cover the money he had
taken. This was a mistake: the district auditor wanted to know
why he had borrowed the money. If his nerve had held and he
had not secured the loan, the prosecution told the court, 'it
was quite conceivable that he would not have been brought to
justice'. The magistrate inquired of the representatives of
Wembley Council whether they had taken all proper precau-
tions to prevent such frauds and received the significant
answer that an employee in the chief clerk's position would
normally have been expected to be above stealing.[15]

Towards the end of the war the system of local authority
controls seems to have broken down in certain areas, especially in parts of London. On a separate issue the district
auditor for Fulham noted how in 1944 the procedure in the
department responsible for the checking and passing of payment of accounts relating to war damage repairs was defective. He gave an instance: on one occasion a tradesman was
paid twice for the same consignment of tarpaulins he had
supplied to the council – an overpayment of £676 10s. The
tradesman had discovered the error, not the council, and he
had promptly refunded the full amount. This was incompe-
tence, not fraud, but the implications were disturbing. The
district auditor noted, for example, that 749 tarpaulins used
to protect houses damaged by enemy action had 'mysteriously'
disappeared: they were worth £5,568 and represented nearly
half the total in the borough.[16] Tarpaulin, in common with all
forms of material, was greatly in demand at this time.

The breakdown in controls was also observable in other
areas of municipal responsibility. For instance, large quantities of furniture and household goods were rescued from
bomb-damaged houses and taken to council stores to await
collection by the owners. However, a proportion was not
claimed and after a period of three months councils were
permitted to use this furniture to assist people who had lost
everything in the bombing to set up new homes. The potential
for abuse here was considerable and in some north and east

London boroughs (Hackney and Poplar certainly;[17] possibly others) depredations of the stock of property became something of a scandal. In October 1941 nine persons were charged with either stealing or receiving goods from Hackney Council's store. In the course of the hearing it became clear that certain council officials and girl secretaries had had almost a free run of the place, and that a file containing details of who got what had unaccountably disappeared. Not surprisingly, the magistrate (Hopkin) commented unfavourably on the way the store had been managed, and suggested that there ought to be an investigation.[18] At any other time the evidence of municipal mismanagement and what appears almost to have been licensed pilfering on the part of higher council officials would have attracted considerable attention, but the blitz of the autumn and winter of 1941 obliterated such concerns. Hackney Council duly announced that an inquiry would take place[19] but that seems to have been as far as the matter went.

When the wartime shortages of food are recalled, it is not perhaps surprising that the distribution system should have come under attack. Two serious cases occurred in the Hornchurch–Barking area alone. The first, in early 1943, involved the food control executive officer for Barking, a wholesaler and three retailers. The official and the wholesaler were jailed for three years; a grocer for nine months; two others were each fined £250 including costs. The racket emerged around that most precious wartime commodity, sugar.

The looseness of the controls for the issue of sugar was demonstrated by the variety of methods the official discovered to circumvent them. In his relations with the grocer, S., he was able to make out sugar permits in the man's favour without any of his subordinate clerks knowing (to none of which S. was entitled and about which no record was kept). He also secured permits which had already been issued and increased the figures in S.'s favour; suppressed permits and made out new ones for larger amounts, and gave to S. permits issued in the names of other retailers. With the aid of the wholesaler, S. was able to draw the sugar. The prosecution stated that they did not know the extent of the frauds and, not surprisingly, in the light of this, the defendants endeavoured to play down their financial gains. S. said: 'I have made no extra profit on any of this excess sugar.' The executive officer on 'one or two occasions . . . borrowed' £5 from S. which he did not repay.

However, two of the defendants had been sufficiently worried by the impending prosecution to try to persuade employees to give false evidence. One man's nerve seems to have failed and he made 'an amazingly frank statement' about what had been going on, on which the prosecutions were based.[20]

The second case, in September 1944, involved the allocator of Hornchurch Butchers' Retail Buying Committee. It also revealed that the various records, documents and miscellaneous slips of paper that officialdom required in order to function had been extensively falsified. Meat was distributed throughout the country by the Ministry of Food and the butchers in each area (fifty in Hornchurch) were grouped together in district committees. B. was the allocator for the Hornchurch district and his duty was to apportion meat among the various butchers in line with their entitlement. What happened then was all too predictable. B. increased the amount of meat supplied to one butcher (who appeared in court alongside him) at the expense of the others and falsified the accounts accordingly. Each butcher lost only a small amount of meat, but when these amounts were multiplied by 49, the quantities going to number 50 were considerable.

B.'s system was so nimble that when the Ministry of Food eventually modified their procedures he was able to devise new frauds to cope with the changes. He was let down, however, by his butcher associate, who failed to destroy his records, and the two were prosecuted largely on the basis of this evidence. Although the prosecution went to 'considerable trouble and expense and had checked thousands of invoices and masses of schedules' in the process of building up a case, the defendants were only fined, even though B. had a previous conviction for embezzlement in 1933.[21]

Thirdly, there is evidence to suggest that a centre of fraud emerged in the very strong position the relevant ministries acquired in the process of allocating contracts. If companies could not secure orders from the government, then they were unable to go into production: this put dishonest officials at a great advantage.

In June 1944, a radio production officer at the Board of

Trade, who visited firms engaged in radio work to arrange supplies, attempted to extract from the managing director of one company a payment of £25 a month in return for using his influence to channel orders and spare parts to the company. The director went to the police and thereafter acted on their instructions.[22]

The fine imposed here, £70, was also surprisingly light. It may be that the magistrate was impressed by the plea of the defence that the official was 'a man of irreproachable character, who came from a very respectable family'.

In other cases the prosecution had to persuade one of the participants to a corrupt bargain to testify against the others in order to be able to proceed to court. In 1943 a company was actually established in order to take advantage of the 'fine' opportunities the war had created. At the instigation of a professional engineer, two financiers decided to set up an engineering business. Their first object, however, was not the usual one of finding labour and plant, but rather to make useable (bribable) contacts at the relevant ministry (in this case Aircraft Production) to ensure that orders would be forthcoming, and at a major company (Plessey's) for which the new company would carry out subcontract work. It was not revealed in court exactly how these matters came to light, but the principal witness for the prosecution was the professional engineer who had been instrumental in setting up the company. It was a situation that appalled the recorder, Sir Gerald Dodson:

'The irony of this case was that the person chiefly concerned [the professional engineer] now found himself in possession of a flourishing business. That business was conceived in corruption, fed on corruption, and had prospered on corruption. But this man is not before the court, so nothing can be done about him. The prosecution have made use of him, so he enjoys the invidious safety which is acquired by somebody who first makes use of and then tramples underfoot his fellow conspirators. No words can be too strong to describe his part in the transaction, but I cannot pass any penalty upon him.'

Perhaps for this reason the sentences imposed on the defendants were lenient – fines, not jail. The chief buyer at Plessey's was fined £550 plus costs and the Ministry of Aircraft Production official £50.[23]

The most serious wartime frauds of all, however, emerged

in the building industry. The 'cost plus' system of payment used for the settling of contracts was particularly vulnerable to fraud. In its usual form the building company sought to charge the body paying for the contracted work with the wages of non-existent workers, or of workers who had worked only a proportion of the time claimed. There were other forms of fraud carried out by workmen on their own account with the connivance of the employer, and the total amount embezzled probably ran into several million pounds. Cases occurred affecting both local authorities and government-controlled bodies. A sample of six (in Birkenhead, Romford, Bromley, Ilford, Stratford and Sittingbourne) illustrates what was happening. The highest single fraud mentioned in the charges was £1,372 in Birkenhead; the smallest £22 10s, and they range in time from May 1940 to November 1944. All but one of the six defendants had been conducting repair work for a local authority – either ARP construction or first-aid repairs to houses damaged by bombs (the exception was a subcontractor for the Admiralty). In these cases employers either put in claims for the payment of persons who had not done any work (in one case a 'clerk' who was in fact the mistress of the builder; in another the builder claimed for his domestic cleaner and his dancing teacher; but most claimed for employees engaged on other contracts); or they exaggerated the wages they had been paying. For example, 'the defendants had jointly certified that a man named Halligan, an apprentice plumber, had, during the week ended January 27th, worked 70 hours and was paid 1s 6½d an hour, his wages for that week amounted to £5 9s 4½d . . . Halligan's actual rate of pay was 7d an hour and . . . he received £1 10s 0½d.'[24] The extra went, of course, into the builder's pocket.

The defendants in these six cases were exposed in one of two ways. Either someone in the company informed ('one of the workmen reported the matter . . . to a supervisor of War Damage Repairs in the Corporation';[25] a clerk with the company wrote anonymously to the architects) or the offences came to light in the normal process of tax gathering. For instance, questions began to be asked about one company after a tax inspector wrote to a workman about tax that he had not paid. The money concerned had indeed gone in on the builder's forms, but it had never been paid to the employee.

One firm actually maintained two sets of wage books in the office, one a truthful account, the other for inspection by visitors. However, a CID man appeared unexpectedly with a search warrant and he discovered that the difference between the two books amounted to some £58 a week in the builder's favour.[26]

The defence in these cases invariably pleaded lack of intention: either the defendants had been 'recklessly careless' or they had made a mistake ('anyone can make a mistake')[27] under the pressure of wartime conditions. All eleven were nonetheless found guilty and jailed, for various terms of between three and fifteen months. All were either company directors or managers.

How prevalent such 'cost plus' fraud was is impossible to ascertain but judges and magistrates clearly felt obliged to make examples because 'these offences relating to false time sheets were far too prevalent in the country at the present time',[28] while defendants invariably saw themselves as unlucky victims: 'Why pick on us? There are plenty of firms doing it.'[29]

Even to bring a prosecution at all required a strong sense of public duty. In one case the defendants were engineers engaged on a £20,000 contract for the Admiralty and had included in their claims to the Admiralty domestic staff employed in their own homes. The engineering overseer from the Admiralty revealed his dilemma in court when he spoke up for the defendants, stating that their work 'was of a specialised character and had been carried out in a most satisfactory manner. Both . . . had done everything they could to assist the war effort, even working night and day to get a particular job completed.' If they went to jail their contribution would be at an end. The judge (McClure) conceded that point, nevertheless he jailed them for twelve and nine months respectively.

In his review of the war years the Chief Constable of Liverpool gave some idea of the scale of 'cost plus' fraud in his city and the problems it posed for the police. The use of this system 'for nearly all Government work led to endless abuse. It became the financial interests of the employer to increase costs and many frauds were carried out in different ways. The largest, by which thousands of pounds a month were obtained for the pay of fictitious workmen, resulted in the police recovering £300,000 of the illicit gains, the extent of which will never be fully known'. Furthermore, employers connived at 'many minor frauds' committed by their workmen. 'Prosecutions were instituted against workmen who received double overtime for working all night when in fact they were sleeping in their homes. In the ordinary course the employers would have been expected to see that the work was done, but as they were paid a percentage on all wages it was not to their financial interests to do so.'[30]

Thus white-collar crime in the building industry flourished in response to the circumstances of the war, and the ending of those circumstances presumably also ended the crime (at least in its wartime form). Whether the war was similarly responsible for the increase in white-collar crime generally is a more difficult question. What is certain is that many of those involved pleaded the war in explanation of their behaviour. It had greatly reduced normal business and governmental supervision, because of the shortage of staff, and people had been 'tempted'. Furthermore, the wartime inflationary spiral hit middle-class incomes particularly hard.

The problem of the reduction in supervision was a big one. Romford Council made a typical complaint: municipal officials had not been able to check all the individual builders' accounts and so 'had to rely upon the honesty and integrity of building firms and hope that they would not take advantage of the difficulties with which . . . the Council was contending'.[31] Other concerns also did not 'check things properly; a cogent reason' was 'the tremendous amount of work that had to be done'.[32] The problem extended to private companies: there was 'naturally less supervision of employees . . . in wartime . . . than in normal times'.[33] Some builders had seen an opening and exploited it, just as many shopkeepers, businessmen and traders had seen 'possibilities' in the black market. Such people took an aggressive approach to the criminal potential of business: perhaps they had always done so, the exigencies of war merely offering them greater scope and opportunity. Others were defensive, seeking to protect their incomes from erosion. Explanations along these lines were often given in court.

In one case, a 52-year-old clerk, who had had 'an honourable career' in West Africa (including spending a period as British Consul in the town where he lived), was prosecuted for embezzlement. He argued that his wage of £9 a week became inadequate to his needs after 'his house in Brixton was bombed. His wife had to undergo an operation, and when her doctor ordered her to live in the country' he was obliged to take a (two-guinea-a-week) house in Guildford, and also add to his expenses by travelling each day to his place of work in Peckham. In three years he defrauded his employer of £1,120; the magistrate jailed him for six months.[34]

In a second case the defendant was a cashier in Kensington with twenty-three years service at his firm who had, in 1943, falsified invoices and over a period of twelve months robbed his employer of £51. His pay was also £9 a week, and he pleaded 'the difficulties of a middle-class man with a sick wife, two young children at a secondary school and a large income tax deduction from his salary'. The magistrate fined him £100.[35]

Defendants offering these and similar explanations were clearly trying to formulate their appeal in terms that the usually middle- and upper-class occupants of the bench would understand: they would be familiar with the financial 'plight' of the salaried classes at this time. As the second case illustrates, some magistrates were indeed persuaded to be lenient.

Thus, during the war, crime had ceased to be 'almost exclusively a proletarian phenomenon', and it is at least arguable that, as far as the salaried were concerned, it had ceased to be so for precisely the same reason that over the years had driven many proletarians to turn to theft: an inability to make ends meet in any other way.

CHAPTER SEVEN

Betting, Gaming and Drink

In May 1944, the London County Council prosecuted a London cinema company, Original Classics Ltd, for allowing unaccompanied children under the age of sixteen to attend screenings of two films, *The Son of Frankenstein* and *Tower of London*. They were supposed to be excluded from the first altogether, whilst if they attended the second, it was to be in the company of an adult. An LCC inspector had noticed children there on their own who 'appeared' to be below the age limit. The magistrate (Hopkin) remarked that the title of the second film sounded 'quite innocuous' but counsel for the LCC replied 'I may say . . . that the two main characters in the film are taken by Mr Boris Karloff and Mr Basil Rathbone, who generally appear only in horror films.' He further insisted that the court be guided by the British Board of Film Censors' decisions on category. Although some of the children present in the cinema had probably experienced at first hand the rather greater real-life horrors of the London blitz, counsel persuaded the magistrate to accept his case and the company was fined £10 including costs. The prosecution made the front page of the local newspaper.[1]

The decision to initiate such a prosecution might have seemed surprising even in the most tranquil years of peace, but its taking place during the spring of 1944 requires an explanation. Six months later, an unrelated and, on the surface, totally contrasting prosecution resulted in the jailing for three months of the manager of a club in Chelsea. He was also fined £800. The club had broken the rationing and licensing laws: non-members had been able to buy drinks at the bar, paying 3s for a nip of whisky, while a restaurant sold black-market steaks at 6s and eggs at 3s each. In another part of the club, rooms were available 'for immoral purposes'. A porter carried a tariff which indicated how much each of the girls present would charge if a guest wished to spend the night with her. The police experienced some difficulty in keeping observation on the club because entry was restricted to members of the US forces – no British troops were allowed in. British *girls*, however, were welcome, and evidence with which to prosecute the manager was provided by a woman police officer.[2]

The link between these two prosecutions lay in the fears of many members of the general public that traditional standards of behaviour were breaking down, and that the law must be invoked to restore them (or at least prevent the situation deteriorating still further). The cinema company and the Chelsea club therefore represented opposite extremes of the same problem and threatened particularly two groups in society which were held to be especially vulnerable: juveniles and young women.

The war was thus aggravating a tension that existed in English life over leisure-time activities. The ambiguity of much of the legislation, combined with an erratic policy on the part of the police when enforcing it, or failing to do so, added to the problem. Finally there was a class bias in the laws which emerged most strongly with respect to betting, and this in itself encouraged many people to ignore them. The antiquated licensing laws had also been widely flouted before the war, and much police time was spent tracking down and punishing offenders. Clubs which set out deliberately to ignore the rules did flourishing business, while numerous public houses gave the official closing times a very wide interpretation.

The pressures and undertones present when the laws *were* enforced can be discerned from three prosecutions in Brighton in the summer and autumn of 1939. All three dealt with clubs which broke the licensing laws and the greatest number of summonses (105 of them!) was issued against Brighton Conservative Club. The police had visited the club on *thirteen* occasions, buying drinks, playing billiards, gathering evidence. Drinks were always sold well after time. The case gave the Bench, dominated by Conservative worthies, some uncomfortable moments and the club secretary was eventually fined £38.[3] It was a noticeably more lenient sentence than was imposed in the two other cases.

Both these clubs were struck off. In one of them three gaming machines were in use (the largest coin they took was a shilling); in the other, there were a number of automatic machines. This club (Jimmy's Club) was not only struck off, the premises were disqualified for twelve months, yet (apart from the gaming machines) the circumstances in all three cases were similar.[4] Fortunately, the court hearing concerning Jimmy's Club revealed something of the pressures that lay behind these prosecutions.

The police had examined the books of Jimmy's Club and the court was informed that, as a result of 'taking an unfair advantage' (selling drinks after hours, etc), it had made a fair profit whereas many of Brighton's publicans experienced difficulty in showing any profit at all. The town was grossly overstocked with public houses and competition with the clubs for customers gave them all 'a particularly difficult time'. The licensees were well represented in the local Conservative Party and, through it, on the Watch Committee and the Bench. Pressure on the police to take some remedial action was considerable and indeed successful, but this had the unintended result (for the pressers) that, in order to maintain their reputation for impartiality, the police began investigations into the Conservative Club, the prosecution of which followed the disqualification of Jimmy's Club by precisely three weeks.

In addition to the pressures brought by vested interests like the licensing trade there were also those coming from the self-appointed guardians of public morality. These bodies were vigilant, self-confident and aggressive in the late 1930s, and they exercised considerable influence in small and medium-sized towns. But even in London they were able to make themselves felt. For instance, a feature of 1930s night life was the emergence of fly-by-night clubs and bottle parties to which entry was by introduction only and at which drinks were supplied at exorbitant prices. A body calling itself 'The Public Morality Council' devoted a part of its energies to suppressing such places and its 1939 annual report detailed an impressive rate of success.[5]

Some 67 clubs and bottle parties had been reported to the
Council of which 35 had been 'convicted' or 'remedied', while
action was pending against 15 and another 11 were under
investigation. Onlookers might well have wondered why, with
so many deplorable social problems confronting them in the
1930s, the Council should have preoccupied itself with the
desire of members of the public to drink after hours at exorbitant prices. It was a question that the Council had evidently
discussed: The 'complaints' against these clubs (the Council
insisted that it only intervened because of 'public disquiet')
'range from the presence of and use by men and women for
undesirable purposes or practices, to conduct in the clubs,
and, in some cases, undesirable entertainments, or the fact
that the premises are not licensed'.

The police took a rather curious line on this. A drive against
bottle parties was initiated in the late 1930s: by January 1939
admission was almost impossible unless the would-be reveller
knew the organisers, for, as one explained, 'the days when you
could run bottle parties wide open are over. We never know
who's who any more. All sorts of people are employed as
informers.'[6] Yet the police had denied all knowledge of a
campaign. 'Police activity is constant,' they stated. 'Where
there is evidence of an offence, we take action.'[7]

It was a disingenuous statement: the police certainly regu-
lated their activity and also the rate of prosecutions for certain
offences. This was particularly noticeable over brothel-
keeping during the war. Indeed, they had been known to
allow certain types of offence to be committed in the belief
that, if they cracked down, the criminals would turn to other,
more serious, crimes. The Chief Constable of Essex, in the
early 1930s, refused to 'clean up' the local racetracks, despite
the notorious pickpocket gangs that operated on them, believ-
ing that if the gangs ('confirmed' criminals) were deprived of
racecourse 'loot' they would turn instead to housebreaking
and burglary.[8]

The clubs the police raided in London on the eve of war
varied a great deal.[9] For example, the Bethnal Green Progres-
sive Club was struck off and the premises disqualified for
twelve months, for serving drinks after hours; it catered for a
working-class clientèle, the profits were poor, and the magistrate conceded that 'there was nothing of the West End club

about the case'.[10] Three months earlier the Walham Green
Social Club, Fulham, had been struck off and disqualified for
six months. Drinks had been served to non-members and the
police claimed that 'a good deal of drunkenness went on'
there. On the other hand, fair sums of money had been
invested in the club (£3,000, the defence claimed); it had
2,000 members and there was 'no suggestion of immorality'.[11]
In May, the Gunter Grove Social Club in Chelsea was struck
off and the premises disqualified for twelve months. 'Observation on several days in March showed that anyone could
walk into the club and buy drink.' The place was running at a
slight loss, according to its books.[12]

These clubs all catered exclusively for the working class:
'The members were decent, hard-working men who, with
their wives and children, were in the habit of spending their
evenings there. Attached to the club . . . were a loan club and a
football team.'[13] This preoccupation with working-class clubs
was to become an important element of public policy during
the war; it was matched by a drive against clubs which permitted (or encouraged) immorality, or catered for gambling on
the part of the 'new' rich. Prosecutions of clubs catering for
the 'established' rich, however, tended to be infrequent. For
instance, in June 1941 a 'well-known Scottish racquets player
was prosecuted for breaches of the licensing and gaming laws
at the squash club he owned and managed in west London.
The prosecuting counsel stressed that 'he did not press for the
striking off of this club because it was not the usual type of
pothouse which was so often before the Court, it was a well
appointed Club and apart from the gaming machines and the
service of alcohol to non-members [which had been sufficient
reason for courts to strike off other London clubs] there was
no suggestion of drunkenness or disorder.' The magistrate,
Sir Gervais Rentoul, heard the case in the appropriate spirit.
He drew attention to a newspaper cutting and remarked, 'I
see the police were defeated in their [racquets] match with this
club', which caused some amusement in court. Rentoul fined
the owner £35 including costs and adjourned the summons
for striking off on the understanding that the club would be
conducted properly henceforth.[14]

This bias in the policy of some courts was later to be sys-
tematised by the defence regulations; the bias regarding bet-

ting was contained in the legislation itself. Betting was in effect a criminal offence anywhere but on the race track. Parliament had endeavoured to permit the wealthy to bet freely but had tried to satisfy the anti-betting lobby by making it very difficult for the poor to do so. The latter could only place a legal bet if they went to the racecourse, which meant taking time off work and losing pay. Placing money bets in the street was illegal, though credit bets could be telephoned or posted. It was obvious at which section of society the legislation was aimed, but the poor were as determined to bet freely as the rich, and bookmakers were equally anxious to meet this desire. It was a potentially dangerous situation: a popular pastime from which a good deal of money could be made was illegal – precisely the mix that led to the growth of organised crime and police corruption. And indeed, the only instances of such crime on the American model developing in England at this time occurred in racing and betting. That the English variety remained a pale reflection of the American was the consequence of a combination of social pressures, the fact that the police had established a considerable measure of control over the criminal community, and the lack of appropriate experience on the part of that community.

Nonetheless, during the 1920s and 1930s, a number of gangs vied for control of the race-tracks. They offered 'protection' to bookmakers and attempted to secure a proportion of the profits of the betting industry. Epsom and Ascot were the courses most affected, and gangs of some size were based in Leeds and Birmingham as well as London. There ought to have been sufficient 'loot' for all, but the gangs squandered a great deal of energy on internecine 'warfare': they seemed as anxious to demonstrate 'toughness' and 'daring' and thereby establish a claim to be 'boss of the turf' as to make money.

There was one major exception to this rule, the Sabini gang. These were Anglo-Italians based in Saffron Hill, London, and they prospered by showing more imagination and consistency of purpose than their contemporaries. Their financial strength derived from traditional racecourse extortion rackets (selling sticks of chalk to bookmakers at 1s each, or race cards worth 2d at 2s 6d) and employed their resources to move into the protection racket in the West End, taking over gaming parties, and 'cleaning' windows. They also attempted

to bribe and compromise policemen. Their income was substantial by English, if not American, standards: Darby Sabini
was said to be making £20,000 a year by 1926.[15] They were
able to reap advantages from the political situation because
two contrary trends in British society were coming into conflict from the late 1920s. Gambling was an increasingly popular activity, and therefore 'big business', at a time when the
pressure groups opposed to it retained sufficient political
muscle to prevent liberalising of the laws.

Gambling expanded fast after the First World War. Football pools, which had barely existed in 1926, were taking some
£30 million annually ten years later. This eclipsed the expan-
sion of betting on horse and greyhound racing, but the latter,
which was a new sport, experienced formidable growth. In
only three years from 1927 to 1929, attendance at tracks in
London alone rose from three to eight million.[16] With large
sums of money moving into legitimate gambling (and
unquantifiable amounts going to the illegitimate varieties) it is
hardly surprising that criminal elements were attracted.
Horse racing had indeed had a criminal fringe since its begin-
nings as an organised sport. In the 1920s and 1930s there had
been a number of doping scandals, whilst confidence men and
even the occasional racing journalist had conspired to
defraud bookmakers. On several occasions considerable sums
had been stolen. But the most profitable activity was not the
confidence man's dramatic coup, it was the regular and systematic organisation of illegal street betting.

By the 1930s (if not long before) a criminal machinery had
been established for the organisation of illegal betting that was
efficient in that it protected the men at the top while providing
the courts with suitable candidates for punishment. Most, if
not all, working-class districts were covered by the agents of
the bookmakers, and the police barely scratched the surface
of the lawbreaking. Between 1935 and 1939 an annual average of 14,578 persons was dealt with at courts in England and
Wales[17] (a typical London street bookmaker could easily
handle 2,000 betters in the course of a week). These persons
were mainly customers; as for suppliers – 230 search warrants
were issued in the Metropolitan Police District alone in 1939
and fines of £7,000 imposed.[18] But the background organisers
went untouched.

The pattern was well established. Look-outs were posted whose duty it was to warn the person taking bets of the arrival of the plain-clothes police. These look-outs would make themselves familiar with the faces of as many as possible of the police whose job it was to control street betting, even attending court to hear them give evidence. The bookmaker's agent would hire a shop or a private house and word would pass round the neighbourhood that at certain times on certain days he would be available there to take bets. Hundreds of people would patronise him. In only half an hour on one day in April 1939, forty-seven people entered such a house in Fulham. 'Ten of them handed something' to the agent 'who was standing in the passage, just inside the doorway. The remainder entered the house, and emerged after a few moments.' Sometimes the police would keep watch on such an agent during the course of several days (in this instance, four) before launching a raid. If the look-outs were sharp enough, they succeeded in warning the agent in time: 'Further down the street, the front door of a small house ... slammed shut and was bolted on the inside, but the police managed to force their way in. A man, inside, tried to escape via the garden but the police caught him, and they also caught the look-out.' When they searched the ground floor of the house they found 'on a table ... a paying-out book and six books of betting rules, also a mid-day paper and a morning paper open at the racing page'.[19]

This agent was fined £10 for keeping and conducting premises as a betting house but he did not live there. He had an arrangement with the tenant, a woman, who was also prosecuted, though the charge against her was dismissed. All the same, the police raid had given her a scare and she ended their agreement, so the next time the agent was arrested, three months later, he was actually standing in the street to take the bets. Caught with him was his look-out who had been riding a bicycle 'in the vicinity, and twice raised his hands as a signal that police officers were approaching'.[20] But the 'big man' behind the agent (the bookmaker) was not prosecuted, even though he took the profits and paid the fines.

There was of course a limit to the number of prosecutions agents and look-outs could sustain: if they appeared too often before the same magistrate prison might well be the consequence. So they moved on to another district (if the city was large

enough) or to a different town, utilising the numerous contacts of the bookmaking fraternity.

For the bookmakers it was a cumbersome and inefficient
system: much more convenient to bribe the police to 'turn a
blind eye'. They knew they had the support of a substantial
section of public opinion and the police knew it too. During
the war two market stall-holders and a café proprietor were
accustomed to take bets in Watney Street, Stepney, and one
day in 1944 plain-clothes police watched them do it. But when
they moved in to make arrests the men 'loudly protested their
innocence' and 'a crowd of people gathered in a few seconds'.
One of the betting agents shouted out 'we don't want any ——
Gestapo here' and called for help which, the police admitted,
he looked like getting: 'The crowd became much thicker and
rather menacing.'[21]

Measured by the numbers who participated in it, gaming
was a much less popular activity than off-course betting,
though in terms of social class the range of persons who
indulged was very much wider. Gaming clubs and parties
catered for all sections of society, from the inhabitants of
Mayfair to groups of the unemployed spinning coins on
Hackney Marshes. At the lower end of the scale was the
Pavilion Bridge Club in Shepherd's Bush, run by a family in
their own home. Whist and rummy were played for stakes of
up to 5s, and there was a charge of 2s for each game.
Working-class and self-employed persons were present on the
night of the raid, as were four 'housewives'. The police moved
in, it seems, after they had received a number of complaints,
six written and four oral, one from a woman 'who said that her
husband gambled away his money and kept her short of
food'.[22] A similar club in Brighton (a temperance club!)
charged a membership fee of 1s p.a., and also made a small
charge for playing cards and snooker. Police kept watch on
the place for three days, 'listening on a landing outside the
door at intervals'.[23] The amount of police activity against
gaming in one of the tougher districts of London can be
assessed from the *Hackney Gazette* which, during the first five
months of 1939, reported six raids; altogether 140 persons
were prosecuted.

At the opposite end of the scale was the Gateways Club,
King's Road, Chelsea, which in 1939 functioned as a gaming

house. It had 700 members and was 'very tastefully decorated. The walls had been to a large extent decorated by the members themselves – well-known artists, doctors, and professional men – and the membership was really a good class of person.' The defence admitted that it was 'unfortunate' that gaming machines were installed but 'those using them were well able [to afford] to do so'. Significantly, although the magistrate fined the proprietor £50, he did not order that the club be struck off immediately, deferring a decision for three months to see how the place was conducted in the meantime.[24]

The impact of the war on the argument about gaming and off-course betting was to strengthen both sides in their belief in their case. Opponents of liberalisation of the laws argued that they had 'history' on their side: the country's life-and-death struggle demanded that people should sacrifice their appetite for pleasure for the duration and, indeed, that yet further curbs should be imposed. Advocates of change, however, declared that the public needed and deserved greater opportunities for relaxation in wartime. The policy of the police was to continue to enforce the law and indeed – as their activity had always been 'constant' – to make it even more constant.

The principal obstacle they had to overcome was shortage of resources. The Government supported them with vigour, even though the wartime coalition included members not renowned for the abstemiousness of their private lives. But in home policy, Herbert Morrison and Sir Stafford Cripps exercised considerable influence, while the Government generally was impressed by the Treasury argument that it was necessary to close as many outlets for wasteful expenditure as possible in the hope that the money would be directed to saving. An attack on gaming, off-course betting and illicit drinking would have that purpose. Whether in fact such an objective could be secured by any system, even of a thorough going totalitarian type, is questionable; certainly people in wartime England who wished to gamble continued to do so whatever the authorities intended.

In the early stages of the war the police believed they had the situation firmly under control. The Commissioner of the Metropolitan Police commented in his report for 1939 on 'the impression of London in wartime produced by the reports in certain newspapers' which suggested 'that it had become completely demoralized. Vice was said to be flourishing – the number of night clubs, drinking dens and "gambling hells" to be increasing beyond all bounds, gangsterism and racketeering were said to be rampant . . . Actually nothing could be further from the truth. There was no noticeable increase in any of the activities mentioned and, in some respects, the position was unusually good. The harm done by these exaggerated reports is obvious enough. At home they add needlessly to the anxiety and apprehension inseparable from war conditions, and abroad they provide welcome food for hostile propagandists.'[25]

Wartime statistics seemed to confirm the point – at least as far as drink was concerned. Drunkenness declined sharply in London, despite the direct impact of the war on that city, as well as in England and Wales generally, and aggravated drunkenness also diminished:

Proportion per 1,000 population in the Metropolitan Police District arrested for simple drunkenness and drunkenness with aggravation (A); number of persons found guilty of non-indictable drunkenness offences (B); * *number of persons found guilty of disorderly behaviour (including use of violent, obscene or abusive language) in the streets and public houses (C)*[26]*

	A	B	C
1938	2·265	52,661	17,379
1939	2·069	51,012	14,735
1940	1·930	44,699	13,342
1941	2·023	38,680	12,761
1942	1·392	25,900	11,963
1943	1·434	25,747	11,870
1944	1·234	21,295	9,631
1945	1·228	19,368	7,805

*England and Wales.

The decline in all three categories was dramatic, though such statistics must be approached with caution. Arrests were of course made by the police and there may have been a change of policy during the war. The *Police Review* certainly recommended one, arguing that prosecutions for simple drunkenness should 'be given a rest in wartime'.[27] Furthermore, getting drunk was in itself harder, as severe shortages of beer occurred, while many spirits were often out of stock altogether, and those supplies that did appear often had their

alcohol content reduced. At the same time many people had
more money to spend while the nervous strain of the time sent
crowds to seek refuge in the pubs. On balance it seems probable that 'a lower police profile' combined with the decreased
strength of alcohol made some contribution to the decline in
arrests for drunkenness, though it is unlikely that they
accounted for a fall of well over half between 1938 and 1945.
The decline was a real one, if not as great as the statistics
suggest.

The police did not slacken their drive against clubs and
pubs which broke the licensing laws; if anything, the reverse.
Even in the closing winter of the war, when police manpower
was most stretched and flying-bomb attacks a regular occurrence, prosecutions for after-hours drinking in Tottenham,
Bethnal Green and Hackney took place at a rate of about two a
week. Fines ranged from £1 to £5 and in one well publicised
case a policeman with fourteen years' service was caught
drinking at the bar with the licensee.[28] As for clubs, in the
Metropolitan Police District in 1942 there were 152 prosecutions, in 1945 only 31; the difference between the two years
being accounted for by Defence Regulations 44C and 55C,
which added considerably to the powers of the police. Regulation 55C enabled them to object to the registration of a new
club, and it was used extensively. No longer did they have to
spend many hours gathering evidence of law-breaking
against the club. The Commissioner of the Metropolitan
Police commented that 'with the amount of easy money in
war-time London and the shortage of goods for sale on which
to spend it, this Defence Regulation has saved the situation'.[29]
In theory, the kind of club aimed at was the Ninety Club, in
Clapham, which was closed in October 1942. This place was
'frequented by men and women of the lowest order, and
troops of the Allied Nations [sic] ... A young woman ...
made spasmodic noises on an accordion ... anyone could get
admittance by giving three rings on the bell, and they could
then drink to their hearts' content. The people ... were
mainly of the worst possible type: thieves and women of the
lowest order. The conversation was foul, and some dancing
went on with women high-kicking in scanty clothing ... the
place was in effect an unlicensed public house.' It had had two
previous incarnations as a club (both had been struck off) and

was now making a substantial profit. The premises were disqualified for five years.[30]

Yet whether all the clubs closed were of this type is debat-
able. Regulation 55C may well have provided a good reason to
shut down many places purely in order to restrict outlets for
'easy money'. Police now assessed them on such slight evidence as their names. The *Police Review* in August 1941 commented adversely on the number of clubs and bottle parties
available in the capital and noted the names of some of them –
'Boogey-Woogey', 'Hi-de-Hi', 'Paradise', 'El Morocco' –
adding that 'the names give some idea of their real character'.[31]

Maintaining a firm control over the nation's night-life was
thus considered sufficiently important a task to justify the
devotion of considerable police resources to it. For instance, in
two prosecutions of public houses in Chatham in 1943, the
police in the first case kept watch from 8 February to 5 March,
and in the second from 8 June to 13 July. In the first pub
'sometimes there would be as many as six or more prostitutes
. . . They would either sit down or gather round the serving
bar, and when a serviceman came in they would walk up to
him, and address him in endearing terms, and suggest that he
should offer them and their friends drinks. Sometimes the
man would buy drinks, and after a while one of the women
would retire with him to a dark alley opposite [the pub]. She
would then return to the bar after a while with or without the
man, and then perhaps go out later with another man.' In the
second pub, during a visit by an Inspector and two other
policemen, 'there were four such women in the saloon bar and
one in the public bar, contacting sailors, begging drinks . . .
and soliciting. As the [Inspector] entered one of the women
recognised him and said in a loud voice: "He's a —— copper.
Someone wants to crown him", and pointed at the witness.
Whereupon two Australian sailors began to jostle him,
offered to fight him and used obscene language. The licensee
was standing behind the bar, but made no attempt to interfere, and on one occasion was grinning.' The licensees of both
pubs (one of them the widow of a Superintendent in the Kent
Constabulary) were fined £10.[32]

Supplementing such prosecutions were numerous others in
which it is difficult to detect very much, if any, evidence of

'crime'. Police warnings were even issued to pubs which permitted 'a certain amount of singing of popular songs . . . and
instead of the normal words being sung obscene words are
substituted'.[33]

A similar process occurred over betting and gaming. The
war does not appear to have seen a marked increase in the
public participation in either; indeed at its start there was a
sharp fall in prosecutions and, although the number rose
steadily thereafter, the total in 1945 was still only half the
pre-war level.

Number of persons prosecuted in magistrates courts for betting and gaming offences[34]

Annual average						
1935–9	1940	1941	1942	1943	1944	1945
14,578	3,659	4,308	5,913	5,754	6,042	7,595

These changes were largely the result of the police orches-
trating the rate of prosecutions, rather than mirroring a significant decline in the incidence of betting and gaming compared with 1935–9. There was one possible exception – 1940
– when horse racing was banned for three months.

Public opinion was probably more hostile to betting and
gaming during the war than for many years previously, and
indeed, in 1942, an opinion poll showed that half those questioned wished to see horse racing stopped altogether.[35] However, when the individual prosecutions that make up the
statistics are examined they show, firstly, that a proportion of
offences seem to have been largely technical and prosecutions
instituted in order to demonstrate continuing police presence, and, secondly, that the authorities tended to take a harder line with working-class and 'newly rich' offenders than
they did with upper-class ones. Thirdly, there is evidence to
suggest that the police were failing to come to grips with the
core of professional crime in both betting and gaming.

The anti-betting and gaming lobby was still able to bring
considerable pressure to bear during the war. In July 1943 an
amusement fair, which had been established in Wembley in
connection with the 'holidays-at-home' scheme, was raided.
The police found that games of the roll-a-penny type were
being played for cash prizes. This was the flaw: *cash* prizes.
The law permitted gifts, but gifts in wartime were hard to

find. The police stated in court that they believed 'these people have made genuine efforts to obtain prizes' but the magistrate commented that 'we can pay too big a price for amusement and there are some people who object to gambling. The police, of course, acted on information received . . . You have been acting as a money box when people should have been putting it into National Savings.' He fined the fifteen defendants 7s 6d each.[36]

In a second incident, in May 1943, Fulham Council proposed to hold a draw to collect money for Merchant Navy Week. They had issued 3,000 sixpenny tickets and hoped to raise in all £1,000. According to the Mayor, the tickets sold like 'hot cakes' and only a few books were left when the local police asked to examine one of them. Shortly after this the Mayor was visited by a Scotland Yard official and a police inspector who told him that the scheme came within the category of a public lottery and must be abandoned, otherwise action would have to be taken. The nature of the objection was that tickets were on sale to the general public; if the lottery had been private (for example confined to the employees of a business firm) it would have been legal. The Mayor pointed out that the Council had organised a similar scheme the previous year for Russia Week and the police had not interfered. The answer came back that on this occasion a member of the public had gone to the trouble to point out that the scheme was a lottery. The Mayor had no choice but to send out letters cancelling the draw and offering people back their money.[37]

The point made by the magistrate in the Wembley case, that the money should not have been gambled but put into National Savings, was a common theme in betting and gaming prosecutions. During the war a minority of people grew rich, some of them honest businessmen, tradesmen and shopkeepers, and some not. Wartime racketeers and black-marketeers became very rich indeed, but in a society in which many outlets for conspicuous spending had been shut off. It was a potentially dangerous mixture, and added to it were those elements in 'high society' who had traditionally gone abroad to pursue their taste for gambling and fast living. The 'established' rich and the 'new' rich were now obliged to seek their pleasures in England, and they found no shortage of suppliers.

Private parties emerged which people were able to join by invitation. One was run by 'Madame Estelle', a 47-year-old riding-school proprietress who gave roulette parties in her Oxford Street flat. When the police raided they found twelve persons playing roulette, with Madame Estelle acting as croupier. Chips on the table had a value of about £100. She took the profits, after supplying a meal and liquor.

Such parties hovered between social meetings of friends and serious gambling; the war pushed many of them firmly into the latter category. They were joined by others which endeavoured to recreate Nice and Monte Carlo in wartime Kensington or Chelsea. One was conducted by a retired engineer in a flat at Prince of Wales Terrace. He employed a croupier and three waiters and when the police raided it in November 1941 they found twenty people seated round a roulette table with chips worth £1,160 stacked up before them. The engineer admitted that the place 'was run on the lines of a miniature casino' and said that he took the bank against the other players. His counsel pleaded in his defence that 'the party was attended by people who in normal and happier times would have gone abroad at this time of year to enjoy a little gambling at the casinos in the South of France'. The magistrate (Rentoul) said that 'this might be described as a reasonably respectable party. It is not one of the gambling hells run to lure young people and fleece them of their money. It seems to be admitted that those who took part were responsible people who knew what they were doing and were prepared to risk their money for the sake of the game. Doubtless in normal times they would have gone abroad . . . to indulge their gambling propensities without any infringement of the law.' He fined the engineer £100 (plus £20 costs), the croupier £10, and the waiters £5 each.[38]

On the other hand, when the police raided a gaming club in the Commercial Road in August 1940, 'there was a general grab for the money on the table': fifty-five men were playing faro. The place was not 'a gambling hell', it was 'rather well fitted and contained two billiard tables, a well stocked refreshment bar and a hairdressing saloon'. The club manager, however, had five previous convictions for gaming offences and this time he was jailed for six months; two others present were fined £50. One of these men, a gown manufacturer from Finchley, had been acting as croupier. The magistrate (Harris) said to him, 'I'm surprised at a man of your position coming down to spend your time in trying to rake more money out of your fellow men by gambling. [Your motive is] the accursed lust for gain which impels all these people.'[39]

This pattern of response harshened later in the war. In the first four months of 1944 four cases were reported in the *Hackney Gazette*. Altogether 113 people were present, and if names can be relied upon as an indication, two of the clubs catered for Jews, one for gentiles and one for a mixed clientèle. Significantly, shopkeepers and small businessmen predominated (nineteen of them) although there were also clerks (seven), labourers (five) and soldiers (three). In one instance, the police kept watch on the establishment on three days (including Christmas Day and Boxing Day) before carrying out a raid on New Year's Day.

The police presented a picture of these clubs catering for criminal and semi-criminal elements who had suspiciously large amounts of money to gamble. In one case the people attending were 'of low repute. A number of men with criminal records frequent this place purely and simply for gambling. It has a very undesirable effect on the neighbourhood, and has done so for a number of years.'[40] In another, the police found on the accused a total of £578 (though £382 of it belonged to a fishmonger). The police stated that they had been pursuing this particular gaming party for some weeks, but the organisers (who had 'very heavy financial backing') had moved the party from address to address.[41] In the third case, of thirty-eight people arrested, eleven were discovered to have police records, and they had a total of £1,538 on them. The magistrate, on being told this, exclaimed: 'Do you mean to say that in these days of national savings these men could find nothing better to do with their money than take it to this club?'[42] Pertinent to these remarks are those made by another magistrate (Blake Odgers) in the prosecution of a number of men who had been convicted of betting at a boxing match held in a Stoke Newington cinema. 'I think the wickedness of this sort of thing is that here we are in a war, and we have had to stick it for nearly six years. You, all of you, ought to know that every spare pound ought to go either to war savings or be put into the bank, and here you are going off with hundreds of pounds between you to a boxing match . . . and not only betting yourselves, but encouraging other people to bet. I cannot help noticing that nearly all the defendants took the oath in the Jewish fashion, and cannot help remembering what people of that race and creed have gone through during these years. I think it is disgusting that people of the same race and creed who have not had the bad time they have had should behave themselves in this way, instead of doing what they can to finish off the war.'[43]

A complex set of attitudes lay behind such comments. Firstly, it was not simply a case of 'one law for the rich, another for the poor'. Magistrates tended to distinguish among the rich themselves. Some East End gamblers were certainly rich but the money was 'new' and had often been made out of the economic circumstances created by the war. The 'established' rich were accustomed to 'high living' and knew how to cope in such situations (in theory), but the 'new' rich were not and did not (again, in theory). Hence the former were in effect excused whilst the latter were treated not to fines which they could easily afford, but to public arraignment and humiliation. In this respect the courts were performing a traditional function, providing 'the perfect stage for acting out society's ceremonies of status degradation'.[44]

Working-class clubs were also the object of a hostile campaign during the war. Partly this was because such activities as gaming posed a threat to the income and well-being of the working-class family, a point that was often emphasised during prosecutions ('there had been several complaints against the Club, to which [working] men had been lured and deprived of large sums of money', etc.).[45] But there was a second motive, arguably more important, that particularly affected working-class drinking clubs. This was the danger that they would interfere with the 'efficient prosecution of the war' by encouraging or permitting drunkenness among the working class. Regulation 44C was specifically designed to close such clubs. Chief constables were empowered to do this (or change the opening hours) if a club was visited by people engaged on work essential to the life of the community or if drunkenness at the club interfered with their ability to work. The police would decide what was meant by 'drunkenness', acting in concert presumably with the employer (who would naturally be engaged on tasks 'essential to the life of the community'). Correspondence relating to the closure of such clubs (and the police shut considerable numbers) cannot yet be examined but the *Police Review* drew clearly the implications of the regulation at the moment when it was introduced. 'No peacetime Government has been willing to tackle the question of amending the law relating to clubs. This reluctance is largely due to the strong feeling that manifestly exists in the minds of the supporters of working men's clubs that if club law is altered so as to give the police the right of entry and far greater powers of oversight, it is the working men's clubs, rather than those which cater to a higher social order, that would suffer interference. The working man will have none of it on those terms.'[46] The war, and Regulations 44C and 55C permitted precisely such interference, and so effectively that the Commissioner of the Metropolitan Police suggested that there was a 'strong case' for making them permanent.[47]

The war tended also to strengthen the position of the professional criminal, in the London underworld especially. The memoirs of policemen and criminals, newspaper and court reports collectively give a picture of the underworld flourishing as never before and of the police experiencing great difficulty in controlling it.

At the start of the war the emergency itself gave the police a bonus in that the Sabinis, as enemy aliens, were interned. That was the end of their period of ascendancy: they did not recover their hold after release (and Darby Sabini died in obscurity in Hove in 1950). Into the vacuum moved a number of would-be underworld monarchs, of whom Billy Hill and Jack Comer eventually emerged as the principal contenders.

Hill's vigorous account presents a picture of the underworld moving efficiently and thoroughly to the black market as soon as the war started. This seems questionable in view of the slowness with which professional thieves developed lorry and warehouse theft, but certainly, by the fourth year of the war, thieves, the black market and the underworld were flourishing together. 'All thieves were so prosperous', Hill writes, 'that they adopted a sort of competitive spirit to display their wealth by dressing up their wives and girl friends in as expensive jewellery and clothes as they could buy – from the black

market of course. By common consent, Monday was regarded
as truce day. It was the day after the week-end working . . .
usually we all had bombs to spend, and we congregated in a
club in Archer Street. What with all the villains in their
genuine Savile Row suits and their wives and girl friends
wearing straight furs and clothes by the best West End dress-
makers, that club looked like the Ascot of the Underworld.'[48]

Hill's power, it seems, derived from his skill at 'fixing', his
diplomatic tact in handling the various criminal gangs, his
willingness to be ruthless when threatened, and his insight
into the mentality of the police with regard to the underworld.
He traded on the belief held by some senior members of the
Metropolitan Police that a certain level of criminality was
inevitable, in which case it was advisable to deal with a known
quantity rather than an unknown one. To this end, Hill followed a policy of keeping violence to the minimum ('now,
whatever goes on in the underworld, the law will never stand
for people being wounded') and preventing gang wars. He
implies that channels of communication existed whereby the
police were able to indicate to him what was permissible and
what was not ('it was . . . made clear through the grapevine
that if the matter [a gang feud] was not settled soon, and
settled in a peaceable way, the law would get to work. Well, the
law could close down every speiler, almost every drinker in the
West End . . . I, the guv'nor, stood to lose most').[49]

Hill's income derived to a considerable extent from gaming
and other clubs. By 1943–4 he had developed techniques
designed to limit the penalties of the law when such places
were raided, while the underworld had acquired a 'police
force' of its own: professional criminals who were employed to
keep the others 'in line', to collect gambling debts, and such-
like.[50]

By the end of the war the authorities were confronted by
ever-rising levels of professional theft, lorry hi-jackings, and
warehouse raids, and they turned to the desperate expedient
of conducting night-time round-ups in central London in the
hope of catching criminals in possession of the tools of their
trade. Newspaper reports cannot conceal the failure of such
operations. The *Evening Standard* describes one in January
1946 in which the police closed all the Thames bridges from
Hammersmith to Blackfriars, together with the main roads to

the north-west and west. Some 300 police questioned persons moving in and out with the result that precisely fourteen arrests were made – for such offences as unlawful possession of petrol and unauthorised possession of an army vehicle. But the 'drive' had been intended to trap 'black market operators and car thieves'.[51]

Billy Hill comments on a similar round-up carried out in December 1945: 'They questioned every living soul they saw within the boundaries of Mayfair and Soho . . . they checked thousands upon thousands of service passes and identification cards. From eight o'clock at night they worked until the early hours. I think they might have tumbled about half a dozen deserters . . . Identity cards? They were as pieces of paper we could get any day we liked. Army passes? We could print them if you wanted them . . . which all goes to show how organised we were, and handicapped were the law in trying to fix us.'[52]

At the same time allegations were made that the police were taking 'short cuts' to try to overcome some of these handicaps. Protests that the evidence they offered in court was false were made from time to time, but there was a striking cluster of such incidents between 1945 and 1947. For instance:

February 1947:[53] Boxer and vinegar merchant accused of breaking into warehouse at Clapton Park and stealing cloth worth £2,400. When arrested one said, according to police, 'you seem to know all about it, but you can't prove anything' while the other added, 'all right. Nobody saw where we came from.' But in court both men claimed that the remarks attributed to them 'were not at all accurate'.

November 1947:[54] Seven men charged with breaking and entering at Hackney Wick and stealing £8,300 worth of consumer goods. When Inspector Glander gave evidence of a conversation with one of the men, he and a woman at the back of the court 'violently protested'. When Inspector quoted the man as saying 'he knew the "squeak" had gone in' and 'how many of us have you got?' the man shouted 'Lies! May I be struck down, I didn't say anything like it.'*

---

* These are condensed summaries of the newspaper reports.

Six further instances, all involving East End criminals, were reported during 1946–7. It may be that the newspapers were reporting such trials more fully at this time, in view of the public concern about the increase in large-scale thefts, but if the police had been 'embellishing' or fabricating evidence (and this has not been proved) it was in order to convict men they were convinced had committed crimes. As regards betting and gaming, however, there is evidence that misconduct went further, and one of the authorities for this view was Lord Trenchard. When he became Commissioner of the Metropolitan Police he found that the taking of bribes from bookmakers by police was the commonest form of 'graft'. He endeavoured to suppress it, compelling officers suspected of dishonesty to resign.[55] The difficulty lay in proving corruption when there were only two parties to the arrangement. When a bookmaker from Clapton was prosecuted in 1943, it was stated in court that he approached a police sergeant in a public house in Dalston and said, 'You know what we want. Tommy is taking them at Queensland Road and you can easily turn a blind eye' (the reference being to a man taking bets on a street bookmaking site). 'We can give you £2 a month until the flat racing season starts, and then increase it to £5.' The bookmaker added that if the sergeant 'wanted a job now and then' he would 'stick a man up for him' – presumably arrange for an associate to be arrested and prosecuted. The confident language the bookmaker was alleged to have used in making his approach is as interesting as his defence. He 'had been in the position of a man who acted as an informer for the police in relation to betting houses and things of that kind, and had been used by the police. Being a bookmaker himself he apparently thought that by offering a bribe he could avoid being brought in too often.'[56] But why should he draw that particular conclusion from having been an informer? One would have expected him to draw the opposite conclusion if all the police had been as honest as the sergeant in this case obviously was.

All the sergeant was required to do was 'turn a blind eye' (and for a monthly sum in the flat racing season nearly equal to a week's wage); whether there was more serious corruption can still not be known. However, during a case heard in August 1942 at North London Police Court some disturbing allegations were made against two CID men.

A 31-year-old commission agent and a 41-year-old engineer were prosecuted for being suspected persons loitering with intent to commit a felony. The CID men gave evidence that they saw them one morning at 10.15 'try the doors of a motor car and afterwards look into two motor cars'. They followed the men for the rest of the morning as they went to various car parks trying the handles of cars and vans. They were singularly unsuccessful: in nearly two hours (they were arrested at noon) they did not find a single vehicle to steal. The defendants denied these allegations and the commission agent claimed that on the morning in question he had been at his office carrying on his work as a bookmaker. There he had been seen by a GPO telephone engineer at the time when he was alleged to have been trying to steal a car, and this engineer came to court to confirm his claim.

The agent then told the court the following story: he had recently started a bookmaker's business which encroached on that of one already established. Three days before his arrest he was summoned to Upper Street police station and there 'warned not to open a bookmaker's business on the other man's territory . . . He was told that if he did so there would be trouble'. This suggestion that certain members of the CID not only 'licensed' bookmakers, but also assisted them in their business by driving away rivals (by prosecuting them on false charges) was not accepted by the magistrate, and the agent's previous convictions told heavily against him. He had once been arrested with the engineer, and had also in 1935 received a three-year sentence for car theft (of course, if one sought to bring a false charge against a man with a record, the case would look more convincing if it accorded with his previous convictions). Both men were jailed for a month.[57]

Yet the case is made interesting by the particular story the agent produced. Many untruthful tales offered in court were highly stereotyped, and the war added a number of appropriate variations. The commission agent's story had, if nothing else, the merit of originality, but there was perhaps more to it than that. 'Licensing' by some members of the CID of pornography dealers and drug pushers was to assume the proportions of a major scandal during the late 1960s, and in the early 1970s several senior policemen were jailed for precisely this kind of activity.[58] It is at least worthy of note that similar accusations concerning the betting industry and the CID had been made as early as the 1940s.

CHAPTER EIGHT

Prostitution *

In 1940 an anonymous autobiography was published with the title *Nell or I had no choice. The Diary of an 'Unfortunate'*. In it 'Nell' recounts her life in London, tells how she came to be a prostitute and explains why she has taken to print. She paints a vivid and gloomy picture of prostitution in London in the late 1930s. The path which led her to the streets started in childhood, in the home of her parents who lived in Notting Hill and took in paying guests. These were mainly men and Nell appears to have been the sort of child who much prefers adult male company to that of other children, whatever their sex: she makes no mention of playing or of friendships with her age-mates. By her thirteenth birthday she is 'very much in advance of [her] years and thoroughly at home in men's company'; she also knows the 'facts of life', having wheedled 'the most intimate details' from her mother's two maids.[1] By the time she reaches seventeen both her parents have died, leaving her a little money but not enough to live on. One of the paying guests, a doctor, takes an interest in the orphan and rapidly detects her disinclination to work for her living. He courts her, takes her out and wines and dines her, a courtship which reaches its culminating point when he slips a pill in her drink: 'I had strange dreams of being held in a vice and being powerless to struggle against some unseen force.'[2]

Nell and the doctor live together for a time but he soon tires of her and thereafter she is 'handed round' among a number of married men; without exception they let her down; she attempts to become 'moral' but finds the trials of a single girl in London, without relatives, friends, or references, too

*This chapter concentrates of female prostitution, and follows the *Chambers Dictionary* definition of a prostitute as one who hires out for 'indiscriminate sexual intercourse'.

much. She is reduced to working in a tea-shop: her legs swell up. She consults a doctor who tells her she must find easier work; shortly after that she makes a friend, Connie, who knows of precisely such a job. They prosper for a brief period but their looks quickly fade: Connie is thirty and Nell twenty-five. From then on the path goes relentlessly downwards. Connie becomes pregnant and needs an abortion, but customers are hard to find and money is short. 'We shall have to think about going to Ma Hackett.'[3]

Ma Hackett insists that the girls live in, makes them work six days out of the seven, and pays 2½ per cent which means they are lucky to receive 15s at the end of the week. Eventually Connie has a row with her and she throws them both out. There is now only the East End left. They struggle along for a while, but Connie becomes ill, cannot work, and at last kills herself by jumping in the river. Nell, meanwhile, has sunk to the lowest depth of all: she accepts a blind date and he turns out to be black. 'This monstrous creature, with his full thick lips, white flashing teeth, and horrible flat nose, seemed more like an animal than a man. Give my body to this nigger I couldn't.'[4] She flees in terror to the nearest pub.

In no time she is down and out, not yet thirty but looking fifty. Her story is almost over: by chance she encounters a benevolent upper-class lady who gives her shelter at her home in Devon. There is only time enough remaining to Nell for her to write her life story, as a lesson and warning to others, before she dies.

Perhaps the most striking fact about this 'autobiography' is that, although it may just possibly represent a plausible account of the life of a single individual, as an indication of what life was like on the eve of the war for the generality of prostitutes in London, it is almost wholly inaccurate. Yet it is one of only three or four books published in England at this time which purport to deal seriously with prostitution. The subject by and large was shunned, and academics felt obliged to apologise when they introduced it into works of scholarship.[5] The climate of the time opposed the publication of accounts which suggested that prostitution paid, yet the bulk of the police and court evidence suggests that in the late 1930s the earnings and living conditions of prostitutes were better than they had been at any time within living memory.

One policeman, Inspector Sharpe, who in the mid-1930s
was head of the Flying Squad, estimated that most London
prostitutes worked about four hours a day (or night), and
received fifteen to twenty visitors during that time. They
charged from 10s to £1 per client, which represented a weekly
income of from £80 to £100 at a time when many London
shopgirls were paid a weekly wage of about £2. Nor were these
prostitutes the 'elite' of the profession (call-girls with flats in
Mayfair, maids, and motor cars); they were ordinary London
streetwalkers and Sharpe once counted seventy-six of them
standing along a single stretch of roadway near Piccadilly.
Few, if any, arrived there as result of pills dropped in drinks
or of the machinations of 'an old woman with a hypodermic
needle'. And as for Ma Hackett's, most talk of white slavery
was 'rot'.[6] Although there must have been individual casualties, the life of the average prostitute was not short, isolated
and impoverished: indeed the reverse seems often to have
been the case. One observer noted that for some women
prostitution represented a way of rising in the world: 'If they
had gone straight they must have contented themselves with a
seventy-shillings-a-week husband and a semi-detached house
in the suburbs. They would have had to pinch for their cheap
finery, and within a few years a brood of squalling children
would have surrounded them. On the streets they make five
times what a husband could have brought them, and three-
quarters of their talk is of their money . . . You will hear
boasting of flats and ponces, too, and half the boasts are true.
There is a woman of thirty-odd whom I meet in Piccadilly
often who looks like a little servant girl. She has a pug-face and
wears the plainest taffeta frocks: before she went on the game
she was married to a fifty-shillings-a-week railwayman and
had five children. Now, she told me, she kept a five-pound-
a-week flat and a maid. I was sceptical at first, but I have been
there and it is not a lie. There is a tall, ungainly girl, nearly six
feet high, who plods down the pavement with a scrap of
mangy fur round her collar. "D'you know, dear," she says, "I
keep two places and two telephone numbers, one for lumber
[clients] and one to live in. I give my ponce twenty pounds a
week." '[7] Prostitutes who worried about the future and
the impact of ageing on their earning power need only
look around and observe the women of fifty, with legs 'like

Grecian columns' marching clients home, to be comforted.

Prostitutes lived irregular lives, but not isolated ones. A woman police officer commented: 'They are a friendly lot, ready to help one another, exchanging clothes with each other, and even loaning small sums to a rival down on her luck and out of business for the time being.'[8] The social framework that existed among them was likened by a researcher into the subject to 'trade union status' which they were prepared to enforce by 'threatening violence toward any woman who goes below the agreed minimum rate for their neighbourhood'. She adds: 'The basic unit is often the family, consisting of the prostitute, the ponce and his, her, or their children. Local, geographically cohesive groups may form in this society, but transcending them is the fact that the woman's status is now defined, she belongs to the group of prostitutes, and is able to talk about "us".'[9]

Prostitutes appear to have divided into three main groups in England in the late 1930s:* those who did not solicit in the streets, but relied upon introductions and arrangements by telephone to obtain clients; those who did solicit outside but took clients either to their own flats or to houses of assignation; and those who both solicited and had sexual intercourse outside. As they grew older prostitutes tended to move from the first group to the second, though the situation was always changing.

A period of illness in particular could oblige a woman who was accustomed to receive all her clients as a result of appointments to go out and hunt for them in the streets. Once she had built up a regular clientèle she would cut down street walking and perhaps give it up altogether.

The first group is the hardest to find information about: as such women did not streetwalk they did not often attract the attention of the police. It is nonetheless plain from a number of court cases in the late 1930s that the call-girl business was a thriving one. Houses and flats in the fashionable districts of

---

* Most of the information in this chapter refers to London, partly because this was the country's major centre for prostitution, but also because reliable information for the provinces is difficult to unearth. The local press, except in London and to a lesser extent Brighton, Rochester and Bath, shunned the subject. There does not, however, appear to be any reason to believe that provincial prostitution differed to any great extent in style (though it certainly differed in scale) from that in London.

west, central and north London were luxuriously furnished for clients who sought discretion and comfort and were prepared to pay for them.

A dress designer rented an expensive apartment near Grosvenor Square: men would phone her there and ask her to find them a girl. This she would do by ringing up one of her contacts, then both man and woman would meet at her flat. The police noted that the women 'were of smart appearance and young', the men 'very much older and seemed to be of some position'. The extent of the clientèle is suggested by the names, addresses and telephone numbers of 52 women which the dress designer kept in a book – which also contained similar information on 154 men.[10] The organisers of such establishments were usually prepared to cater for a variety of sexual tastes: a raid on an 'elaborately furnished flat' near the BBC in Langham Place revealed, besides the usual packed address book, pornography and 'three flagellation canes, one of which had tin tacks secured in the end, a birch and two whips'.[11] Businesses of this kind, conducted in semi-private, must have been very difficult to detect: the police relied on information from neighbours or from the underworld before they could move in to break them up. It seems unlikely that a large proportion ran foul of the law before the war started.

Most prostitutes solicited in the streets. For clients who could afford it several expensive establishments were available, usually private hotels. London had a number of these in the late 1930s; Brighton had at least two, and there were probably others in the larger provincial cities. Some of these hotels were very comfortable indeed. At one in the Marylebone Road, rooms at 'the front of the premises were luxuriously furnished, and the back rooms were furnished in good taste'. The police noted that the hotel was 'kept scrupulously clean, and an unusually large quantity of bed linen was ... used to ensure this cleanliness'. The hotel functioned solely as a brothel:* genuine travellers with luggage were turned away. The only food in the place at the time of the raid

---

* The mid-Victorian type of brothel, where prostitutes were available on the premises for inspection by visiting clients, seems largely to have ceased to exist by our period, despite Ma Hackett's. As far as the law was concerned, any house or flat to which two or more prostitutes took clients was a brothel, the term being applied interchangeably with 'premises used for the purpose of habitual prostitution'.

was a dozen eggs and half a pound of butter. The staff of three (manager aged sixty-three and two maids in their twenties) catered for prostitutes paying short visits with clients: the police counted twenty-six different women calling at the house during the period of observation.[12]

Most clients could not afford the fees charged in establishments like these but a great many cheaper facilities were available, divided into several types. Firstly there were apartment houses, split into separate flats, each of which was let to a prostitute. Some lived there, others merely used the place for 'business'. Certain streets in London contained a number of these houses – Upper Berkeley Street, for instance, 'in a good residential part of the West End' and conveniently near to Marble Arch. One house, in 1939, contained fifteen separate flatlets managed by a steward and stewardess. The weekly takings *according to the books* were, at £22, only half those at the hotel in the Marylebone Road, even though 14 prostitutes took 103 men there during the five days of police observation.[13] The rents of flatlets appear to have been low in the late 1930s, even to prostitutes, and the owner of this house was obliged to go recruiting among them in order to obtain tenants. He would approach girls in the street, ask them if they were comfortable where they were and tell them he had a place where they could stay without questions being asked.

Other prostitutes preferred to take self-contained flats, sometimes sharing with a friend, partly to save on rent and partly as a form of protection in the event of a difficult or dangerous client. Often unwittingly the tenant ran the risk of prosecution for brothel-keeping. One case, also from 1939, involved a 26-year-old waitress who rented a 'comparatively small' flat which she kept 'in a fair state of cleanliness' in Baker Street. She paid what was then the 'very substantial' rent of £3 15s for it and shared in order to halve the cost.

The magistrate warned the waitress that if she 'chose to pursue that form of life' she must take care not to break the law, that is, share with another prostitute.[14] This friendly, even cosy relationship was the wonder of foreign visitors to London's police courts. The American broadcaster and critic, Alexander Woollcott, was asked on a visit to Bow Street what struck him there as being most different from the US courts and he answered: 'The old-world courtesy with which your

magistrates treat your whores.'[15] This aspect of court life was
to change as wartime conditions caused London prostitutes to
increase in number and gain in confidence and as patronising
them ceased to be a luxury only the better off could afford
and became, with the rise in real wages, a possibility for an
ever larger proportion of the male population.

A third type of indoor accommodation was provided by
shopkeepers, caretakers or private householders who would
make available to several prostitutes one or more rooms which
the women could use when they found a client. There were
numerous such premises throughout London and a large
number in Brighton and Bath: many were near railway stations, barracks and tourist attractions. On busy days the prostitutes often arrived to find the room occupied and police
observers then noted them walking their clients round the
block till it became available. Such places had the advantage
that there were usually other people in the house which provided a form of protection for the prostitute, but there was
little incentive for the owner to keep the place clean. If they
found dirt or vermin present the police usually brought evidence of it to court to strengthen their case; where fairly
large-scale prostitution was involved (in hotels and apartment
houses) the owners usually ensured cleanliness, but lower
down the scale keeping the rooms clean was seen as an added
expense.

One such establishment was run by a 47-year-old general
dealer who let rooms in his house in the Hampstead Road to
four prostitutes. He was, however, unusual in the preparations he made against the event of a police raid. He resorted to
the 'revolting device of getting a small boy to admit the
couples' while he and his wife kept in the background. For a
time this procedure worked and the police found it 'extremely
hard . . . to get the evidence they required'. When eventually
they did decide to launch a raid 'the two boys escaped by going
into the garden and over the wall at the back' while the general
dealer tried to warn his visitors what was happening by shouting 'Police! Police!' It did him no good: he was taken to court
and sentenced to six weeks hard labour. Two other features of
this case were unusual. Firstly the dealer had a record (of eight
previous convictions, mainly for larceny). Only a minority of
people prosecuted for brothel-keeping had made previous

appearances in court, and when they had it was generally for a prostitution offence. Secondly, he knew he was breaking the law.[16] It is clear from their reactions when police read out warrants to them that many of the persons questioned had only the haziest idea of the law. This was particularly true of prostitutes prosecuted for sharing a flat with another, thereby keeping a brothel. Their response is typified by the French Canadian who exclaimed 'Can't you do that in this country?' when the police raided his house.[17]

The third group of prostitutes did not have a place to take clients to: they solicited and had sexual intercourse in the open air. Many were either very young or ageing women, at the beginning or the end of their careers. George Orwell noted that the Trafalgar Square prostitutes sold their favours for sixpence a time, although towards morning they were reduced to accepting a cup of tea or a cigarette.[18] It would be a mistake, however, to imagine that all women, or even a majority, who worked outside were down-and-outs. Many prostitutes who temporarily lacked a room would turn to the parks; others actually preferred to work there. They saved on rent and had a good excuse not to concede some of the demands of clients – for instance that they should undress. In London the parks – and particularly Hyde Park – were major centres for prostitution, for women regularly solicited at Marble Arch and along the Bayswater Road. Not surprisingly, police activity in the parks was usually intense, although there were lulls. One of these, in the early 1930s, followed a series of scandals (the most notorious of them being the Savidge case) which brought the police a very bad press. The number of prosecutions fell dramatically for a time[19] but by the late 1930s the police were once again paying serious attention to the parks. However, the outbreak of war and the introduction of the blackout in a sense turned all London into a massive Hyde Park. There had been over 3,000 arrests for prostitution in the Metropolitan Police District in 1938; in 1939 there were only 1,865, and in 1940, 1,505.[20]

Prostitution, already thriving, was entering what prostitutes later recalled as the 'years of plenty'.[21] The war changed the pattern of English prostitution in three ways. It transformed it economically. Demand outran supply and prices rose accordingly while the time the prostitute spent with each client was reduced. Secondly there was a marked deterioration in the cleanliness of brothels. Thirdly, after the initial lull, the authorities mounted a fierce campaign designed to make it as difficult as possible for prostitutes to carry on their trade. All three reached points of peak development in 1943–5 but the ground was prepared during the three previous years. The war required huge armies; it caused substantial population movements, both planned (the evacuation) and unplanned (the blitz); it created a generalised state of anxiety and deep fear of the future; and it established, particularly in London, a shifting cosmopolitan population of refugees, deserters, and, most important of all, foreign military. The arrival of the Canadian and, later, US armies coincided with and contributed to a radical alteration in sexual attitudes. This process was one that the authorities viewed with growing concern.

Prices rose almost from the outset. To some extent this was part of the general inflationary spiral that the war sparked off. Rents fluctuated: between the declaration of war and the onset of the blitz, the exodus from London and particularly from the West End opened up to prostitutes many 'respectable' apartment houses that had previously excluded them. The 'appalling slump in flat letting'[22] explained why some prostitutes were paying as little as 10s a week for the loan of a room, but this situation changed once the bombing got under way. By the end of 1941, prostitutes were paying 30s a week for rooms in Marylebone while men visitors to a hotel near St Pancras were charged sums between 10s and 13s by the night porter.[23] Some brothel-keepers had started to impose a levy on women according to the number of clients they had. Although in 1941 this poll tax was still small (2s 6d per head) it was later to grow considerably.[24]

In 1942 rents rose further. A brothel over an empty shop in the Edgware Road commanded from 30s to £2 a week each from the four women who made use of it, even though the place was in 'filthy condition';[25] whilst the twelve rooms of a house in Upper Berkeley Street were let at rents from 25s to £2 15s.[26] These rents were presumably quoted from rent books when they were detailed in court; increasingly prostitutes paid a supplement in cash. The 'real' rents of accommodation to prostitutes will thus probably never be known accurately. These increasing costs were passed on to customers, though the 'short time' does not yet seem to have become the rule. Police observers at a *maison de passe* which they raided in 1943 noted that some couples 'stayed for short periods and some for the night'. This case provides an indication of how much money proprietors were making at this stage of the war: annual takings amounted to about £3,800.[27] The American invasion of southern England assisted the process: in thirty of the forty-seven couples observed in this case the man was a US soldier, some of them accompanied by 'very young women'.

Many had been picked up in the sleazy clubs that throve in wartime. Although extraordinary measures were taken by the authorities to suppress such places, many nonetheless managed to maintain a fly-by-night existence for a few weeks or months. Some were night-clubs-cum-brothels. One, near Coram's Fields, was a hotel with a club in the basement. Prostitutes solicited in the club and took men up to the hotel. The police were presumably expecting a big haul when they raided the place but they chose the wrong time: only two of the fourteen bedrooms were occupied, one by an elderly man on his own, the other by one of the club's barmaids. However, as two couples arrived while the police were still in the building they managed to secure a conviction against the proprietress.[28] Likewise a club near Paddington Station was visited by merchant seamen, British and Canadian soldiers, and 'loose women'. Police officers, keeping watch in plain clothes, observed 'acts of indecency' and were themselves solicited.[29] Such cases attracted considerable press interest, a sign that editors were seeking to draw their readers' attention to the moral condition of the capital. Court officials did not miss the point: one magistrate remarked on the 'public outcry that magistrates were not dealing severely enough with these cases'.[30] It was a deficiency that was soon to be remedied.

During 1943 the American invasion bid up the tariffs charged by prostitutes as well as those for most other services. Prosecutions in 1943–4 provide numerous instances where £3 and £4 had been paid;[31] by May 1945 US soldiers were being charged £5 for a 'short time'.[32] Since British soldiers could not match rates like these there may have been a differential tariff, although no documented references to one have been found. The high pay of the US military was well known, indeed notorious: US Army sergeants, for instance, received approximately four times the pay of their British equivalents.

Rising prices did not restrict 'turnover'; indeed, quite the reverse. As the Allied armies gathered in southern England in preparation for the invasion of France, the military visited prostitutes in droves. Police observers outside the brothels painstakingly conducted head counts: 33 US or Canadian soldiers in one case (one of them accompanied by a girl of fifteen),[33] 42 in another, 35 in a third, and 29 in the fourth.

The record appears to have been held by a disorderly house in Brighton to which 14 girls (one of them aged fourteen) brought 154 servicemen.[34] One madam pleaded the war in her defence. 'The boys belong to a bomber crew,' she declared to the police. 'They might all be killed tomorrow. Surely you don't mind them having a good time with the girls?'[35]

What this meant for the individual prostitute is suggested in a memoir by one of them, Marthe Watts, although accounts by prostitutes tend to be unreliable (though perhaps not more so than the recollections of others concerned with crime, whether gangsters, lawyers or policemen). Marthe Watts, a Frenchwoman, had drifted into prostitution while a teenager in Paris and had pursued her profession in several of the large cities of southern Europe and northern Africa. Her autobiography is refreshingly free of the self-pity and moralising which often mars accounts by English prostitutes. She regarded prostitution as her calling and felt no shame about it – at least before she moved to England. She arrived shortly before the war broke out, having made an arranged marriage with an elderly Englishman called Watts in order to obtain a British passport. Eventually she became involved with one of the Messina brothers (Gino), which is presumably why her account attracted the interest of a publisher.

At the time of publication (*c*. 1960) the Messinas were the most notorious and unpopular criminals in Britain (at least as far as the press was concerned). Marthe Watts portrays Gino as a brutal, jealous, greedy pervert but fails to provide a convincing explanation as to why she continued working for him even after he had been sent to prison (for twenty-six months) and was 'looking forward to a great celebration when he came out'. Indeed, during those twenty-six months, she claims she earned £22,000 (this was in 1947): 'I was very pleased with myself when I told him that.'[36]

The section dealing with the Messinas is indeed the least satisfactory part of the book, and nowhere more so than in her discussion of the origins of what she calls 'the ten minute rule'. This, she alleges, Gino introduced because he was afraid that if men spent more time with his girls they would demonstrate greater sexual prowess than he and would take the girls from him.[37] But prostitutes throughout London were introducing ten- or fifteen-minute rules at this time for the precise reason that Marthe Watts herself notes – the 'vast seller's market in the commodity we had to offer'.[38] They sought to get rid of each client as quickly as possible. Every minute spent off the street meant that customers were lost. Marthe Watts's most heroic effort was, appropriately enough, on VE Day, when she succeeded in taking home forty-nine clients, working through the night until six o'clock the following morning.[39]

It is not surprising that she made over 400 appearances at Bow Street during her career as a West End prostitute. Nor was her large number of arrests unusual: one survey in the late 1940s revealed that one London prostitute in seven had between sixty and a hundred convictions.[40] In order to hurry their clients along many made their rooms as bleak and comfortless as possible: one American, when he saw Marthe Watts's hard wooden bed, exclaimed, 'Huh, a workbench!'[41] 'Speed up' had finally arrived in the oldest profession.

The 'all-night' arrangement also ceased to be a feature of wartime prostitution: men could no longer afford to pay for it.[42] Consequently, even the most ramshackle outfits – like the disused shop and attic near Euston managed by a 'coloured barber' called Charlie – produced (by the standards of the time) small fortunes. Charlie attempted to protect himself against prosecution by training his male visitors (usually black US soldiers) in a question and answer routine:

Charlie: 'You have all come to see me?'

The soldiers (in chorus): 'We have come to see Charlie!'

The implication was that they had not come to see Charlie's girl friends. The police duly recounted this to the amusement of the court, yet they also produced Charlie's post-office savings book into which, in two months, £250 had been paid. His rent for those two months was £24.[43] Similarly, a house in Upper Berkeley Street made £2,600 in 1944 (annual rent £250); one near Oxford Street made £4,000; whilst 1945 produced five cases where the annual income exceeded £3,000. The takings at a house in Argyle Street were in excess of £7,500 while another in NW1 earned a clear profit (after rent and rates had been deducted) of over £13,000.[44]

Easy money drew more and more women on to the streets. It is impossible to estimate how many: the absolute minimum is the number 'known to the police' but what that number amounted to does not appear to have been published. A second method of estimating is to base it on the number of women arrested, the way chosen by *The New Survey of London Life and Labour*. This suggested that the proportion of the whole number of prostitutes who came before the courts was approximately one-fifth.[45] This gives a figure of 3,000 for the number of prostitutes in London in 1931, based on the total of 600 women arrested during that year. Provided that the ratio of 1:5 remained constant, it seems there must have been about 6,700 prostitutes in 1946, based on the 1,342 arrested. The number of prostitutes in London had thus more than doubled in fifteen years.

Among these new recruits were a number of very young girls – fourteen- and fifteen-year-olds. The police drew attention to such instances when cases came to court. Girls running away from home, and others whose homes had been broken up by the war, either because of evacuation or bombing, were drifting on to the streets. Other recruits included the wives of men in the forces who in peacetime would perhaps not have become involved in prostitution. One was the wife of an army sergeant: when the police raided her house they found it full of prostitutes and soldiers.[46] Many such cases might well have escaped the attention of the police but for some unusual occurrence. For instance, a sergeant in the Royal Engineers unexpectedly turned up at his house in Camden Town in December 1944. He 'opened the door with his key . . . in the front room he saw two negro soldiers in bed with two women. In the Morrison shelter in that room were five of his six children.' His wife was in another room, the door locked. The sergeant eventually compelled her to open it and she 'appeared . . . in her pyjamas. In bed in the room was a coloured soldier.' The sergeant was granted a separation order; the children were taken into custody by the LCC; their mother was sentenced to two months hard labour.[47]

By the end of the war space on the pavements in areas of London frequented by prostitutes was running out, so much so that interlopers ran the risk of violence from women already there. A newcomer was obliged therefore to go to an area where pavements were less thoroughly covered (but which were presumably less profitable because men preferred to hunt in districts which had 'a reputation') or she relied on her pimp (if she had one) to clear out an established prostitute.[48] This could be a risky procedure because the injured party might try to obtain revenge by informing on the man, with the result that he might be prosecuted for living on immoral earnings. Alternatively she could buy a beat from a prostitute who was retiring. In the mid-1940s the buyer paid the seller a percentage of her earnings for an agreed number of months, while the seller undertook to ensure that there was no trouble from girls with neighbouring or overlapping beats.[49] Another solution was to buy a motor car and cruise for clients, but during the war this was not a possibility.

Taxation and conscription also presented prostitutes with problems. By 1941 conscription* had become almost unavoidable unless a woman had a young family, but prostitutes found they could usually discourage the relevant department by writing 'prostitute' in the occupation panel of the preliminary call-up papers: the authorities did not want them mixing (and recruiting?) in the ranks.[50] A similar declaration generally silenced the taxman, who was apparently reluctant to make demands on the earnings of vice.[51]

The final two years of the war thus saw a 'boom' in prostitution which persuaded the authorities to take drastic action to suppress it. However, the relationship between the police and prostitutes during the 1930s and 1940s was somewhat ambiguous. Robert Fabian gives the policeman's view:

'One night you would walk down Frith Street, say, and everything would be exactly as it was the night before. Tomorrow there would be a new face on the corner . . . You would stop and say, "We haven't met, have we?" and before

---

* The conscription of women was announced in December 1941; unmarried women between the ages of twenty and thirty were called up. By 1943, Angus Calder states (*The People's War*, p. 383), 'it was almost impossible for a woman under forty to avoid war work unless she had heavy family responsibilities or was looking after a war worker billeted on her'.

she could reply, out of the adjacent shadows would glide her protector, who would naturally be standing near to look after her on her first few nights. "G'evening, Guv'nor," he would say, amiably if a bit apprehensively, "this is Ursula – she's a Polack. Ursula, this is Mr Fabian, Chief of the Manor – you don't give him any nonsense, and he'll treat you fair".[52]

Prostitutes saw the relationship in a rather different light: 'I had reached the top of the street when a constable who had been pursuing me with giant strides snapped his fingers. "Hey, I want you," he said. I said: "I haven't solicited anyone." "They all say that." "I'm not all the women in London. I thought you were supposed to warn us first." He made no reply. He simply said: "Come along." '

At the police station another constable spoke to her. ' "Don't get distressed. You all have to take your turn." ' The police used to arrest prostitutes on a rota basis ('You're coming in now, and we're taking Anna tomorrow and Betty on Sunday and Jane on Monday.') Prostitute folklore held that it was 'asking for trouble' not to plead guilty to a charge of soliciting – the police 'would mark you down otherwise'.[53] Prostitutes tended, in effect, to regard fines as the method the authorities chose for taxing their earnings.

Police would sometimes take unorthodox action when dealing with brothel-keepers who permitted or encouraged prostitutes to rob their clients, as Superintendent Arthur Thorp describes. He would take the victim of such a theft to the house where it had occurred 'ostensibly . . . for identification purposes'; once there he hinted 'in a veiled roundabout way' that the victim might like to 'work over the place. Then, while we weren't looking, he would put his boot through the washbasin, tear down the electric light fittings, etc. It didn't take the real owners long to realise that at this rate crime didn't pay.'[54]

Obviously, the police did not prosecute in every case of soliciting, brothel-keeping or living off immoral earnings that they discovered. They used considerable discretion. They would also know, if it should be decided to 'clean up' London, where to go and whom to arrest. That a deliberate decision to shut down brothels and houses of accommodation was taken, probably in 1942, seems clear from the following table:

Number of persons dealt with summarily by magistrates courts for brothel-keeping in England and Wales[55]

Average of 1935–9	1940	1941	1942	1943	1944	1945	1946
198	142	258	343	624	944	843	250

The rise in the number of prosecutions between 1940 and 1944 may be striking, but the table measures increased police activity rather than a dramatic change in the number of such houses. The campaign bore down heavily in London, but statistics of summary prosecutions were not published for the Metropolitan Police District during the later stages of the war. Figures do exist, however, for England's second city, and these show both the small scale of brothel-keeping in Birmingham and the wartime rise in prosecutions. The peak year there also was 1944.

Number of persons proceeded against for brothel-keeping in Birmingham[56]

Average of 1935–8	1939	1940	1941	1942	1943	1944	1945	1946
3·7	16	5	14	NA	17	40	NA	13

NA = not available

By 1944 police resources were coming under considerable strain from a combination of growing crime and the sudden worsening of the bombing caused by the V.1. Both developments had most impact on the capital. Police chiefs responded to concern about the deterioration by pleading shortage of resources, so the decision to divert so many of them (and gathering evidence in brothel-keeping cases was a time-consuming process) seems surprising.

That a deliberate decision to 'clean up' the brothels had been taken seems clear: the question is, by whom?

During 1944 London magistrates as a group certainly became more hostile to people accused of offences involving prostitutes and, further, there was a marked trend to harsher sentences. This may indicate that the word had gone out that a tough line should be taken in such cases, but the procession of brothel-keepers through the courts – one magistrate in June 1944 complained that such cases were coming to his court at a rate of one a week, an unprecedented number[57] – created a momentum of its own and magistrates were responding by making examples. One commented on the 'public outcry' that brothel-keeping cases were not being dealt with 'severely enough', while another declared that 'this . . . sort of place brings London into disrepute, and the sooner such places are stamped out the better'.[58] A third put the blame firmly on the prostitutes, not the clients: 'Girls like you are a very great menace to many otherwise excellent young men who are serving their country.'[59] Consistent with such remarks were the sentences meted out: in the districts of north London covered by the *Paddington News*, the greater use of the prison sentence by magistrates in 1944–5 is marked:

Sentences imposed in brothel-keeping cases

	Number of cases	Fines of £10 and under	Fines of between £11 and £50	Fines of between £51 and £100	Prison
1939–41	6	3	3	0	0
1942–3	10	2	7	1	0
1944	7	0	2	0	5
1945	20	1	7	4	8

Although in examining individual cases it is sometimes difficult to establish why one defendant was sent to prison and another fined, when the circumstances of the two cases appear very similar, certain trends do emerge. Firstly, if the house was very profitable, either prison or the maximum fine was imposed. There are six such cases and three defendants were imprisoned and the other three fined. One magistrate, when sending the defendant to jail, commented that the week's takings of his house amounted to more than the maximum fine of £100.[60] Secondly, if children lived in the brothel, the defendants were invariably imprisoned. Thirdly, in all three cases where the defendant was black (two in 1944 and one in 1945) he was jailed. Previous convictions, however, did not necessarily mean that prison would be the sentence for a second or even a third offence. Courts were aware that the person standing in the dock was often no more than an employee of the owner and, although magistrates made strong threats about the action they would take if the 'real culprit' was brought before them, very few were ever prosecuted.

With small fortunes being made out of prostitution it is not surprising that professional criminals and racketeers should become involved. By contemporary American standards such men were small fry, but 'big' money meant, for instance, the danger of corruption, especially among the poorly paid and overworked police force. A journalist who worked on the Messina case in the late 1940s alleges that it was precisely this factor – bribery of policemen – that the Messinas employed successfully to ensure they were not prosecuted. It required the press furore about their activities to force the authorities to take action against them.[61]

The police certainly knew how these *souteneurs* operated. They relied on a clause in the relevant act on brothel-keeping which includes the word 'knowingly' – premises were 'knowingly' used as a brothel – so they made sure they did not know. They established a chain of middlemen between themselves and the women – usually at least two: the manager of the 'house', who would agree to take the consequences if anything went wrong (he would be amply rewarded), and an estate agent, generally either an employee or a confederate. If the police started to make inquiries the landlord replied that letting was in the hands of the estate agent and he had no idea who the tenants were. The estate agent's books (or the manager's) would show carefully doctored rents, as would the rent books of the prostitutes: the actual rent was paid in cash. In an emergency – if the police did appear to have a case – the landlord promptly evicted the girls, declaring that he had discovered (to his horror) how the premises were being used. He had taken immediate action to clear up the scandal himself.

In 1945 the owner of thirty-five apartment houses in various parts of London was prosecuted, though the charges he faced related to only one of them, a house in Kentish Town. He was found guilty, principally on the evidence of one of his tenants, a prostitute with the alliterative name of Christine Christie. Her evidence described how the landlord 'let the rooms to me. He said if I wasn't a prostitute he would not let the rooms to me. I said I was one. He said if I did not continue taking men to the premises I would have to stop living there. I paid the rent every Monday and it was part of the agreement that I gave him an extra pound for every man I took there. He used to come to the premises every day to collect the extra pound and I had a man there every night.'[62] Not surprisingly, after this evidence of exploitation, the landlord was sentenced to three months hard labour. However, on reflection, Christie's evidence seems questionable. Would the owner of thirty-five apartment houses go in person *every day* to collect money from a prostitute? Further, if as seems to have been the case he lived elsewhere, how did he know how many men she took to the house? Did he rely on her telling him the truth? Christie alleged that he had the same kind of relationship with other girls in the house but none of them came forward to support her. Perhaps the police had good reason to believe that the landlord was a brothel-keeper on some scale but lacked the evidence to prove it. Prostitutes are notoriously vulnerable to police pressure.[63]

In a number of other cases the decision to prosecute seems surprising. These involved two prostitutes sharing a room or apartment: the woman whose name was on the rent book had broken the law and such cases were taken to court often. For instance, of thirteen brothel-keeping cases reported in the *St Marylebone Record* in 1944, six were of this type. Yet, to bring those six cases to court, the police had to spend approximately 180 hours gathering evidence.* It is cases such as these that give the clampdown on brothel-keeping the air of a morality campaign:

1   15 January, 1944. Prostitute aged 23 fined £25 for brothel-keeping. Police observation from 27th to 31st December. Accused took 7 US soldiers to premises and another prostitute took 8.
2   11 March, 1944. Prostitute aged 24 fined £25 for permitting her flat to be used as a brothel. Four days police observation during which accused and one other prostitute took 9 US soldiers home.
3   3 June, 1944. Prostitute aged 37 fined £40 for knowingly allowing premises to be used for the purpose of habitual

* Calculated on the basis of one of the cases in which police kept observation for 35 hours over four days.

prostitution. During three nights police observation she and one other prostitute took 14 men to the flat.*

They also provide a clue as to police policy. Montgomery Hyde has described the process with reference to police campaigns against homosexuals: 'Promotion in the junior ranks of the force has always depended to a considerable extent upon the number of convictions a particular officer has been able to secure, and when the news filters down to the lower ranks that the authorities are interested in a particular type of offender the inference is obvious, especially as in this instance it was easier and, incidentally, safer and less troublesome for a police officer to catch a homosexual [or a prostitute] than a burglar.'[64] Hence all those hours spent by policemen hanging around prostitutes' flats counting male heads, during the summer and autumn of 1944 when thousands of their contemporaries were risking their lives in the invasion of Europe.

One side-effect of this campaign was a pronounced deterioration in the quality and cleanliness of accommodation used by prostitutes. In the cases reported in the *Paddington News* between 1939 and 1941, police rarely mentioned that the premises were dirty; a typical comment was that the place was kept in a 'fair state of cleanliness'.[65] However, when the decision was taken to shut down the brothels, the first targets were those known to the police (unless they had, as Duncan Webb alleges,[66] arranged for police 'protection' against prosecution). As clean premises were shut down, others less clean replaced them. Action by the police seems to have been more effective in this respect than that by the enemy. In one house the bedding consisted of mattresses, dirty and rotting, supported on boxes;[67] in another the prostitute herself claimed the 'dirty and verminous' condition in her own defence. People, she stated, would refuse to use such disgusting rooms, so how could they be a brothel?[68] Indeed, with a campaign against brothel-keeping in progress, there was no incentive to keep premises clean. This deterioration could hardly have failed to be a factor contributing to the wartime epidemic in sexually transmitted diseases.

* Condensed summaries of newspaper reports.

Prosecutions for brothel-keeping fell sharply from their wartime peak in 1944 and 1945. It seems that the campaign had succeeded in its object and that the bulk of brothels had been closed, because the campaign against prostitution now shifted its focus to prostitutes soliciting in the streets.

Number of arrests for soliciting in the Metropolitan Police District[69]

1938	1943	1944	1945	1946	1947	1948
3,062	2,279	1,526	1,983	4,289	4,784	5,363

The number of arrests in London thus doubled from 1945 to 1946. In part this must have been a function of the ending of the blackout – prostitutes were once again exposed to street lighting, which also revealed all too plainly that prostitution had become much more prevalent during the war. There were more women on the streets and they were more confident and aggressive in their approaches to men. But there was an additional development which alarmed the authorities: the range of men who were able to afford the services of prostitutes had become much greater. The war had witnessed a rise in demand that proved to be permanent, and the supply of women had grown to meet it. A similar phenomenon had occurred after the First World War, but the rapid fall in wages after 1920 and the rise in unemployment had cut this development short. But real wages did not fall after the Second World War. Men who in the late 1930s could not afford to pay the 10s or £1 that prostitutes charged (average wages then being approximately from £3 to £3 10s) were now able to do so. At the same time the departure of the US soldiery caused a fall in prices. Furthermore, wartime military service proved to be a great disseminator of information on this as on many other topics: men knew where to go to find what they wanted. The problem proved to be particularly intractable: if prostitutes could earn the fines they had to pay when they were taken to court from a single customer, how could their street activities be controlled? Only, it emerged in the late 1950s, by driving them off the streets altogether.

CHAPTER NINE

Violence

In Graham Greene's novel *The Ministry of Fear*, published in 1943 but set during the blitz, the principal character, Arthur Rowe, looks in a newspaper for reports of a murder he believes he has witnessed. He does not find them. 'Not even in the smallest type under a single headline was there any reference.' He tries to explain this astonishing omission by referring to the pressures of the war itself. 'Nobody troubled about single deaths . . . in the middle of a daily massacre. Perhaps a few elderly men in the C.I.D., who were too old to realise how the world had passed them by, were still allowed by patient and kindly superiors to busy themselves in little rooms with the trivialities of a murder . . . "Old So-and-so," he could imagine a senior officer saying, "poor old thing, we let him have a few murder cases now and then. In his day, you know, we used to pay quite a lot of attention to murder, and it makes him feel that he's still of use. The results – oh, well, of course, he never dreams that we haven't time to read his reports." '[1]

The murder Rowe believes he has seen is not reported because it has not in fact occurred, but the view that the police were grossly overstretched during the war and could not maintain their peacetime standards was frequently offered as an explanation of their failure to limit the rise in crime – though not, it must be stressed, to excuse defeat in clearing up incidents as serious as murder.

Murder statistics assume particular importance because they tend to be the ones most closely scrutinised by advocates of 'law and order' for evidence that serious crime is growing and that drastic action is required to stop it. For the wartime period, the murder statistics present in fact a comforting picture: there were only six more murders in 1945 than there had been in 1939:

Number of murders known to the police of persons aged one and over in England and Wales[2]

1939	1940	1941	1942	1943	1944	1945
135	115	135	159	120	95	141

The 'tougher punishment' lobby was not put out of countenance by this stable pattern, and in fact it does give a mislead-
ing impression of the general wartime trend in serious crimes
of violence. For example, a domestic brawl in which a husband
hits his wife with a hammer could be classified under one of
several headings. If it could be proved that he said before he
hit her 'I am going to kill you', the offence might be recorded
as an attempted murder; if he said nothing or his words were
not heard then it would probably not be defined in this way. If
he fractured her skull, the attack might be 'a felonious wounding', whereas if he merely knocked her out he might find
himself in court on a charge of indictable assault. If she
dodged the hammer altogether, then the attack could well be
treated as a non-indictable assault.[3]

If we take the wartime figures for two of the more serious
crimes of violence – felonious wounding (which included
most acts that endangered life, especially shooting and
wounding with grievous bodily harm) and malicious wounding (inflicting grievous bodily harm without intending to do
so) – they show the following trends:

Number of crimes known to the police (England and Wales)[4]

	Annual average 1935–9	1940	1941	1942	1943	1944	1945
Felonious	286	237	272	279	329	403	545
Malicious	1,639	1,539	1,638	1,718	1,950	2,332	2,737

Thus the number of felonious woundings nearly doubled
during the war (much of the rise being concentrated in the last
two years) and, whilst the increase in malicious woundings was
not so sharp, once again the period 1943–5 showed the most
worrying changes. With serious crimes of violence it is almost
certain that the statistics did demonstrate broadly what was
happening: it is unlikely that many violent assaults went
unreported. The worsening position towards the end of the
war coincided with a serious wave of professional thefts, with a

booming black market, and with the police crack-down on prostitution, but although the surge in violence accompanied these changes it appears to have had separate origins.

The professional criminal preferred to avoid using violence where possible, and in particular he shunned the use of firearms. Guns kill but razors do no more than wound yet 'make their point'.[5] 'I never chivved [knifed] anyone unless I had to,' Billy Hill writes. 'There's no point in cutting up people if it's not necessary. And I would stand for plenty of liberties before eventually I did use the knife.' And as for murder: 'Only mugs do murder, as I've said before.'[6] The London gangs of the 1930s conducted running feuds with one another but apparently avoided the use of *both* knives and guns. On occasion wounds were inflicted that were serious enough to put people in hospital but even then the injured rarely informed on their assailants to the police.[7] Other members of the gang were expected to secure revenge. When a powerful London receiver (whom the police never caught) was badly knifed by a thief, Chief Superintendent Gosling immediately sought him out in the hope of persuading him to talk. But the receiver made it clear that he was going to handle the matter in his own way.[8]

Much of the wartime rise in violence, therefore, was not caused by professional criminals but grew out of the social conflicts of the period. Where it did occur in the pursuit of criminal ends, it tended to be in inverse ratio to the professionalism of the criminals involved.

There was an important exception to this. Robberies carried out by Americans and Canadians were often accompanied by assaults on victims and the use of guns. When two Americans raided a shop in the East India Dock Road one April afternoon in 1943 they managed to steal £84 10s, but only after striking the shopkeeper sixteen times on the head with the butt end of a ·45 service revolver. They then rushed into the street, their clothes spattered with blood.[9] Three months later, in Brixton, two Canadians robbed a cinema of £20 15s after overpowering the commissionaire, 'striking him blow after blow' and knocking 'him unconscious with an instrument'.[10] Robberies such as these received headlines in the newspapers as further examples of 'the lawlessness abroad in the streets of London' but they were to a considerable extent a feature of the North American 'invasion'. After the end of the war, as Britain's allies returned home, the number of violent robberies declined and the use of violence in the pursuit of theft even became 'rather rare'.[11]

There appear to have been three main sources of violence in wartime England (apart from the war itself). Firstly a sharp increase in woundings from 1943 coincided with the build-up of troops in preparation for the invasion of the Continent. Friction occurred among soldiers of the same army (particularly between US whites and blacks); between individual soldiers and groups of soldiers belonging to different armies; and between the military and the civilian population. That so many young men had been trained in military skills was a feature that contemporaries noted and worried about: they feared especially that commando training might predispose young men to violent behaviour and make them callous to the value of human life. John C. Spencer inquired into this aspect of military training and concluded that 'there seems very little evidence for such a view', adding that 'it is important to remember that a great many of the men convicted of the most violent offences never received this kind of training at all, but generally were given dull routine tasks in barracks and holding units'.[12]

It was in the great cities that conditions deteriorated furthest, with, as particular sparking points, the pubs and cafés that stayed open late at night; the cramped and overcrowded air-raid shelters, the public services (suffering relentless erosion, especially in transport), and the never-ending queues. Adding to the tension was the presence of numbers of refugees and minority groups from Europe and the British Empire. Furthermore, families were broken up with the conscription of fathers and husbands and the evacuation of children, and the ensuing marital and domestic problems sometimes exploded into violence. So indeed did marital difficulties in peacetime, but the disruption caused by the war enormously increased the number of families at risk.

To begin with the military: the most serious conflicts occurred between British and American troops, but the latter also suffered considerable problems of their own.[13] There seems to have been an importation into England of patterns of racial conflict prevailing in the American south and in such

cities as Chicago and New York. When these spilled over into
riots involving British soldiers, magistrates were confronted
with a difficult problem.

In September 1943 three privates in the Canadian Army
were drinking in a London pub when two soldiers belonging
to a regiment from British Honduras entered with an English
girl. One of the Canadians went up to them and said that 'that
sort of thing is not allowed where I come from' (according to
the black soldiers he said, 'Go and take a ride . . . where I come
from black men don't go out with white women'). When the
blacks retorted that they were as good as whites a fight started
and 'glasses began to fly in all directions and glass-topped
tables were used as weapons and were smashed to smithereens
on the counter . . . When the police arrived in force the
soldiers were fighting on the floor.'

In court it emerged that two of the Canadian soldiers were
in fact US citizens from Kentucky where, a Canadian Army
official explained, 'there was very strong feeling between
blacks and whites'. The magistrate (Rentoul) declared he was
'quite satisfied that the trouble arose as a result of an offensive
remark made to the coloured soldiers'. He told the Canadians
that 'these coloured men are British subjects and they are
serving and doing their bit just as you are. You have no right
to vent your prejudices or interfere with them in any way.
Whether these men are coloured or not they all have their
rights and must be treated properly or decently. It is the whole
basis on which our civilisation and our Empire rests.' After
this ringing statement the fines imposed (1s plus £5 costs)
seem somewhat tame but the magistrate had to resolve the
dilemma of punishing the offender without impeding his
value as a soldier. Magistrates tended to lean in the latter
direction, especially when the men were volunteers, as was the
case with these US citizens.[14]

Judges and magistrates were worried by the increasing use
of firearms. When two Canadians were jailed for robbery with
violence in 1943, one of them pleaded for leniency because 'I
should hate to be in prison when the war ends. That would be
the biggest disgrace I could bring on my family.' The judge
(McClure) agreed and added 'That makes my duty a very
hard one, but . . . there was a pistol. It is getting far too
common in this country.'[15] By the end of the war magistrates

were prepared to jail men merely for the possession of firearms[16] for the police warned that the problem 'was becoming serious'. Guns were in much more general use in the United States and there were numerous incidents in which Americans used firearms where Britons in a similar situation would probably have used their fists. For instance, a US soldier in a Wembley pub in 1945 'engaged in an argument with a woman' and got his face slapped. He attacked her and 'was ejected by two servicemen'. He later reappeared, brandishing a pistol, and managed to shoot an English soldier in the leg. He was tried by US court martial, reduced in rank, and sentenced to six months hard labour.[17]

The fact that he was not tried by an English court – despite wounding an English soldier in a London pub – introduces a vital point about the relationship between the American armed forces and the English during the war. George Orwell had some barbed comments to make on the subject: 'It is difficult to go anywhere in London without having the feeling that Britain is now Occupied Territory', he wrote, and he criticised particularly 'the agreement by which American troops are not liable to British courts for offences against British subjects – practically "extra-territorial rights". Not one person in ten knows the existence of this agreement; the newspapers barely reported it.'[18] According to Norman Longmate, the agreement had its origins in the decision of the US Government that American public opinion 'would not take kindly to the idea that all offences against the law of the United Kingdom committed by United States troops were liable to be tried by the British civil courts'. The reason for this attitude was the American view that 'as they were helping this country [Britain] by sending troops here it would be up to [HMG] to give the United States' authorities exclusive control over these troops'.[19]

It seems an astonishing situation; American troops had not come to Britain out of the kindness of American hearts, nor had their Government declared war on Germany in a frenzy of support for the British. The United States had entered the war against Germany because Hitler's Government *had declared war on them*; and US troops were sent to Britain because it was the only point in north-western Europe from which an invasion of the Continent could be launched. The

British Government nonetheless conceded the demands made by their ally, a measure of how desperately they needed American help, and an indication that they were already behaving as their clients. Similar privileges were not extended to the Canadians, who *had* declared war in support of the British, and one curious result of this was that newspaper reports for the period give the appearance that Canadians were responsible for very much more crime than Americans, despite the disparity in the size of the armies of the two countries.

Where civilians were the victims of American criminals, Norman Longmate states, 'good sense' prevailed and the American offender was 'often' handed over for trial in an English court.[20] If this was so, the newspapers do not appear to have reported such cases. In eleven incidents in London between 1943 and 1945, in which an English person was the victim of violent American attack – these included the murder of a man; the assault on the shopkeeper who was battered sixteen times on the head with the butt-end of a loaded revolver; and the attempted murder of a City police constable by a US air force sergeant[21] (surely as highly charged an offence from the English point of view as could have happened) – all the offenders were tried in American courts. On some occasions, the fact that the English might have an interest in cases involving US troops was contemptuously dismissed by the Americans. When an American soldier killed a military policeman and then committed suicide in Leicester in 1944, the US military authorities brusquely announced that 'all the investigations' were being made by them and stated that 'the matter was purely a military one, and had nothing to do with the civilian authorities' despite the fact that the murder occurred at closing time outside a pub in the city centre.[22] The Leicester City Coroner duly announced that 'in the circumstances' no inquiry would be held. The incident might never have been reported in the press had not numerous English people witnessed it.

The result was that something resembling a conspiracy of silence grew up between the British and American authorities and lasted for the duration of the war; if it hastened the end of that war by promoting good relations between the Allies then that is its best defence, and the contemporary press silence was perhaps justified. Certainly the broad pattern of relations between American and British troops seems to have been good (perhaps because they did not mix very much), but conflicts did from time to time break out.

The sight of a GI with a young woman on his arm seems to have been particularly infuriating to some Englishmen. One eighteen-year-old youth from Feltham 'saw a Yank with a girl. I went up, took a fancy to have a go at him and let him have it. I knocked him into a ditch. I punched him on the body but not on the face and left him in the ditch.' Magistrates were well aware of the potential political repercussions of such events: 'These people come over here to help us win this war and you assault them in this way. We cannot allow this sort of thing.' Yet the punishment the magistrate imposed was surprisingly lenient: a £2 fine, even though he threatened the boy with imprisonment if he repeated the assault.[23] He was fortunate. When two English soldiers were found guilty of assaulting and robbing a US soldier (of £10) in Leicester in 1944, they were jailed for a month and sentenced to nine strokes of the birch. They offered what was becoming a standard defence in such cases, attempting to play on supposed English grievances against the GIs. 'The American soldier . . . made some display of his money and [one of the defendants] resented his attentions to a young woman who was with him.' He 'struck the American because of remarks he made about the young woman'.[24] In another case in 1944, three young Englishmen were jailed for systematically robbing at least seven US soldiers. Their method was to wait outside Ilford railway station at night, posing as a taxi service, and offer lifts to GIs who were anxious to return to their billets. Instead they drove them to a lonely spot and robbed them. They claimed they had decided 'on an orgy' of robbing GIs because 'it was so easy'; the judge, however, drew a political dimension to the crime when he sentenced the ringleader to twenty-one months in prison.[25]

The Americans had ample grievances. There is no doubt that many English shopkeepers, café proprietors and hoteliers overcharged them, and some establishments maintained one tariff for Americans and another lower one for the English. One inquiry carried out by the North Midland Price Regulation Committee into boarding houses discovered that whereas most 'good-class' hotels had only increased their charges since the start of the war by about 10 per cent, there were boarding houses which charged visiting Americans up to 700 per cent above the pre-war tariff. Others were cheaper but offered them squalid sleeping conditions. 'Me and my partner', one American Mercantile Marine complained, 'paid 30s . . . for a room and breakfast. There were two other sailors with us in the same room.' Before the war such semi-doss-houses had been lucky to obtain 3s 6d a bed per night. The Committee decided the profiteering was 'widespread', especially where Americans were concerned, but claimed that it was difficult to investigate specific complaints because boarding-house keepers took the precaution of not giving receipts.[27]

Once an outbreak of violence between English and Americans took place there was always a danger of it turning into a 'running battle'. Pub conflicts in the tougher areas of the big cities had a tendency to generate considerable violence, and newcomers on both sides would inherit a vendetta from their predecessors in the area. One battle, which occurred around the Commercial Road in 1944, ended in murder.

This fracas combined features from several types of violent outbreak that were likely to occur in wartime. 'There was a fight between a tall white man and a coloured man'; English civilians watching the Americans started 'to throw glasses at them'; some of the Americans arrived prepared for trouble (one showed a girl he met before the incident a knuckleduster he was carrying); while the victim himself left home on the day of his death saying he was going out for a drink and his wife did not appear to be particularly concerned when he failed to return. 'He did spend a day off away from home occasionally,' she said when the police called ten days later to inform her that he had died.[28]

The increasingly international mix of the population at this time, especially in London, was accompanied by a growing intolerance on the part of some sections of the population.[29] A bill poster from Battersea Park found himself in a fight after he argued with two Canadian soldiers in Sloane Square one evening at closing time. 'You damned Canadians are no good,' he was alleged to have told them. 'All you do is come over here, drink our beer and enjoy yourselves with our women.'[30]

Another Canadian got into a fight after asking the doorman at a club in Knightsbridge why he was not in the army, called him 'a Jew' and told him he ought to be serving his country.[31] It would be possible to multiply similar incidents almost indefinitely.[32]

Trains and buses were frequently the scenes of trouble. When a dispute about change broke out between a bus conductor and a South American seaman (accompanied inevitably by an English girl) the following exchange occurred:

Conductor: '—— foreigner!'

Seaman: 'I am a foreigner, but I am fighting. Why don't you go and fight?'

Conductor (to the girl): 'Why do you go out with foreigners?'[33]

Men of military age in any civilian capacity were vulnerable to similar taunts. When a policeman approached a driver whose lorry had stalled the driver commented 'I fought for you —— in the last war' and a fight began.[34] The sentences imposed in the four superficially similar cases described here were, however, very different. The Knightsbridge doorman (whose home was in Brick Lane, E1, a notoriously tough spot) inflicted the most damage and the Canadian had to have five stitches put in his head. The magistrate nonetheless concluded that the prisoner 'had to put up with a great deal of provocation' and bound him over for twelve months. The bill poster from Battersea Park, 'an elderly man', was still suffering from severe shock thirty-six hours after the Canadians assaulted him (and a witness insisted that both participated) but the magistrate dismissed the charge against one, though he sent the other to a month's jail. The magistrate who was most incensed by the evidence given in court was John Harris, who told the lorry driver, 'You seem to have behaved like a wild beast. If there's something that makes me wild, it's spitting and kicking. Kicking is something that Englishmen do not do. If you had been in normal health, and if the police officer had not stood up for you in a way that you do not deserve, I should have sent you to gaol, and with hard labour.' However, he discharged the man.

The South American seaman was punished most severely, although the bus conductor he fought suffered no more than minor injuries. The judge (McClure) jailed him for four months, even though he conceded that the seaman had acted under great provocation. If he had not, the judge added, the sentence would have been twelve months.

The most serious sparking points among civilians during the war – to judge from court evidence – occurred in queues, whether at shops,[35] for trains or buses,[36] or outside air-raid shelters;[37] actually inside the shelters themselves;[38] and between shopkeepers and tradesmen and their customers. Many of these incidents involved women and they seem to have had less serious consequences in terms of the injuries inflicted than in fights between men.[39] In most cases, slapping and hair pulling seem to have been the extent of it, and many as a result never reached court. Of those that did, magistrates tended simultaneously to warn future offenders convicted of a similar offence that they would be punished severely, while imposing only nominal fines on those actually before them.[40] In many of these cases a policeman had in fact been on the spot or nearby when the incident took place.[41]

Finally the war created or exacerbated many family difficulties and a number of these erupted into violence. The divorce rate more than doubled during the war[42] while some people simply ignored the marriage laws altogether and acquired a second (or even a third) spouse while still legally married to the first. The rise in prosecutions for bigamy was startling:

Number of crimes of bigamy known to the police, England and Wales[43]

Average of 1935–9	1940	1941	1942	1943	1944	1945
320	366	795	1,107	1,179	1,046	1,135

The greatest increase took place betwen 1940 and 1942, and it was in February 1942 that Judge Singleton, noting that eight out of eleven cases to be heard at Essex Assizes were in respect of alleged bigamy, commented on the difficulty judges faced in sentencing in such cases. 'They realise, and they are often so reminded, that an able-bodied man is of more use in the Navy or Army than he is in prison, and yet they have to remember that if such offences are passed over lightly, that fact may itself encourage other people to think lightly of the crime, and may lead to a further increase in it.'[44]

Some 5,600 cases of bigamy occurred between 1940 and

1945, but the precise impact of the war cannot yet be established, nor can we yet answer such questions as whether courts
discriminated between serving men and civilians, and between 'husbands' and 'wives'. This is also the position with
regard to abortion, which similarly showed a sharp rise during
the war, *at least as far as police knowledge of what was going on* is
concerned.

Number of crimes of procuring abortion known to the police
England and Wales[45]

Annual average						
1935–9	1940	1941	1942	1943	1944	1945
156	110	171	344	461	649	464

It is very probable that this rise reflected a real increase in
abortions during the war. Greater police activity may have
increased the proportion known to them, but it is extremely
unlikely – given their stretched resources between 1943 and
1945 – that it accounted for all, or anything like all, the
fourfold rise that took place between 1935–9 and 1944. As for
sentences imposed, and whether these differed compared
with before the war – there is evidence to suggest from a study
of violence in the family that courts tended to take as sym-
pathetic a view as possible when dealing with violent husbands
who had been 'betrayed' by their wives.

This sympathy for husbands who attacked wives who had
'let them down' while they were away 'fighting for their country' even extended to cases of murder. In 1942 a lance-
corporal shot his wife dead at their home in Fulham.

The husband was a Cypriot who had come to Britain in
1929. He married in 1935 and he and his wife had two children. When he was called up his wife and children were
evacuated to Norfolk, where she began to go out with other
men. Eventually she asked for a divorce. The husband 'was
very distressed'. He 'explained the situation to his command-
ing officer . . . obtained seven days' compassionate leave and
went home carrying with him his service rifle and, against
orders, five ball cartridges'. He found the flat empty so he
waited for his wife in the dark. She and her lover arrived
home some hours later and it 'seemed that they had been on a
spree'. The evidence about what happened next was closely
debated in court. The prosecution had already conceded that

'if a man finds his wife with a lover and in his fury and red anger kills one of them on the spot, the charge may be reduced to manslaughter', so this point became the central plank of the defence. The couple, counsel claimed, went immediately into the bedroom where a struggle took place in which the wife was shot. The husband told the police, 'I did not intend to kill my wife. I love her and only intended to frighten her.' Nonetheless, the bullet he fired passed through her forearm into her body, 'killing her almost at once', then continued through the kitchen and lavatory, through a partition, finally ending in the garden. An important element in the husband's defence was provided by his diary, extracts from which were read out in court, for example: 'when I see every other man getting letters and parcels from home and I do not, I get depressed'.

The jury found the defendant guilty of manslaughter, not guilty of murder, and the judge (Asquith) allowed that he had had some provocation in sentencing him to fifteen months jail.[46]

In another very similar case, however, which occurred in the summer of 1945, a 34-year-old soldier was accused of murdering his wife. In his absence she had led 'a grossly immoral life' and eventually became pregnant. She wrote to tell him about it; compassionate leave was granted, and the couple met'. She asked him to say the child was his '. . . he refused to do this and left'. They appear to have met again on the following two days, but on the second day they had a row and the husband stabbed her. 'I only meant to scar her so that nobody else should have her, but she struggled and I stabbed her in the wrong place.' He then went out into the street 'with the blood-stained knife in his hands and said to a motor-driver, "Get the police. I have just done in my missus." ' In the police car he 'kept repeating, "To think it was an Italian she was going with" ' and his sister-in-law testified that 'his wife's infidelity was the main subject of his conversation the whole time . . . he said that what had happened to him was the general fear of all the men in Burma'.[47] The jury reached the same verdict as in the Fulham case (defendant not guilty of murder though guilty of manslaughter) but the judge (Charles) objected strongly to this verdict. He argued that it established a dangerous principle if a husband whose wife had been unfaithful while he was away in the forces returned and killed her and was then in effect exonerated by the court. He jailed the man for five years. 'If manslaughter it be . . . it is a bad case of manslaughter . . . If you had not been so sorely tried I should have been bound to give you a very, very heavy sentence.'

In these cases, perhaps more than in any others, the punishment could vary decidedly, depending on who was the judge. Charles took a hard line (he was also a vigorous advocate of the merits of hanging, flogging and birching); other judges, such as Norman Birkett, believed that they had a duty to view such cases as sympathetically as possible.

For instance, in October 1942 a 32-year-old soldier from Poplar discovered that his wife had been 'carrying on' with another man while he was in the army and he stabbed her, the wound penetrating her lung. She was still in hospital at the time of the trial. The police told the court that the soldier 'bore an excellent character both in the Army and in civilian life' and Birkett made the following comments: 'While you were serving your country you were betrayed and humiliated in circumstances which can be described as quite revolting . . . It was only at the last, when you were humiliated beyond endurance, your home broken up, and the welfare of your child disregarded, you did that for which you stand in the dock today.' The soldier pleaded guilty to a charge of wounding his wife with intent to cause grievous bodily harm and Birkett sentenced him to two days prison, which in fact meant his immediate discharge.[48]

Such sentences could represent a dangerous precedent, as Judge Charles had observed. Some judges and magistrates therefore took pains to distinguish carefully between the case before them (in which there might be mitigating circumstances) and the generality of assaults, which deserved the most severe punishment.

In these instances the soldier husbands had assaulted their wives; when they attacked their male rivals, some courts, in the ensuing prosecutions, tended to resemble tribunals of morality rather than courts of law. In June 1946 a Fulham soldier waylaid and beat up a man he accused of associating with his wife while he was fighting overseas. Defence counsel had to try to explain an attack in which the rival was punched 'so savagely' that his dentures were broken, his lips lacerated, and his body 'covered in bruises'. He was able by deft questioning of the victim to extract from him the fact that he had 'associated' with his attacker's wife and that further 'there might have been some justification for the assault'. Such words of sympathy as the magistrate expressed were directed at the defendant, whom he bound over, advising him 'to treat the matter as past history and try to forget'.[49]

In other prosecutions, magistrates went further in their comments. In 1944, when a gunner assaulted the man who was having an affair with his wife, the Chairman of Tunbridge Wells Bench, Sir Ronald Gowers MP, made it clear who he thought the real culprits were. The gunner had said of his rival 'I felt like killing him' and Sir Ronald Gowers seems to have experienced a similar emotion. He said to the victim, 'Don't you think you richly deserved everything you got? Here you are, in a cushy job, and here was a man serving his country, and you take advantage of his absence by seducing his wife. Do you think you are a man?' The charge was dismissed but, before the victim and his mistress were allowed to leave court, Gowers had these remarks to make: 'The Bench wish me to say that this man . . . is a nasty blackguard, and a man deserving of the contempt of all decent people. The Bench also desire me to say that we regard the wife as a very nasty individual. There are too many worthless wives, who take advantage of their husbands, and carry on with other men.'[50]

The most frequent casualties of disputes within families, and of the dislocated circumstances of the war, were children, and the period witnessed a sharp rise in prosecutions for cruelty and neglect:

Number of persons found guilty of cruelty to and neglect of children, England and Wales[51]

1938	1939	1940	1941	1942	1943	1944	1945
932	751	671	968	1,413	1,612	1,721	1,643

Once again, the rise did not represent a real change in the incidence of cruelty and neglect so much as growing public awareness and concern that there was a problem. The most dramatic alteration took place between 1940 and 1942, precisely the period in which the evacuation was bringing the realities of life in the urban slums before the attention of many middle-class and country people. Some horrifying cases of neglect were exposed in court. In June 1945 a Birkenhead woman whose husband had died of 'bomb shock' in 1941 was prosecuted for neglecting her children. 'David . . . was wearing only a jersey and trousers, which were in filthy condition. He had no underclothing or shoes. The boy's head was covered with septic sores, in which were traces of lice . . . Albert had septic sores on his elbows and heels, and his head was verminous with lice. Stanley had septic sores on his ears, arms and toes . . . there was a fowl running about the kitchen . . . the children were so hungry [the policeman] went out and bought some food which [they] ate ravenously.'[52] In August of the same year the wife of a soldier was prosecuted for neglecting her children who were suffering from scabies 'in a moderately advanced stage'. The four-year-old was 'plastered with excreta from the waist downwards. She was clothed only in a filthy vest, and the bedding was covered in excreta.'[53] A year earlier a young London woman had 'constantly neglected' her baby, 'and when his bodily condition became serious she was afraid to take him to hospital . . . when she brought the child in . . . after its death . . . the body was wasted and emaciated, and large areas of the skin were raw and wet and undergoing putrifying changes. There were also maggots in the body.'[54] This woman was jailed for two years; the two others for three months each.

Cases such as these – and they were not exceptional occurrences – would have been treated seriously by the courts at any time, but there was a second category of prosecution in which the war seems to have played a crucial role. In a case from Coggeshall, in Essex, an NSPCC inspector received complaints that the evacuee mother of a family of three children 'went out at night' leaving them 'locked in the flat. She walked the streets hour after hour, and went to dances at night. She was often out until midnight "on her pleasures".'

Defendant: 'I deny that I go to dances every night.'

P.C. Lewis: 'When there are dances at Coggeshall you go to them.'

The woman's soldier husband spoke up for her in court: 'The war is to blame for this; my wife has been left on her own.' Nonetheless she was jailed for three months with hard labour.[55]

In Bath, in April 1944, three mothers were fined for neglecting their children. The police described one as a 'good time woman' while the others were said to have gone out with US soldiers. The prosecuting counsel added that the Chief Constable 'asks me to say that the police have received far too many complaints of women leaving their children to the tender mercies of the world and going out in the evenings, leaving the house locked up. This has become so prevalent in Bath that it is causing endless trouble to the police.'[56] Watchful neighbours observed the comings and goings of mothers and the visits of soldiers, and notified the police or the NSPCC. Accounts concerning the supposed promiscuity of the mother sometimes received greater attention than the evidence that she had neglected her children. The son of one Bath woman talked to an NSPCC visitor about his 'American daddy and sailor daddy' and it was this that made the newspaper headline, not the fact that the child was discovered in a cold flat in March wearing only a vest.[57]

Some anonymous letter writers not only informed the authorities about their suspicions, they also wrote to husbands serving in the armed forces, even as far away as France or Italy. One such husband was given compassionate leave and arrived back at his home in Birkenhead in time to find a man there, whom he 'flung into the street'. His wife shared her home with another woman, whose husband returned from France at the same time. Both were found guilty of neglecting their children and jailed for three months, but in such cases it is sometimes difficult to tell at what point a prosecution for neglect or cruelty ended and one for immorality began.[58]

Three main motives lay behind this type of prosecution. Once again the authorities sought to prevent standards of behaviour deteriorating and invoked the law in order to bring exemplary prosecutions that would catch the attention of the press. Courts punished such offences more harshly at the end of the war than they had done before it. There was a slight rise in the proportion of offenders jailed, but a substantial one among those given the longest sentence magistrates imposed:[59]

Percentage of offenders who were found guilty who were:

imprisoned: 1938 men 32·8, women 39·0; 1946 men 35·8, women 40·9
jailed for between
three and
six months: 1938 men 7·4, women 6·5; 1946 men 14·2, women 12·4

Secondly, the growing public concern about child cruelty and neglect, among slum dwellers especially, increasingly took the form of punishing the parents. It was a curious idea that this represented a way of solving a serious social problem, but not only was it applied with greater vigour but some authorities believed that still harsher punishments were required. One police doctor even spoke in favour of flogging 'delinquent' parents.[60]

Finally, the neglect of children was perceived as directly related to what was increasingly regarded, from the mid-1930s onwards, as the country's most serious criminal problem, that of juvenile delinquency. It seemed only too obvious that the neglected or abused child would grow up to become the juvenile offender and the adult criminal. It was therefore necessary to take remedial action as early as possible in the child's life if there was to be any hope of diminishing the amount of juvenile crime. But was there such a problem on anything like the scale that contemporaries suggested?

CHAPTER TEN

Juvenile Delinquency

In *English Journey*, published in 1934, J. B. Priestley described a tour he made of England. He was struck principally by the misery of the depressed areas of Lancashire and the North-East and he made a vigorous plea that something be done about 'the England of the dole'. But he also noticed 'the new post-war England, belonging far more to the age itself than to this particular island. America was its real birthplace,' he suggested. This new England could be found along the arterial and bypass roads and its outstanding features were 'filling stations and factories that look like exhibition buildings . . . giant cinemas and dance-halls and cafés, bungalows with tiny garages, cocktail bars, Woolworths, motor-coaches, wireless, hiking, factory girls looking like actresses, grey-hound racing and dirt tracks, swimming pools, and everything given away for cigarette coupons'. This new England was 'essentially democratic . . . You could almost accept Woolworths as its symbol . . . The young people of this new England do not play chorus in an opera in which their social superiors are the principals; they do not live vicariously, enjoy life at second-hand, by telling one another what a wonderful time the young earl is having . . . they get on with their own lives . . .'[1]

George Orwell noticed the same phenomenon: 'After 1918 there began to appear something that had never existed in England before: people of indeterminate social class. In 1910 every human being in these islands could be "placed" in an instant by his clothes, manners and accent. That is no longer the case. Above all, it is not the case in the new townships that have developed as a result of cheap motor cars and the southwards shift of industry.'[2]

The most prominent characteristics of the stereotype are Woolworths, Dagenham, the motor car, the radio, *youth*.

Together they symbolised a development that Orwell welcomed rather more readily than Priestley, who regretted the 'cheapness' of the new England – 'Too much of it is simply a trumpery imitation of something not very good even in the original – but neither felt the alarm that some of their contemporaries expressed about future developments. Harold Nicolson, for instance, believed that the war sealed the fate of the 'cultured' classes, who were doomed to 'have to walk and live a Woolworth life hereafter'.[3] His wife, Vita Sackville-West, wrote to him, 'I hate democracy. I hate la populace. I wish education had never been introduced ... I wish la populace had never been encouraged to emerge from its rightful place. I should like to see them as well fed and well housed as T.T. cows, but no more articulate than that.'[4]

However, the 1930s witnessed an increasing self-confidence on the part of the T.T. cows, a growing articulateness, especially among the younger ones. The origins of the trend probably lay in the East End, among the lively and fashion-conscious Jewish community. The styles they pioneered were rapidly adopted by their gentile neighbours and soon spread to the surrounding circle of lower-class districts in north and east London. The *New Survey* had observed the process as early as 1931: 'Visible signs of class distinctions are disappearing ... The dress of the younger generation of working men and women, so far from having any distinctive note of its own, tends merely to copy, sometimes to exaggerate, any particular fashion current in the West End. In the same way paint and powder, once regarded in this class as the mark of the prostitute, are freely used by respectable working girls ... In fact the whole demeanour of the different social classes has tended towards a closer approximation in the past generation.'[5] So far so true, but the *New Survey* missed the point that exaggeration of fashion style in itself constituted a distinctive note.

Many contemporaries, especially among the older and better-off sections of the community, were disconcerted by these developments. They feared that England was in danger of 'Americanisation' and identified the cinema, dance halls, cafés, and certain sea-side resorts as accelerating the trend to a democratic, lawless and promiscuous society. The young in particular were regarded as both advancing the tendency and most susceptible to its attractions. Control of them therefore became an object to be sought: it was imperative to halt change at its roots.

As young people were expected to behave increasingly badly, they were closely watched. The authorities knew what to look for and duly found it: the statistics showed a relentless rise in juvenile crime.

Number of indictable offences in respect of which proceedings were taken against juveniles[6]

	1933	1934	1935	1936	1937	1938
Manchester	338	487	648	885	904	914
Liverpool	1,013	1,492	1,788	2,055	NA	1,650

Thus, in only four years (1933–6) there was a rise of 162 per cent in Manchester and one of 103 per cent in Liverpool. Thereafter the upward movement slackened considerably in Manchester while in Liverpool there was a fall of 19·7 per cent between 1936 and 1938. Nonetheless, the increase in both towns *since 1933* was serious and caused gloomy comments and predictions to be made. The Chief Constable of Liverpool wrote in 1936 that 'as regards Liverpool . . . over 25 per cent of those charged with the more serious crimes started their career as juveniles . . . it is . . . only reasonable to assume that when the juveniles of today reach manhood there will be an increase of adult crime'.[7] This point of view was supported by the editor of a leading journal on police affairs: 'There is . . . very little comfort to be drawn from any section of this report . . . some at least of [its] opinions are widely shared by Police officials all over the country . . .'[8]

These anxieties soon found their way into the popular press, emerging in sensational headlines. Yet it was questionable whether in fact the statistics as presented gave a true picture of what was happening. Even pessimistic chief constables sometimes sounded a cautious note.

The Chief Constable of Manchester regarded the situation as 'very unsatisfactory' but he also advised the public to take into account alterations that had been made in the law. 'A big change' was the Children and Young Persons Act of 1933*,

---

* This raised the minimum age of criminal responsibility from seven years to eight, and extended the jurisdiction of the juvenile court to young persons up to their seventeenth birthday.

which 'did much to stimulate interest in the problem of
Juvenile Delinquency . . . As a result, delinquents, who in the
past might have been dealt with in other ways, are now
brought before the court'.[9] In what other ways, it might be
asked? The Education Officer of the London County Council
observed that 'whereas in the past the station or other officer
may have administered a rebuke or correction on the spot
[now] his successor . . . accepted a charge.'[10] An Assistant
Secretary at the Home Office stressed the same point: there
was 'abundant evidence' to show that since the 1933 Act prosecutors were 'less reluctant to bring offending children
before the courts' and he proceeded to generalise: 'Experience shows . . . that each time a new statute relating to the
young has been put into effect, the immediate result is an
apparent rise in the number of offences. This "rise" is not due
to any "wave" of crime among juveniles, but to a desire on the
part of those concerned with putting the law into motion, to
make use of the new method of treatment.' He summed up
thus: there was 'no justification for jeremiads about a decay in
the moral fibre of the young'.[11]

These views were certainly not accepted by many of those in
a position of authority who were professionally concerned
with juvenile crime, although few went as far as Captain
Popkess, Chief Constable of Nottingham in 1937. He
lamented the doubling of juvenile delinquency in only three
years, which was such an unfavourable contrast with the position in Germany. There such crime was notable for its 'almost
complete absence', a development he attributed to the 'youth
movement' of the Nazi regime.[12]

What was in fact required was a more careful questioning of
the statistics themselves. The Commissioner of the Metropolitan Police, for example, warned of the danger of relying on
the crude figures without relating them to changes in the size
of the population at risk, and variations in the extent of police
vigilance. However, such analysis carried out with the view of
establishing the position in the capital showed that not only
had the number of juveniles charged risen, so had the number
as a proportion of the total juvenile population. Furthermore,
increased police vigilance and a greater tendency to charge,
he argued, could not account for all the increase. His conclusion was that there had been a real rise in juvenile crime.[13]

If that was so, then the problem was to explain it. Most contemporaries with an interest in the subject located the responsibility firmly within the context of social change. Increased liberality (or indifference) on the part of parents was seen as the major cause. The Chief Constable of Liverpool suggested that 'the sense of parental responsibility has notoriously declined', an opinion shared by the Chief Constables of Preston ('laxity of control in the home circle') and Leeds ('growing laxity of parental control and the unsatisfactory nature of home life').[14] The 'lack of opportunity for employment in wage-earning occupations'[15] was a point that was mentioned fairly often, as was the paucity of facilities for young people in the working-class districts of the great cities. 'Many children are sent out of their homes especially on Saturdays and Sundays merely to get rid of them. Where they go and what they do is a matter of complete indifference so long as they are not in the way' (Chief Constable of Plymouth).[16]

Others went further and referred to the emerging acquisitive consumer society of the 1930s: 'There never was a time like the present when blatantly obtrusive advertisements and incitements to participate in "get-rich-quick" schemes of all kinds were so rife and manifest . . . Parental example in recent years, illustrated . . . by open indulgence in gambling on football pools, horses and dog racing . . . must have definitely harmful influence on their children' (Chief Constable of Bradford).[17] The Chief Constable of Leeds observed that 'young people nowadays have much more freedom of thought and action . . . coupled with the excitement of modern life, its many attractions and many temptations [which together] led many a youth into crime'.[18] Likewise the Chief Constable of Huddersfield regarded the 'greater degree of freedom' of the time as harmful in its influence on the young.[19] Such statements of generality, however, did not go very far in explaining the connection between broad social trends and the individual child actually committing a delinquent act. It was left to Sir Philip Game to be more specific and he picked out two developments as directly encouraging juveniles to commit crimes: the movement to open display in stores and shops, and the proliferation of automatic machines and easily stealable consumer goods like bicycles, which were often left unattended and unlocked.[20]

As for remedies, these were inherent in the comments that the chief constables had made. Youth must be controlled, its free time filled up, and 'anti-social' outlets ('action') shut down.

The Chief Constable of Preston welcomed 'any effort which could be made by the clergy of the various churches and schools by taking steps to organise gymnasium clubs at the schools, and the promotion of other forms of culture and sport, so as to provide an outlet for the exuberance of spirit natural to youth'.[21] The *Police Review* advocated the establishment of boys' clubs along the lines of a successful one in Norwich 'in order that the freedom and activities of juveniles may be directed in the proper channels ... Much of the mischief is due to lack of interesting occupation and consequent boredom.'[22] The Commissioner of the Metropolitan Police described how a promotion examination for police officers had elicited 'the remarkable consensus of opinion' that want of employment and leisure interests were the chief causes of juvenile crime, and boys' clubs and similar institutions the 'cure'.[23] This approach was the current orthodoxy, though isolated warning notes were sounded. Clubs attracted only those boys who were 'clubbable': delinquents would not go to such places. In the words of a Home Office memorandum 'The "respectable" club does not attract the undisciplined youth of the streets.'[24] In addition, not everyone was convinced that attendance at a boys' club guaranteed that a juvenile would cease to commit crime. The Chief Constable of Liverpool pointed out that in a three-month period during 1936–7 over 10 per cent of the boys dealt with by courts in the city were found to be members of youth organisations and clubs.[25]

Stricter punishments were also advocated. Sir Cyril Burt, an influential figure at this time, believed that corporal punishment was useful as a last resort in bringing home to young people the nature of pain and should therefore be used for such offences as cruelty to children and animals. He argued also that the birch could be applied effectively on boys over the age of fourteen who were beyond parental control and suggested that the threat of it deterred potential delinquents.[26] The Chief Constable of Leicester advocated the use

of physical punishment on delinquents who had become so
'hardened' that the 'benefits' of the probation system were lost
upon them, while Bacup's Chief Constable related success in
life to corporal punishment generously inflicted in youth:
'Many a man whose career and achievements are now contemplated with pride, had the foundations of his character
laid and consolidated by the well merited and equally well
executed parental "spanking" which accompanied any tendency to what we now term "juvenile delinquency".'[27] Some
councils, indeed, in the early stages of the war, voted to extend
its use. Portsmouth, for instance, passed a motion in May 1940
to give authority to the superintendent of the remand home to
inflict corporal punishment 'when necessary' and there was
no opposition to the principle. The debate revolved around
the question whether a second person should be present during the caning. The seconder of the proposal, a Councillor
Lowe, said 'the one aim of the Juvenile Bench of . . . this city
had been to make little boys little girls . . . They could not
check vicious spirits by kissing them and telling them to be
good boys.'[28] If he was correct in this opinion of the Juvenile
Bench then they had surely been working on the correct lines:
the delinquency rate for girls was everywhere a fraction of
that for boys.

Although corporal punishment had its critics (the Chief
Constable of Plymouth believed it was 'no remedy' for juvenile
crime: 'offenders punished in this way have had to be sent to
Approved School after all')[29], and several commentators
pointed out that 'hardened young toughs' were the persons
best equipped to withstand it, there was a rise in its use in the
early stages of the war. In 1939, only 50 birchings were
inflicted on boys under fourteen, but in 1940 there were 283,
and in 1941 over 500.[30*]

The significance of the war, both as it was anticipated, and
as it actually happened, is thus obvious. Its disruption was
expected to send juvenile delinquency rates soaring; this was
watched out for and it duly occurred. The statistics tell the
story:

* The number fell dramatically, however, after the Hereford birching 'scandal' in
1943, which caused an outcry against the use of the birch. Only 31 birchings were
administered in 1944. There is a full account of the Hereford affair in F. Bresler, *Lord
Goddard* (1977), pp. 95–9.

Number of persons found guilty in magistrates courts, England and Wales[31]

	1939	1940	1941	% change 1939–41
Under 17	52,814	65,771	72,105	+36·5
17 to 21	58,902	61,112	69,096	+17·3

Much energy and paperwork was expended trying to explain this alarming rise. The influence of evacuation was hotly debated. Hermann Mannheim believed that there was 'a great reluctance' in the reception areas to prosecute evacuee children, and in many places this may have been so.[32] But in other towns it seems clear that evacuee children were scrutinised for the least sign of delinquency and immediately rushed to court if they overstepped the limits. Northampton received 17,000 evacuees and its Chief Constable announced that he had taken 'drastic action . . . to curb' their 'criminal propensities'. In a single week in the autumn of 1939 twenty-two 'intractable' and 'defiant' youngsters were taken to court, mainly for stealing (often from chain stores) and receiving.[33] In Oxford in 1941, 30 per cent of the juveniles prosecuted were evacuees while in Cambridge, which received a large contingent of children from London, 50 per cent more juveniles were prosecuted in 1940 than in 1939.[34]

Yet the areas from which the children originated did not experience a corresponding reduction in juvenile crime. There, schools were closed as a deliberate policy, partly to make them available for use for war purposes, and partly to provide 'a further stimulus' to parents to send their children away, or, if they returned, to refuse to let them stay. Inevitably, it proved impossible to pressure many parents in this way with the result that there were still some 80,000 children of school age in London at the end of 1940, and 68,000 in Manchester in April 1941.[35] Thus, large numbers remained to 'run wild' all day. The blackout and shelter life exacerbated the problem. Many young people chose to go to different shelters from their parents, or not to go to any shelter at all. It was widely believed in consequence that numerous youths received an apprenticeship in crime, and girls an apprenticeship in prostitution.

That evacuation, shelter life, bombing, and interruption of schooling should have the most damaging impact on the young was foreseeable and was indeed foreseen. This makes the comments of many persons in authority on juvenile crime particularly difficult to understand. In their attempt to explain what was happening they seemed almost to ignore the war, preferring to trot out once again the worn explanations of the pre-war period. 'Lack of parental control' (the Chief Constables of Middlesbrough, Newark, and Preston)[36] was joined by the return of full adult employment ('both parents . . . at work, and the children . . . allowed to run wild all day and until late hours at night').[37] Many fathers had been called up and were thus unable to supervise, though before the war they had not apparently been much of a success at this. Young people 'gallivanting about the streets at all hours' became a theme, as did the 'dangers to young girls who are allowed to use the streets in this way' (the Chief Constable of Blackpool).[38] The popular press built up a picture of juvenile offenders as 'wasp-waisted loungers, who ape the methods of their film heroes', breaking the law in gangs and with impunity. They need an 'intensive police clean up' to deal with them.[39]

Even more curious was the way in which economic circumstances, *whatever they were,* could be held to explain the rise in crime. Before the war it was argued that delinquency was a by-product of unemployment and boredom; after 1941 the high wages paid to 'mere boys' came to be regarded as a major cause. The Home Office and the Board of Education, in a memorandum, warned of the dangers of paying high wages to juveniles, as did *The Times* and the *Police Review.*[40] 'Raising the wages of adolescents . . . from £3 to £6 a week gave boys far too much money to spend and drunkenness was increasing . . . The wages of these young workers must come down', wrote a probation officer at Southwark Juvenile Court.[41] Yet when commentators tried to explain the precise connection between high wages and delinquency they were often obliged to fall back on platitudes. For instance, Dr H. F. Brisby, the Medical Officer at Leeds Prison, asked 'why is it then . . . that when juveniles and adolescents are earning more money than ever before, crime at these ages should increase? The answer . . . is that too much money without responsibility or the necessity of learning its value leads in some cases, where self-control is wanting, to a lack of appreciation of property rights and values with regard first to one's own property and then to that

of others.'[42] Yet even a cursory glance at the statistics showed
that the largest increase in juvenile delinquency was taking
place among those of school age. In the first twelve months of
the war, the number of juvenile offenders under fourteen
rose by 41 per cent on the previous year, whereas in the age
group from fourteen to sixteen the increase was 22 per cent,
and among those from seventeen to twenty-one only 5 per
cent.[43] These suggestions of a link between high wages and
juvenile crime are perhaps more easy to understand if they
are interpreted as an attack on the principle of paying high
wages to young people (and especially working-class ones)
rather than as an attempt to say something serious about
juvenile delinquency.

Many of the commentators who became so anxious about
'the problem' had lost sight of a significant point: its 'very
trivial nature', even when offences were 'technically indictable'. The Chief Constable of Plymouth stressed the fact that
many arose from 'a propensity for mischief and adventure'
rather than anything more serious.[44] The Commissioner of
the Metropolitan Police also insisted that 'adventure-hunting'
and 'mischief' rather than 'crime in the ordinary sense' lay
behind most juvenile offences. The 'worst' age was thirteen
and most 'crimes' were of the sort that thirteen-year-olds
might have been expected to commit, such as bicycle stealing,
theft from vehicles and automatic machines, or shoplifting.[45]
The Lord Chief Justice, Lord Caldecote, who was no liberal,
warned in 1942 of the danger of treating young offenders as
'outcasts of society . . . for they were more the victims of what
society had done, or failed to do, than offenders against
society'.[46] The date of this interesting comment is perhaps
significant: by 1942 the revelations about the living conditions
in the slums of the big cities, brought directly to the attention
of the middle class in the reception areas by evacuee children,
had had time to sink in.

That there were juveniles who were involved in serious
crime was clear but they were also atypical. Gangs in east
London, Leeds and Manchester perturbed the authorities
while Liverpool's Chief Constable wrote about the 'criminal
gangs' in the seaport, who 'although not organised under one
leader, consist of members who are willing to assist each other
in carrying out crimes, intimidating potential witnesses

against them, or even providing perjured evidence to secure
the acquittal of the prisoner. Members . . . have been responsible for many most serious offences, such as robberies, woundings, breaking into all types of premises and even manslaughter.'[47] Even small towns had their gangs, like the one 'tracked
down' in Maidstone in 1940 which specialised in stealing bicycles. Members took the machines to an allotment shed where
'in a matter of minutes' they were taken to pieces, parts from
other cycles fitted, the 'new' machine given a coat of paint and
sold.[48] But, when the wartime policy concerning the more
serious juvenile offender is considered, it is perhaps only
surprising that there were not many more such gangs.

On the outbreak of the war, the government had decided to
release all borstal boys who had served *not less* than six months
of their time. In all, 2,817 boys were freed. If, as some contemporaries believed, borstals (together with approved
schools and remand homes) were little better than training
schools in crime for some of their inmates, while as regards
the rest, the 'after-care' that was supposed to be provided was
either rudimentary or non-existent, it is possible to appreciate
why so many were reconvicted in such a short space of time.
By September 1946, 50 per cent of those discharged in 1939
(1,419 boys) had been reconvicted, while 56 per cent of the
girls were back inside by December 1943.[49]

Some chief constables did not hesitate to express their
views of such institutions. The Chief Constable of Plymouth
commented on the failures of the local remand home which
made no attempt to segregate youngsters with the result that
'a first offender sent for a short period, the persistent type
awaiting a vacancy in an approved school, the mental defective, the sexual offender and the truant, all find themselves
living in communal conditions. Months sometimes elapse
after committal before vacancies can be found in approved
schools, and in the meantime they remain at the Home . . .
much harm has been done through the existence of these
unfortunate conditions.' Supervision was poor: there were
thirty escapes in 1940 'and in some cases the persistent thief
has persuaded the first offender to escape with him and they
both have commenced to steal and to break into houses'.[50]

During the later stages of the war, social conditions in the
country deteriorated, and crime flourished. It might have

been expected – in view of the comments that had been made earlier – that juvenile delinquency would have increased along with it, as the minority of 'hardened' youngsters busied themselves aiding black-marketeers and professional thieves, while those juveniles whose lives had been disrupted by the war 'took out their grievances on society'. In fact the opposite happened: the number of juvenile offenders declined.

Number of persons found guilty in England and Wales[51]

	1941	1942	1943	1944	% change 1941–4
Under 17	72,105	66,179	67,659	67,636	– 6·2
17–21	69,096	58,721	48,777	46,773	–32·3

The reduction in the number of offenders between the ages of seventeen and twenty-one was no doubt related to war service: many were no longer 'free' to break the law. But the decline of 6,000 in the number of offenders under the age of seventeen between 1941 and 1942, together with the steadiness of the total thereafter, is significant. A change in the size of the population at risk may assist in explaining some of this reduction, but on the other hand, the authorities had been alerted to the problem from the start of the war and there is no reason to doubt that they remained as vigilant for cases *of serious crime* by youngsters as they had always been.

What in fact was happening can be gathered from the experience of individual towns. These show some startling changes both from year to year and from one town to another in the same year. For example, Northampton saw a 19 per cent rise in juvenile crime in 1941 and a fall of 19 per cent in 1942, while in 1946 there was a leap upwards of 83·5 per cent.[52] In the same year, Norwich saw a fall of 31 per cent in the number of juvenile offenders, compared with reductions of 52 per cent in Luton and 40 per cent in Oxford, but only 7 per cent in Liverpool and 6 per cent in Peterborough. The contrast can be presented in another way: as a proportion of the total amount of indictable crime juveniles committed. Here the differences between towns were sometimes particularly large. In 1943, they were responsible for 29·5 per cent of detected crime in Burnley, but 38 per cent in Stockport and 58 per cent in Hartlepool. The following year there was an even wider gap between towns. In Bath juveniles accounted for 9·4 per cent of indictable crime[53] compared with 27 per cent in Birkenhead, 44 per cent in Luton and 50 per cent in Hartlepool. In Burnley they had been responsible for 41·4 per cent of indictable crime in 1944, but only 24·5 per cent in 1945.

These differences do not reflect differences in the amount of juvenile crime in these various towns, but rather a difference *in the approach* taken to crime, and this contrast in turn sheds light on the nature of the offences that were being committed. The war saw in many towns (though by no means all) a marked shift in police policy away from prosecutions to cautioning. Preston's Chief Constable pointed this out when he commented in 1944 that there was a 10 per cent decrease in the number of juvenile offenders and attributed it to an increase in the number of cautions made by senior officers.[54]

In this respect most English chief constables lagged behind one of their Scottish colleagues who had appreciated as early as the mid-1930s the public impact a change in policy could have. Percy Sillitoe, Chief Constable of Glasgow, was in charge of a city whose problems of violence, gang warfare, drunkenness and juvenile delinquency were more serious than in any other large city in the United Kingdom. Yet in 1937 he was able to announce in his annual report that there had been an 'appreciable reduction in juvenile crime': only 1,783 juveniles had been prosecuted compared with 2,323 in 1936.[55] This success coming at a time when so many English chief constables were gloomily reporting ever larger *increases,* naturally drew much attention to Sillitoe, who was already well known for his achievement in breaking criminal gangs in Glasgow and, before that, in Sheffield.

To succeed in an area like juvenile crime where so many others had failed was an added recommendation in his dealings with politicians, and he was to show a similar flair in the way he handled the highly charged issue of women police. Yet whether there was any significant change in the level of juvenile crime in Glasgow is doubtful. What had altered was the method the police used for dealing with the offenders.

The exigencies of war forced many English chief constables to follow where Sillitoe had led. Such was the pressure on resources both of police time (especially in terms of drawing up reports, preparing a case and presenting it in court) and on the time of the courts themselves that a fresh policy was essential. The Chief Constable of Plymouth, also an innovator in this field, described how it worked: 'My desire was to prevent, by friendly talk and advice, their [the juveniles'] appearance in the Police Court. These talks were given in my office in the presence of the parents, and the result has been remarkably satisfactory.' He began his experiment in 1937 and in that year only 109 children were prosecuted compared with 207 the previous year – a change that, if it had been left unexplained, might have given the impression that in a single year delinquency had fallen by 47 per cent. But in fact another 336 boys and girls had been interviewed by the Chief Constable, only five of whom were reported for other offences during that year.[56] If only half the 336 had been proceeded against, juvenile delinquency would have 'risen' by nearly 34 per cent.

This policy was successful in keeping considerable numbers of children out of the courts in later years and during the war spread from town to town, becoming particularly widespread after 1942–3. Thus, in the later stages of the war and the early years of peace the pattern of comments on juvenile crime presents a sharp contrast to the position during 1936–41. Now there was 'a considerable reduction in crimes committed by juveniles' (Hartlepool); 'a definite decrease' (Halifax); 'a slight decrease' (Manchester); 'only a very slight increase' (Leicester); and 'fewer juveniles . . . brought before the Court' (Wallasey).

It was possible to make the change-over from prosecutions to cautioning precisely because so many offences were minor ones. The *Police Review* had suggested as early as September 1940 that wartime demanded a different policy from peace. 'Some aspects of the law usually enforced by the Police ought . . . to be given a rest . . . the Constable who wants work to do will find plenty to keep his hand in in the vital business of enforcing the Lighting (Restrictions) Order and keeping important streets clear . . . The comment is prompted by certain cases that have appeared in the Courts in the last few days – begging, various acts of vagrancy, simple drunkenness, etc . . . we would urge once more that the undoubted and well-established Police discretion to issue cautions instead of applying summonses . . . was never so much in need of use as at the present time.'[57]

This trend did not mean, however, that the courts ceased to deal with numbers of trivial offences. It will be recalled that only a small proportion of indictable crime in 1944 in Bath (9·4 per cent) had been committed by juveniles. It is revealing to examine some of these cases.

During the autumn of the previous year there were signs of growing concern about the 'delinquency' of young girls. Bath had emerged as a centre point for a cluster of large US bases in the west country and this had been accompanied by the usual manifestations of wartime social change: 'good-time girls' and prostitutes had gathered in the town; 'disorderly' houses were established (between February 1943 and the end of the war the police closed down at least five); while the GIs had their customary apparent unsettling effect on the female population generally.

The respectable and law-abiding classes were duly agitated. The Nonconformist churches and 'morality' pressure groups such as the Bath Vigilance and Rescue Association set about organising meetings, co-ordinating protests, and drawing up petitions which soon found their way to the City Council.[58] The local press carried alarming articles, their conclusions pointed up in crisp editorials. 'There are girls in Bath', the town's woman probation officer wrote, 'whose only ideas in life are men, lipstick, and showing as much of their bodies as they can . . . war-time conditions . . . were having [an] appalling effect . . . on some girls in all parts of the country . . . children of school age were becoming utterly spoilt . . . Too much money and many soldiers with money to fling about were . . . factors leading to their downfall.' She had also observed 'a tremendous change for the worse in girls she knows since the raids on Bath last April. Some girls were to be pitied. Some were undoubtedly suffering from sexual mania . . . The trouble was they could get any job they wanted at more money than the job was worth.'[59]

Although this campaign did not persuade the council to introduce any new by-laws, it was followed by a marked increase in police activity concerning young girls. Undoubtedly some were in need of care and attention, like the fifteen-year-old who had run away from home four times in three weeks to 'consort' with American soldiers. A painstakingly detailed account of how she spent Christmas 1943 was read out in court. On Christmas Eve she 'went to a U.S.A. camp party . . . spent the night in a GWR cloakroom; spent Christmas Day wandering the town until 7 p.m., dined with a U.S. soldier; left him at 1.0.a.m.; spent the night in a barn; met a U.S. soldier, went to London with him . . . met another soldier, went to the pictures with him . . . came back to Bath; put on a new dress given her by an American; went to a dance; went to a camp with a soldier . . . went to another "pub" with a soldier, who later was intimate with her'[60] and so on, and so on. The girl was now pregnant and did not know which of at least six members of the Allied armed forces was the father; the court sent her to approved school.

But there were also other prosecutions, such as the following:

1   22 January, 1944. Two girls aged 15 and 16 said by police to have been standing in a passageway in Bath each with a half pint glass of beer in her hand. Asked what it was, both replied 'bitter' and claimed they were 18. Magistrate put them 'on their honour' not to visit public houses but to promise to go instead to a youth club two or three times a week.

2   17 June, 1944. Bath girl aged 14 'stated . . . to have been found with American soldiers at midnight, and to have slept on park benches'. Court sent her to remand home. She was 'carried out of the court kicking and struggling'.

3   26 August, 1944. Bath girl aged 15 placed under supervision order. Police stated that she preferred 'the company of coloured American soldiers to white ones . . . On three occasions had stayed out all night. It was amazing the self-assurance the girl had, and she seemed to know more about sexual matters than some women did at 40.'

4   28 October, 1944. Two girls aged 15 and 16 sent to approved school. The older was said to smoke 40 cigarettes a day and the younger to be 'very fond of US soldiers'. The magistrate remarked of the cigarette smoking 'it is an absolute scandal, because it is a wicked waste of money and the mother has encouraged it'.

5   3 January, 1945. Bath girl aged 16 put on probation. Accused of being drunk and disorderly at 10.40 p.m., of having visited a pub with a friend who had been picked up

by two US soldiers. She was ordered not to continue to associate with her friend.

The remedy of approved school or remand home applied to three of these girls seems out of all proportion to their offences. That it should be imposed might be defensible if there had been strong evidence to suppose that such girls were likely to benefit from a period inside one of these institutions. But it was already known that over 50 per cent of those released at the start of the war had been reconvicted by the end of 1943, and further cases occurred within Bath itself which indicated that all was not well at such schools. For instance, two Bath girls were prosecuted for absconding from approved school in early 1945. Evidence given by the matron of the school in court unintentionally revealed that supervision at the school was poor ('the trouble really started when these girls went for a walk and met some Italian prisoners-of-war whom they kissed'), as well her own naivety ('I don't know why they should want to mix with such men because they don't know Italian') and the opportunities approved schools afforded for the dissemination of precisely the sort of information that the authorities sought to keep from such girls (they had absconded when they heard about the 'good times' others were having).

The magistrate decided to extend their sentence by a further six months.[61]

Sentence to an approved school was supposed to be followed by a period of after-care, but even in peacetime such provision was often rudimentary.[62] After the war began it seems largely to have ceased, while magistrates were forced to balance carefully the merits of fining and sentence to an institution in the light of the growing shortage of appropriate resources for probation. They tended to opt for more fines – with one interesting exception. Young adults (aged from seventeen to twenty) were the only age group in the population whose infringements of the law were more widely punished by prison.

CHAPTER ELEVEN

The Police and the Courts

The Editor of the *Police Chronicle*, contemplating the state of crime in February 1939, was 'glad to notice that in one of our big city Police divisions, at least, concrete evidence and indisputable statistics have been produced to prove that crime is on the wane. This pleasant news comes to us from Liverpool . . . Although the year showed a decided increase in the number of prosecutions for dangerous driving and other motoring offences, there was a marked decline in the total number of cases dealt with by the courts, whilst a decrease was also noticeable in the incidence of juvenile crime. We . . . are favourably impressed . . . with the cheering messages which these reports brought' and 'would like to draw attention to the work of the police'. Their high 'standard of efficiency occasionally merits a few words of commendation'.[1] The message from Liverpool seemed particularly gratifying in that the great seaport had traditionally been a major centre of criminal activity.

During the 1930s there had been a steady rise in reported crime, but the year-to-year changes were not particularly sharp, certainly not sharp enough for the press – which took careful note of the relevant statistics – to raise serious alarm about them.

Number of crimes known to the police in England and Wales[2]

1934	1935	1936	1937	1938	% change 1934–8
233,359	234,372	248,803	266,265	283,220	+21·3

This general increase concealed some interesting variations. In Leeds, for instance, the number of indictable
offences fell by 3½ per cent in 1939 compared with 1938, while
in Manchester and Stoke-on-Trent there were also slight
declines. In some smaller industrial towns even larger falls
were recorded: 12 per cent in Burnley, 11 per cent in Bolton,
13 per cent in Luton. Burnley and Luton, industrially, presented an almost total contrast to one another during the
1930s. The car town was booming, had hardly any unemployment, and was attracting immigrants from all over the
country. The cotton centre, on the other hand, suffered
20 per cent unemployment throughout the decade, as its pre-
dominant weaving sector went into alarming and worsening
decline. Both towns experienced their sharpest spells of failure and success in 1938–9, yet both showed an almost identical fall in indictable crime.

Elsewhere recorded crime increased, most conspicuously in
the Metropolitan Police District.

Total number of reported indictable crimes in the Metropolitan Police District[3]

1934	1935	1936	1937	1938
83,036	80,336	83,777	92,192	95,280

There was a stutter in 1934–5, but between 1935 and 1938
recorded offences rose by over 18 per cent. At the same time it
must be remembered that many of these offences were petty
thefts; in Nottingham, where 68 per cent of indictable
offences were simple larcenies, the Chief Constable suggested
that many could have been prevented if the owners had taken
greater care.[4]

The initial years of war did not produce any marked
changes, while between 1941 and 1943 there was a rise of only
3·9 per cent in recorded indictable crime in England and
Wales.[5] Once again there were wide variations between different cities:

Percentage change in reported indictable offences

	Birmingham	Manchester	Stoke	Birkenhead	Leicester	Leeds	Bristol
1942	+4·7	+ 0	+0	+16·1	NA	+0	−6·75
1943	+3·5	+20·4	+5·1	−12	−24·4	−11·2	NA

Some of these changes from year to year were striking, most notably in Birkenhead and Manchester. The Birkenhead figures, however, may serve as a warning to approach statistics for single towns with caution. There, at the end of 1942, a seventy-year-old Chief Constable was forced to resign and the new Chief made it clear that he thought his predecessor had fallen behind the times ('he proposed to give the public all the police service which is normally given by a fully-manned police station').[6] It may indeed have been the case that the organisational changes the new man introduced did reduce crime, but he also had an incentive to demonstrate the effectiveness of the new broom in a way that observers would most clearly appreciate, that is, through the statistics. Technical changes in recording methods – whether a 'theft' should be noted as such or as a 'loss', for example – could produce quite large modifications in the amount of 'crime'. It seems, therefore, that conclusions based on the totals of reported crime for single towns must be tentative unless the broad trend among them goes in the same direction.

In 1942–3 there was no such clear trend, and even the figures for London were superficially comforting: fewer indictable crimes in 1943 than in 1939:

1939	1940	1941	1942	1943[7]
94,852	93,869	99,533	93,138	91,205

Certainly, the blackout, the blitz and the arrival of the Allied armies had not produced a devastating crime wave. But if the figures are adjusted to take account of changes in population (the civilian population of London fell by nearly two million between 1938 and 1945) it shows a steady rise in crime. In 1938 there had been 10·95 indictable offences per 1,000 population; in 1943 there were approximately 13·2 and in 1944, 15.

Observers, in the middle stages of the war, had thus to separate conflicting strands of evidence, though the doubts they expressed about the extent and nature of the increase in crime were soon resolved. The *Police Review* commented bluntly when surveying the position in 1944 that there was 'substantial evidence of a serious increase in crime in many parts of the country'.[8]

Percentage change in the totals of indictable crime known to the police

	England and Wales	MPD	Manchester	Birmingham	Leeds
1944	+ 11·3	NA	+ 41	+ 9·1	+ 11·2
1945	+ 15·2	+ 24·2	+ 60	−1·1	+ 4·3

The rise in crime in the capital is a special case; but the increase in Manchester is a problem in itself. No direct explanation is offered in the reports of the Chief Constable as to what was happening, but rough clues are concealed in the tables in the reports which indicate that housebreaking, shopbreaking and warehouse raids were the types of crime showing the greatest increase – in other words, the pattern in Manchester resembled closely that in London, and behind both of them lay the insatiable demands of the black market. It may be that Manchester's position at the centre of three relevant trades (textiles, retail and distribution) made it especially vulnerable.

These developments were sufficiently worrying in themselves, but they were accompanied by another trend: the record of the police in detecting crime was – during the later stages of the war – deteriorating almost everywhere.

Percentage of offences detected or 'cleared up'

	1941	1942	1943	1944	1945	% change 1941–5
MPD	30·9	33·7	31·5	28·9	24·6	− 6·3
Leeds	44·4	40·1	46·1	40·9	37·9	− 6·5
Manchester	NA	63·8	53·5	42·9	30·9	−32·9 (1942–5)
Birmingham	54	54	50	47	44	−10
Middlesbrough	73·1	65·2	NA	66·5	59	−14·1
Luton	73	NA	63	60	64·5	− 7·5
Birkenhead	NA	53·8	NA	52·3	45·2	− 8·6 (1942–5)
Stoke-on-Trent	NA	86	NA	80·7	66·7	−19·3 (1942–5)
Newcastle/Lyme	76	NA	67·6	56	47·1	−28·9

There were thus improvements in certain years over the preceding ones in some towns, but the general trend during the war was downwards. Rising crime rates and deteriorating success in detection reflected badly on the police and their spokesmen were quick to draw attention to the problems affecting the force – reduced numbers of staff, deteriorating quality of equipment, and poor pay.

Between 1940 and 1944 there was a reduction of 14,000 in

the number of regular police in England and Wales. During 1945, as men were released from the armed forces, the number rose again, though only by 3,600. The decline had been anticipated, and the authorities sought to supplement the diminishing number of regulars from three main sources, full-time special constables, the First Police Reserve (mainly former policemen) and women.

	Regular Police	Special Police	First Reserves[9]
1940	57,012	25,220	5,725
1943	44,430	25,350	4,655
1944	43,026	17,527	2,568
1945	46,623	12,951	1,646

Thus the number of specials and reserves declined sharply during the war, although they greatly strengthened the force throughout the period, a point not always acknowledged by the regular police themselves.

The police had not been nationalised at the start of the war, but individuals were freely transferred to help constabularies in difficulties. Liverpool, for instance, gained 1,225 in this way, and Coventry 941.[10] The police authority that suffered the greatest strain was the Metropolitan, and the regulars there had declined to 14,925 by 1945, compared with 18,511 in 1938.[11] Merely to restore the position to peacetime levels required the addition of one constable for every four policemen already serving.

As younger constables left to join the armed forces and were replaced (if at all) by older men, the police suffered an increasing problem of sickness, which began to reach a position of crisis in 1944–6. In the Metropolitan Police District, the average age of the force rose from thirty-five pre-war to forty-five in December 1945[12], while the number of days lost through sickness almost doubled from 1938 (181,326) to 1945 (345,671). The most alarming change occurred from 1944 to 1945, when in a single year there was a jump of over 100,000 days lost. If these figures are corrected on an individual basis, they show that in 1938 each policeman lost on average 9·8 days, but in 1945 he lost 23·1 days.

The way many smaller provincial police forces were affected can be illustrated from the situation in Birkenhead. There, in 1945, three sergeants and eight constables (representing 11 per cent and 25 per cent respectively of the strength of those ranks) were discharged on medical grounds. The Chief Constable wrote: '. . . this large number may be due in some measure to the average age of the force being so high and to many of the men having completed at least 26 years patrol duty; or it may be an indication that 30 years of patrol duty are too exacting for the average man . . . A middle-aged Police Force has been growing old. Some were already old by Police standards at the outbreak of war and many have already been pensioned on the grounds of ill-health. Black-out, bombing and war strain have taken serious toll of the health of the remainder, many of whom are waiting to claim a pension as soon as they are permitted to do so.'[13] The *Police Review* concluded in 1945 that 'sickness among the Police is much more prevalent than it was, that recovery takes longer, and that the increased average age of the Force has a lot to do with it'.[14]

The senior ranks came under particularly severe pressure. In the first nine months of 1941 alone, fifteen vacancies occurred, including the Chief Constables of such important constabularies as Birmingham, Hull, and Derbyshire. Of the fifteen, only four were the result of appointments to posts elsewhere; two of the remainder were caused by death, one by resignation and eight by retirement. Some left voluntarily, recognising that the war emergency made it necessary that younger and fitter men be appointed, but others resisted, and some showed considerable skill in mobilising local opinion in their support, but usually to little avail. Home Office pressure was usually too strong. In the event of an invasion it was obvious that chief constables would be crucially important and it was essential that they be fully up to the physical and mental requirements of the task. It was an argument that proved too strong for watch committees, no matter how attached they were to their chief constables.

Shortages of staff in the police were, of course, made up from the special and reserve police, and women. This last group was to provide the focus for one of the most bitter conflicts to affect the police during the war (the other erupted over pay, but here the police were united against their paymasters). From the time that Herbert Morrison became Home Secretary, the Ministry brought increasing pressure to

bear on watch committess and chief constables to appoint
more women police, a campaign that came to a head in 1944.
The power to appoint women police had been established for
some considerable time: Oxford County force had had them
since 1918, but many authorities resisted the idea.

Morrison stated firmly at the start of 1944: '. . . it is my
policy to encourage the appointment of Police women in any
area where they seem likely to be useful'.[15] The issue aroused
strong feelings on both sides of the argument. In March 1944,
for instance, 500 women representing 70 organisations
gathered in London to demand the employment of more
women police and the Archbishop of Canterbury, Dr Temple,
gave as his opinion the view that 'the main obstacle has been
sheer downright, stark prejudice'.[16]

Certainly, some chief constables and watch committees
were bitterly and bluntly opposed to the idea. The Chief
Constable of Salford, Major C. V. Godfrey, announced that
'his views did not differ from those he had expressed to the
Watch Committee as far back as 1927. He was of the opinion
that the less decent women saw of the seamy and sordid side of
a policeman's life the better it would be for them, the community at large, and future generations. "I have not met with
any cases handled by my officers which could have been better
dealt with by policewomen," ' he said.[17] Some members of
watch committees expressed themselves even more strongly.
The Marquis of Bristol, for instance, a member of West Suf-
folk Standing Joint Committee, protested against those who
'want to put women in uniform to go about swanking as
police'.[18] Others were fatalistic (the Mayor of Bury St.
Edmunds: 'In view of the Home Secretary having said it was
essential . . . it was not much good kicking against it')[19] while
still others pointed to the financial advantages as the main
consideration. Hence the Chief Constable of Bedfordshire;
women should be appointed 'because they ranked for a 100
per cent grant from the Home Office. If necessary the Committee could dispense with the service of the policewomen at
the end of the war. He had his own views as to whether [they]
would have the effect anticipated.'[20]

Some opponents adopted a rather more subtle strategy,
declaring in favour of the *principle* of women police but going
on to point out either that there was nothing for them to do or

that the type of work available was unsuitable for women. The Chief Constable of Leamington announced that if he was in charge of 'another place' he might favour the proposal, but as for Leamington 'he thought that a woman welfare officer could do more than a woman in uniform'.[21] The acting Chief Constable of Huntingdonshire said that 'he had an open mind on the subject, and was in no way prejudiced. What concerned him as much as anything else was what they were to do with policewomen in Huntingdon. They might do useful work in the evening visiting licensed houses, but for that they would need to patrol in pairs and be accompanied by a man. If they went alone, particularly on Fridays and Saturdays, he was afraid they would be insulted.'[22] The Chairman of Salford Watch Committee, Alderman Greenwood, made much the same point when he said that 'patrols like those in the dock areas establishments are problems enough for hardened men, let alone for women'.[23] Yet was patrol work the only kind of work that was available to police women?

The experience of Salford provides an answer. Not very long after Alderman Greenwood had given his opinion, the Chief Constable reported that a 'serious reduction ... has taken place during the last twenty-five years or so in the number of men available for street duty'. In 1919, 214 men were so available, but by December 1945 only 140. 'Other duties required the services of 116 in 1919, but 191 in 1945.' Furthermore, he commented, 'this process of cutting down the manpower allocated to beats in order to meet the daily demands of other duties increasingly imposed on the Police ... has had a bad effect upon the incidence of crime'. Administrative work was primarily responsible.[24] Yet, it might be asked, were women incapable of assisting in that kind of work, and also in detective work, where the risk of physical violence was presumably practically nil? It was a particularly dishonest tactic to imply that the only kind of work available to women was the most dangerous. It seems more probable that it was not their unsuitability that motivated the opposition but rather the very idea of them entering the male preserve of the police station.

Some authorities did go as far as putting out an advertisement for recruits, but they then discovered that none of those who had answered was suitable. Some made it even more

difficult for would-be applicants by insisting that only single
women and widows were eligible, and the low wages offered
(£2 17s a week)[25] were a further disincentive. Yet those
authorities which pursued a vigorous recruiting policy were
able to find well qualified women. Kent Constabulary secured
the sanction of the Home Secretary for the appointment of
twenty policewomen, found them, and chose a woman inspector to organise them. But the driving force here was Sir Percy
Sillitoe, Chief Constable of Kent, who by this decisive policy
cemented his relationship with the Home Secretary. Sillitoe
declared, 'I think the argument that policewomen are not
required because they will only be doing welfare work is false,
and is based on prejudice.'[26]

Morrison did not hesitate to instruct recalcitrant watch
committees (like Grimsby's)[27] to appoint women police; when
a lady member of King's Lynn Council congratulated members
of the watch committee on changing their minds on the matter (they had decided to appoint two) there were cries of 'we
were forced!'[28] Yet at the end of the day – and this was the
stormiest controversy affecting the police in 1944 – the fuss
was about a total increase in strength in England and Wales
from 282 in 1940 to 418 in 1945.[29] Although chief constables
and watch committees which opposed the idea had been
obliged to concede the principle, they were still able to resist
the practice. In 1945, after all the debate and discussion, there
were precisely thirty-three more women police in England
than there had been in 1944.

The war saw some substantial though temporary shifts in
the nature of police duties. The first and longest-lasting was
the decline in traffic patrol work. Before the war traffic
offences had accounted for about 67 per cent of non-
indictable crime.[30] Thereafter, each year, the number of cases
dealt with decreased. In 1938, 475,124 persons were found
guilty in the courts; in 1940 there were 208,152; in 1943,
101,337; whilst the low point was reached in 1944: 91,798.
Thereafter, as traffic returned to the roads, so did motorists
to the courts: 148,419 of them were found guilty in 1945.[31]
The decrease in the number of vehicles driven was naturally
accompanied by a decline in car thefts. In Brighton, 129 had
been stolen in 1939; two years later the number was only 16.[32]

It was fortunate that the burden of police duties was

relieved in this way because they had to face onerous and sometimes appalling tasks in other areas. Bombing raids were the most severe of a range of wartime duties that ran from enforcing the black-out to trying to maintain 'law and order' among the huge armies of allied troops, and between them and 'the natives'. The diversion of resources to these various duties was not responsible for the growth in crime – that would have occurred anyway, given the emergence of the black market – but it certainly hindered their efforts to come to grips with the problem.

As regards patterns of crime, there was a marked tendency during the war for crimes of larceny and receiving to be carried out by older people. Larceny, it should be pointed out, dominated patterns of crime in England and Wales throughout the war; together with breaking and entering it accounted for 90·2 per cent of indictable crime in 1939 and 90·2 per cent in 1945, even though the total of such crime rose from 303,771 to 478,394.[33]

In 1946, 69,127 persons were found guilty of larceny offences, compared with 56,092 in 1938; while amongst those whose offences were considered so serious that they required to be dealt with at higher courts* there was an even larger rise – from 1,229 to 1,769. People over thirty accounted for the largest change, as they did with receiving offences.

Percentage increase in the number of persons found guilty between 1938 and 1946: England and Wales[34]

	under 14	14 and under 17	17 and under 21	21 and under 30	30 and over
Larceny	13·6	8·5	9·7	18·3	49·5
Receiving	63·8	64·1	125·6	93·3	186

In crimes of receiving also, the higher courts dealt with more cases: 875 compared with 370 in 1938. With crimes of breaking and entering, on the other hand, younger offenders tended to predominate.

Percentage increase in number found guilty between 1938 and 1946[34]

under 14	14–17	17–21	21–30	30 +
84·4	74·9	140	112	82

* Assize, Quarter Sessions and the Central Criminal Court.

The growth in the number of property offenders during the war is striking; changes in the pattern of sexual crimes and crimes of violence were less sharp, though worrying to the authorities nonetheless.

Percentage increase in number found guilty between 1938 and 1946[34]

	under 14	14–17	17–21	21–30	30 +
Sexual offences	9·2	−3·6	7·9	85·7	57·4
Violence against the person	83	37·5	74·8	61·6	11·7

The Chief Constable of Liverpool summed up succinctly the main developments during the war in that city, typical in this respect of most if not all the important manufacturing and trading centres: 'The raids on the City left many premises very easy to break into, and premises made unfit for occupation provided cover from which to attack adjoining premises and also for hiding stolen goods. The shortages of all kinds of food and clothing made it easy for thieves to dispose of stolen property and also made it worth while to steal what before the war would not have repaid the trouble and risk. Crimes on a large scale were often instigated by operators in the Black Market, and on many occasions a whole lorry load of goods were stolen. Many such large-scale operations were detected by the police and successful prosecutions resulted, but it was seldom possible to obtain the evidence necessary to establish the guilt of the principal offender. Deserters from the Forces and Mercantile Marine were responsible for many offences and were not easy to catch as their visits were often of very short duration . . .'[35]

Complaints from commercial and business organisations arrived frequently. In Hull the Chamber of Trade wrote to the watch committee about thefts from business premises and suggested that police protection was 'inadequate'[36], while in Southampton, also in the autumn of 1945, a discussion took place in the Chamber of Commerce about the number of breaking-in offences committed in the town and it was further suggested that the police force was inadquate for its task.[37] In the light of this, certain fears were expressed that some policemen were inclined to 'cut corners'.

In late 1942, the Recorder of Liverpool, E. G. Hemmerde, transformed these fears into forthright allegations and something of an uproar ensued. Referring to a case of alleged police violence in the city he said: '. . . it is no use telling me that . . . beating up of arrested men in Bridewells does not go on . . . I am certain this sort of thing does happen to extract admissions and something has to be done about it.' A seventeen-year-old labourer charged with stealing claimed that he had been beaten for three hours to extract a confession. He told the Recorder that when he refused to admit what officers put to him one of them said 'we will sweat it out of him' and he was struck on the face with the flat of the hand, and beaten about the body. The Recorder added that he had received many complaints about beatings and that also 'he had had the advantage of hearing evidence of Police officers who had left the Police Force with good records'.[38]

These claims were vigorously denied by Liverpool police while the men named declared that 'they had never seen a prisoner struck in the bridewells or the cells'.[39] Members of the judiciary entered the controversy and Mr Justice Oliver at Liverpool Assizes commended the City Police on their 'scrupulous fairness . . . I am glad to think that the Police, who are so often attacked in a public and irresponsible way . . . have done absolutely the proper thing'.[40] Liverpool Watch Committee duly appointed a sub-committee to inquire into the conditions in which prisoners were held and questioned. It reported in late November 1942 that it was satisfied that adequate protection was provided for persons detained at Liverpool police stations.[41]

This, however, did not settle the controversy. Hemmerde came under attack in the *Police Review*, which demanded either that he substantiate his claims or withdraw them.[42] In fact he did neither, but proceeded to make further accusations. He declared that if the police did not restrain some of the 'toughs' among them they would bring the entire force into 'discredit' and he further charged the lay magistracy with 'lending countenance' to these same 'toughs' because they 'seem to think it their duty to support the Police in whatever they do or say'. He also dismissed the report of the watch committee: 'Obviously no proper inquiry was held at all. All they did was visit one or two bridewells after warnings, and ask the Police officers: "Is it true what the Recorder says" and the answer was, of course, "No." '43

At this point the dispute abruptly and unsatisfactorily ended – as far as the police journals which reported it were concerned. It is possible that if Hemmerde had made his allegations in peacetime the popular press and members of parliament would have taken them up and the issue would have been explored much more thoroughly. But the pressure of war news – the controversy coincided exactly with the Stalingrad campaign – permitted this controversy to disappear. The problem of providing proper protection for persons held in custody, however, did not expire with it, but surfaced again after the war, with equally unsatisfactory results. Ironically, only three months after the dispute in Liverpool had ceased, direct confirmation that such beatings did occur was provided, though not from Liverpool, from Reading. This case provided some revealing and relevant insights into the relations between the police and those families which had a record for lawbreaking.

A sixteen-year-old youth had been walking home with his girl friend one June night in 1941 when two policemen stopped them and asked to see their identity cards, which they could not produce. The girl was eventually allowed to go, but the boy was taken into custody and interviewed about a jewel robbery. When he denied any knowledge of this he 'was struck in the face by . . . three officers and kicked by one of them. He became semi-conscious and when he came to they were trying to wash the blood from his face and clothes.' Medical evidence confirmed that his nose had been broken. The judge (Hilbery) drew attention to the fact that a complete conflict of testimony existed between the boy and the three police officers, who totally denied the assault; and he concluded by making several remarks which followed closely what the Recorder of Liverpool had been saying. He observed that the youth was on probation at the time of the assault and that his family was 'notorious to the Police', who 'were just as liable as anyone else to resentment or to bear grudges. They were liable to take it out of someone who gave them trouble or whose associates menaced them.'44

To these points two others may be added. Firstly, the vigorous assertions of innocence on the part of those police accused of violence are invariably convincing in their strength. Magistrates often drew attention to this as a point in favour of the police. In this case too, 'total denials' were made which were in fact absolute lies. This must raise questions about other similar 'total denials', including those in the case to which Hemmerde referred. Secondly, the action (which was a civil case: the boy sued the police through his father) resulted in an award against the three policemen totalling £90, which seems astonishingly light, in view of the broken nose the youth had suffered. In cases of criminal violence, defendants found guilty had been sentenced to jail, even when the wounds inflicted were very much less serious than in this instance, which seems to be yet another unsatisfactory episode in the continuing controversy about police violence.

Wartime shortages of staff and resources also affected policy applied in the courts; there was a marked shift in sentencing away from probation towards prison in more serious cases and fining in less serious ones. To begin with the higher courts: these dealt with an increasing number of cases, and persons found guilty at them nearly doubled during the war, from 8,612 to 15,848. If these are divided into two main age groups, the 17–20-year-olds, and the adults (21 and over) they show the following trends:[45]

Percentage found guilty sentenced to the following:

17–20	1938	1945	1946	% change 1938–46
probation	35	25	25	− 10
bound over without supervision	18	22	21	+ 3
prison	7	17	19	+ 12
borstal	37	35	33	− 4

(Numbers involved: 1938, 2,004; 1946, 4,274)

21 and over	1938	1945	1946	% change 1938–46
probation	13	8	9	− 4
bound over	15	18	16	+ 1
prison	66	68	70	+ 4
borstal	3	2	2	− 1

(Numbers involved: 1938, 6,367; 1946, 10,842)

Thus, in both age groups, the reduction in the proportion put on probation was almost balanced by an increase in that jailed. There was also a lesser rise in the proportion bound over and

a reduction in that sent to borstal. Even more noticeable is the
harsher treatment meted out to the 17–20-year-olds in 1946,
compared with 1938. The same pattern was revealed in sentencing in magistrates courts:[45]

Decisions in magistrates courts in percentages

17–20-year-olds	1938	1945	1946	% change 1938–46
probation	45	24	26	− 19
dismissed or bound over	24	21	20	− 4
prison	7	13	13	+ 6
fined	17	38	36	+ 19
committed to higher court with view to borstal sentence	3	2	2	− 1

Once again the reduction in probation was balanced by a rise
in fining, but the doubling of the use of prison is the most
interesting element. Moreover, this age group was singled out
for the greater use of this punishment. This was not so with
adults (even though they had a worse record for larceny,
receiving, and sexal offences) or the 14–16-year-olds:

Decisions in magistrates courts in percentages

Adults (21 and over)	1938	1945	1946	% change 1938–46
probation	15	6	8	− 7
dismissed or bound over	25	17	17	− 8
prison	26	23	23	− 3
fined	32	53	51	+ 19
14—16				
probation	51	41	42	− 9
dismissed or bound over	26	26	25	− 1
approved school	13	11	13	+ 0
fined	8	19	17	+ 9

It was a curious trend as only in breaking and entering did the
17–20s account for the largest percentage rise among the age
groups, and there the 21–29-year-olds were a close second. It
seems that the decision to single them out for the greater use
of imprisonment was related to the wartime tendency to see
the young as both responsible for and susceptible to disruptive wartime influences.

Conclusion

The Second World War had produced dramatic shifts in patterns of crime. Rationing, combined with severe shortages, had caused a black market to emerge which was supplied by numerous amateur pilferers as well as by professional criminals who concentrated on stealing goods that were in short supply and on improving the techniques of lorry and warehouse theft. The number of receivers grew, of whom a sophisticated minority organised large-value thefts. The black market did not create more than a tiny circle of black-marketeers as such, but it did encourage countless numbers to participate in black-market deals, as buyers or sellers, including many businessmen, traders, shopkeepers and their customers whatever their social standing. Wartime patterns of crime continued to prevail in the early years of peace. Austerity, shortages and rationing prolonged the lifespan of the black market, which now operated in particularly favourable conditions: the war had been won and the public, with more to spend than ever before, sought the rewards of victory. The 'spiv' set out to satisfy them, as the black market reached its highest point of development in 1946–7.

Figures of recorded crime peaked shortly after at their highest all-time level, in 1948. A brief period followed when the rise levelled off, but the upward trend resumed in the mid-1950s. These fluctuations related to changes affecting the police force and the emergence of the affluent society. The police required time to re-organise and recruit before they were able to cope with the post-war surge in crime. Police chiefs during the war had been confident that 'given sufficient beat strength, assisted by and supplemented by mechanical and scientific aid, the present state of affairs would soon be remedied'[1] and indeed it seemed by the late 1940s that such predictions were being fulfilled. However, within a few years, a boom in the sales of consumer products began and the consequent proliferation of easily stealable goods, together with such developments as the eclipse of the corner shop and the rise of the supermarket, caused the number of thefts, and with them recorded crime, to resume the upward trend. By then the police were obliged to try to attract recruits, and keep the staff they already had, in an increasingly tight and well paid labour market, especially for those highly trained.

During the war the authorities and many members of the general public had been concerned that standards of morality and behaviour were deteriorating. Action was demanded and between 1943 and 1945 taken: even though the police were suffering a staffing crisis they managed to find the resources to mount a campaign against organised prostitution, night-clubs, after-hours drinking, betting and gaming. The young were identified as most vulnerable to the loosening of restraints and also as particularly likely to be influenced by the behaviour of American troops. In fact the exigencies of the war caused the police and the courts to re-evaluate 'juvenile crime' with the result that much of it was recognised to be trivial, not worthy of the attention of the courts. Nonetheless, fears about the repercussions of the war on the young continued to be expressed, though after the war they took the form of an analysis of its impact on those who had spent their formative years under its shadow. One study showed that the highest delinquency rates between 1946 and 1957 occurred among children whose fifth year had been passed during it, while rates for those who had spent their fourth and sixth years during the war were also well above the mean. This theory had considerable influence for a time.[2] However, as the generations born after 1945 proved not significantly less 'delinquent' than those born before, the theory seemed less persuasive.

The greatest significance of the war on long-term patterns of crime was that it speeded up the transition from a low-wage to a high-wage society. Even as late as 1938, two-thirds of British families had *no* capital, while the average wage was from about £3 to £3 10s a week. The war provided high wages, but it failed to deliver consumer goods; professional criminals devoted themselves to making up the difference, as did many amateurs and, indeed, children. These circumstances continued into peacetime. While the 'moral' pressures of the war effort ceased, economic conditions became even harsher, with the 'dollar gap' dominating policy and bread rationed for the first time. During this period such underworld figures as Sidney Stanley, Max Intrator and Stanley Setty came into their own, and they did so, one observer has suggested, because crime came 'close to the people . . . Amateurs turned to [its] fringes, and justice was easy to evade . . . Crime became something that even men of probity could rationalize as their proper defence against the turbulent forces around them . . . It reproduced the conditions of war at minimal risk and with substantial promise of benefit.'[3]

For the criminal, the succeeding years were to see that promise substantially fulfilled.

Notes

In this book certain sources have been used frequently. They are abbreviated as follows:

Met. AR: *Reports of the Commissioner of Police of the Metropolis*
Manch. AR: City of Manchester Watch Committee, *Chief Constable's Reports*
Birm. AR: *The Reports of the Police Establishment and the State of Crime in the City of Birmingham*
Crim. Stats: *Criminal Statistics. England and Wales*
PR: *The Police Review*
PC: *Police Chronicle and Constabulary World*
BA: *Birkenhead Advertiser*
EC: *Essex Chronicle*
ELA: *East London Advertiser*
HG: *Hackney Gazette*
IG: *Islington Gazette*
RCG: *Rochester, Chatham and Gillingham Journal*
RR: *The Recorder,* Romford
SLP: *South London Press*
WLP: *West London Press*

INTRODUCTION

1 RCG, 7 March, 1945.
2 IG, 18 November, 1941.
3 *Kensington Gazette*, 6 March, 1942.
4 IG, 31 May, 1940.
5 Crim. Stats, 1939–45, p. 11.
6 Crim. Stats, 1946, Appendix III B.
7 G. Gibson, *Enemy Coast Ahead* (1955 edn), p. 44.

CHAPTER ONE: MORALE

1 *Brighton and Hove Gazette*, 28 March, 1942.
2 *Hampstead and Highgate Express*, 8 September, 1939.
3 HG, 8 November, 1939.
4 *Harrow Observer*, 26 January, 1940.
5 HG, 6 September, 1939.
6 R. Skidelsky, *Oswald Mosley* (1976), p. 345.
7 WLP, 12 April, 1940.
8 HG, 29 May, 1940.
9 ELA, 15 June, 1940.
10 *Finsbury Weekly News*, 31 May, 1940; 7 June, 1940.
11 RCG, 26 February, 1941.

12 BA, 25 October, 1939.
13 HG, 29 May, 1940.
14 ibid., 26 August, 1940.
15 ibid., 15 July, 1940.
16 SLP, 21 May, 1940.
17 ibid., 2 July 1940; 19 July, 1940.
18 *Finsbury Weekly News*, 14 June, 1940.
19 *Brighton and Hove Gazette*, 16 May, 1942.
20 RCG, 17 February, 1943.
21 RCG, 17 July, 1940.
22 *Hampshire Telegraph*, 5 July, 1940.
23 ibid., 16 April, 1943.
24 BA, 27 July, 1940.
25 *Luton News*, 27 June, 1940.
26 *Kensington Post*, 8 November, 1941.
27 SLP, 19 July, 1940.
28 *Hampshire Telegraph*, 23 June, 1944.
29 *Hampstead and Highgate Express*, 18 April, 1941.
30 EC, 23 April, 1942.
31 *Kensington Post*, 25 July, 1942.
32 A. Calder, *The People's War. Britain 1939–45* (1971 edn), p. 574.
33 EC, 23 April, 1942.
34 *Hampshire Telegraph*, 24 March, 1944.
35 BA, 28 August, 1943.
36 Calder, p. 510.
37 *Leicester Advertiser*, 3 June, 1944.
38 BA, 20 February, 1943.
39 ibid., 15 May, 1943.
40 ibid., 11 August, 1943.
41 ibid., 22 November, 1944.
42 RCG, 5 July, 1944.
43 ibid., 5 July, 1944.
44 *Stockton and Tees-Side Weekly Herald*, 10 January, 1942.
45 HG, 29 September, 1941.
46 *Hampshire Telegraph*, 10 April, 1942.
47 RR, 24 March, 1944.
48 ibid., 25 August, 1944.

CHAPTER TWO: THEFT AT WORK

1 N. Monsarrat, *The Cruel Sea* (1956 edn), pp. 170–1.
2 BA, 13 September, 1940.
3 ibid., 25 January, 1941.
4 ibid., 20 February, 1943.
5 ibid., 18 July, 1942.
6 ibid., 23 February, 1944.
7 *Bootle Times*, 14 January, 1944.
8 BA, 8 February, 1941.
9 ibid., 16 September, 1943.
10 ibid., 7 December, 1940.
11 ibid., 25 June, 1941.
12 *Kentish Mercury*, 4 February, 1944.
13 HG, 20 November, 1944.
14 *Northampton Mercury and Herald*, 10 September, 1943.

15 IG, 10 December, 1943.
16 HG, 18 January, 1943.
17 ibid., 10 November, 1941.
18 ibid., 29 January, 1943.
19 ibid., 13 December, 1940.
20 ibid., 7 December, 1942.
21 ibid., 21 September, 1942.
22 ibid., 17 April, 1942.
23 ibid., 7 August, 1940.
24 ibid., 14 December, 1942.
25 IG, 19 May, 1942.
26 HG, 18 September, 1940.
27 ibid., 12 July, 1943; 19 July, 1943.
28 RR, 15 September, 1944.
29 ibid., 30 May, 1941.
30 ibid., 10 October, 1941.
31 ibid., 31 January, 1941.
32 HG, 3 January, 1945.
33 ibid., 1 September, 1944.
34 IG, 28 April, 1944.
35 RR, 2 January, 1942.
36 HG, 25 September, 1942.
37 RR, 30 April, 1943.
38 HG, 15 May, 1942.
39 IG, 30 August, 1943.
40 RR, 4 September, 1942.
41 ibid., 30 May, 1941.
42 ibid., 18 December, 1942.
43 IG, 19 May, 1942.
44 ibid., 4 December, 1942.
45 ibid., 23 October, 1942.
46 HG, 18 January, 1943.
47 ibid., 18 January, 1943.
48 ibid., 9 August, 1943.
49 IG, 19 January, 1943.
50 BA, 22 February, 1941; 20 Feburary 1943.
51 ibid., 19 March, 1941.
52 HG, 27 November 1942; 7 December, 1942; 18 January, 1943; 29 January 1943.
53 ibid., 17 May, 1943.
54 ibid., 14 October, 1938; 5 December, 1938; 19 December, 1938; 28 July, 1939.
55 ibid., 6 January, 1943.
56 ibid., 5 January, 1942.

CHAPTER THREE: THEFT: MAINLY PROFESSIONAL

1 E. J. Hobsbawm, *The Pelican Economic History of Britain: Volume 3. From 1750 to the Present Day. Industry and Empire* (1969 edn), pp. 254–5.
2 Met. AR, 1936–8; Birm. AR, 1936–9.
3 Met. AR, 1944, p. 5.
4 Manch. AR, 1939.
5 Met. AR, 1936, p. 49.
6 Birm. AR. 1937.
7 Met. AR. 1935–9; Birm AR, 1935–9.
8 F. D. Sharpe, *Sharpe of the Flying Squad* (1938), pp. 144–9.

9 Sharpe, pp. 144–9.
10 Dewitt MacKenzie, *Hell's Kitchen* (1930), Chapter XIII.
11 *Star*, 23 April, 1938.
12 ibid., 11 August, 1938.
13 ibid., 30 April, 1938.
14 *Evening Standard*, 10 January, 1938.
15 *Star*, 10 March, 1938.
16 *Evening Standard*, 28 January, 1938.
17 W. C. Hill, *Boss of the Underworld* (1955), p. 139.
18 Sharpe, pp. 49–58.
19 John Gosling, *The Ghost Squad* (1959), pp. 145–6.
20 Hill, p. 42.
21 Met. AR, 1937, p. 7.
22 Birm. AR, 1937.
23 Met. AR, 1939, p. 8.
24 EC, 13 June, 1941.
25 G. H. Hatherill, *A Detective's Story*, pp. 26–30.
26 John C. Spencer, *Crime and the Services* (1954), p. 125.
27 ibid., p. 125.
28 ibid., p. 134.
29 HG, 28 June, 1946.
30 e.g. HG, 21 January, 1946.
31 H. Mannheim, *War and Crime* (1941), p. 97.
32 Birm. AR, 1941.
33 Charles Raven, *Underworld Nights* (1956), p. 186.
34 *Brighton and Hove Gazette*, 29 June, 1940.
35 *Kensington Post*, 14 August, 1943.
36 IG, 1 January, 1943.
37 Spencer, p. 52.
38 Met. AR, 1945, p. 4.
39 Birm. AR, 1940–3.
40 H. Silcock, *The Increase in Crimes of Theft 1938–47* (1949), p. 15.
41 Met. AR, 1944; 1945, p. 29.
42 *Star*, 7 July, 1944.
43 ibid., 30 May, 1944.
44 ibid., 21 July, 1944.
45 Gosling, *Ghost Squad*, p. 20.
46 ibid., p. 43.
47 Silcock, p. 15.
48 Met. AR, 1944, p. 4.
49 ibid., p. 4.
50 ibid., 1947, 38–9.
51 Manch. AR, 1946.
52 Met. AR, 1938–47; Birm. AR, 1938–47.
53 Manch. AR, 1938–46.
54 *Evening Standard*, 18 January, 1947.
55 ibid., 7 January, 1947.
56 ibid., 1 April, 1947.
57 *Star*, 9 August, 1947.
58 ibid., 28 July, 1947; 25 August, 1947.
59 Met. AR, 1944.
60 Birm. AR, 1947, p. 26.
61 Gosling, *Ghost Squad*, p. 20.

CHAPTER FOUR: THE BLACK MARKET

1 Lord Woolton, *Memoirs* (1959), pp. 230–31.
2 Calder, p. 469.
3 Met. AR, 1944, p. 5.
4 Marshall B. Clinard, *The Black Market* (New York, 1952), p. 27.
5 RR, 20 March, 1942.
6 ibid., 20 March, 1942.
7 ibid., 27 March, 1942.
8 ibid., 29 May, 1942.
9 ibid., 12 June, 1942.
10 EC, 14 August, 1942.
11 ibid., 19 February, 1943.
12 ibid., 19 February, 1943.
13 ibid., 3 March, 1944.
14 HG, 13 December, 1944.
15 ibid., 13 December, 1944.
16 ibid., 27 December, 1944.
17 *Stockton and Tees-Side Weekly Herald*, 31 January, 1942.
18 HG, 7 April, 1941.
19 ibid., 14 May, 1941.
20 ibid., 20 February, 1942.
21 RR, 21 November, 1941.
22 IG, 17 October, 1941.
23 HG, 23 June, 1941.
24 *Wembley News*, 1 January, 1943.
25 RR, 30 January, 1943; HG, 30 July, 1943.
26 IG, 19 January, 1943; 4 December, 1942.
27 RR, 26 September, 1941.
28 EC, 29 December, 1944.
29 BA, 13 September, 1944.
30 *West Herts and Watford Observer*, 15 December, 1944.
31 ibid., 22 December, 1944.
32 EC, 15 May, 1942.
33 *Yorkshire Evening Post*, 1 February, 1945.
34 ibid., 22 January, 1945.
35 J. L. Hodson, *Home Front* (1944) p. 25.
36 A. Noyes Thomas (ed.), *Calling Scotland Yard* (1954), pp. 139–40.
37 *Slough Observer*, 1 September, 1944.
38 *East End News*, 6 March, 1942.
39 Calder, p. 373.
40 HG, 18 December, 1944.
41 *Yorkshire Evening Post*, 1 February, 1945.
42 *West Herts and Watford Observer*, 20 August, 1943.
43 *Willesden Chronicle*, 10 March, 1944; 26 May, 1944; 28 July, 1944.
44 HG, 18 December, 1944.
45 ibid., 22 August, 1945.
46 RCG, 3 May, 1944.
47 HG, 8 October, 1945.
48 *Evening Standard*, 4 January, 1945.
49 ibid., 4 January, 1945.
50 ibid., 23 January, 1945.
51 PC, 18 July, 1947.
52 *Evening Standard*, 18 January, 1945.
53 *The People*, 29 October, 1944.

54 *Evening Standard*, 25 February, 1946.
55 HG, 22 March, 1946; 9 August, 1946.
56 ELA, 5 July, 1946; *Kensington Gazette*, 28 June, 1946.
57 ibid., 3 August, 1945.
58 ibid., 28 June, 1946.
59 ELA, 28 June, 1946.
60 HG, 28 June, 1946.
61 HG, 21 June, 1946.
62 EC, 24 May, 1946.
63 HG, 18 December, 1944.

CHAPTER FIVE: RATIONING

1   Calder, p. 322.
2   EC, 24 October, 1941.
3   RR, 5 September, 1941.
4   Woolton, p. 192.
5   HG, 11 August, 1941.
6   RR, 30 January, 1942.
7   HG, 11 August, 1941.
8   IG, 12 July, 1940.
9   *Slough Observer*, 2 June, 1944.
10 HG, 22 October, 1943.
11 *Leicester Mercury*, 25 January, 1944; 2 February, 1944.
12 Gosling, pp. 55–7.
13 HG, 20 April, 1942.
14 *Kensington Post*, 25 July, 1942.
15 ELA, 1 September, 1944.
16 *Willesden Chronicle*, 28 January, 1944; 25 February, 1944; 16 June, 1944; 7 July, 1944.
17 Calder, pp. 325–8.
18 SLP, 15 September, 1944.
19 *Paddington Mercury*, 24 October, 1942.
20 *Wembley News*, 6 October, 1942.
21 ibid., 27 October, 1944.
22 HG, 29 April, 1942.
23 *Willesden Chronicle*, 16 April, 1943.
24 Raven, pp. 126–7.
25 ibid., pp. 92–3.
26 *Star*, 22 July, 1944.
27 *East End News*, 7 January, 1944.
28 ELA, 30 June, 1944.
29 Birm. AR, 1947, p. 26.
30 WPN, 13 November, 1942.
31 SLP, 22 August, 1944.
32 ELA, 17 July, 1943.
33 ibid., 1 October, 1943.
34 *East End News*, 16 October, 1942.
35 e.g. ELA, 6 September, 1941.
36 Sydney Horler, *London's Underworld* (1934), pp. 90–100.
37 ibid., p. 100; R. Thurston Hopkins, *Crime and Money* (undated), pp. 6–11.
38 e.g. *Finsbury Weekly News*, 8 March, 1940.
39 Hill, pp. 142–3.

40   *East End News*, 13 February, 1942; *Manchester Guardian*, 24 March, 1942; 4 April, 1942; 30 April, 1942; 13 May, 1942.
41   *Evening Standard*, 10 April, 1947.
42   HG, 22 February, 1943.
43   ibid., 17 February, 1943.

CHAPTER SIX: WHITE-COLLAR CRIME

1   T. Morris, *The Criminal Area* (1957), pp. 165–70.
2   cf. Bruce Lockhart's account of Nancy Astor's efforts on behalf of one of her sons, in R. Bruce Lockhart, *The Diaries of Sir Robert Bruce Lockhart* (ed. K.Young), vol. I: 1915–1938 (1973), p. 177.
3   WLP, 21 August, 1942.
4   ibid., 7 March, 1941.
5   *Westminster and Pimlico News*, 7 November, 1941.
6   ibid., 14 November, 1941.
7   *Kensington Post*, 16 September, 1944.
8   cf. Hill, p. 140.
9   *Daily Herald*, 25 April, 1944.
10   RR, 16 April, 1943.
11   RR, 14 November, 1941; 13 March, 1942.
12   ibid., 14 November, 1941.
13   *Ilford Recorder*, 26 March, 1942.
14   RR, 30 January, 1942; 13 February, 1942.
15   *Wembley News*, 11 May, 1945.
16   *Kensington Gazette*, 19 April, 1946.
17   HG, 1 December, 1941.
18   ibid., 20 October, 1941; 24 October, 1941; 10 November, 1941.
19   ibid., 1 December, 1941.
20   *Ilford Recorder*, 15 April, 1943; 4 February, 1943.
21   RR, 1 September, 1944.
22   *Willesden Chronicle*, 23 June, 1944.
23   SLP, 16 May, 1941.
24   *Ilford Recorder*, 20 May, 1943; 8 April, 1943.
25   BA, 25 March, 1942.
26   ibid., 25 March, 1942.
27   RR, 2 October, 1942.
28   *Ilford Recorder*, 26 November, 1942.
29   ibid., 2 November, 1944.
30   PC, 31 May, 1946.
31   RR, 2 October, 1942.
32   *Ilford Recorder*, 12 November, 1942.
33   SLP, 7 May, 1943.
34   ibid., 7 April, 1944.
35   *Kensington Post*, 20 March, 1943.

CHAPTER SEVEN: BETTING, GAMING AND DRINK

1   HG, 17 May, 1944.
2   *Kensington Gazette*, 10 November, 1944.
3   *Brighton and Hove Gazette*, 21 October, 1939.
4   ibid., 7 October, 1939; 8 July 1939.
5   *Evening Standard*, 16 February, 1939.

6 *Evening Standard*, 27 January, 1939.
7 ibid., 27 January, 1939.
8 G. H. Totterdell, *Country Copper* (1956).
9 HG, 3 February, 1939; *Kensington Gazette*, 26 May, 1939.
10 HG, 9 June, 1939.
11 *Kensington Gazette*, 10 March, 1939.
12 ibid., 12 May, 1939.
13 ibid., 10 March, 1939.
14 ibid., 13 June, 1941.
15 Norman Lucas, *Britain's Gangland* (1969), pp. 17–27.
16 C. L. Mowat, *Britain Between the Wars 1918–1940* (1955), p. 249.
17 Crim. Stats, 1939–45, Table B.
18 Met. AR, 1939.
19 *Westminster and Pimlico News*, 29 April, 1939.
20 ibid., 21 July, 1939.
21 ELA, 25 August, 1944.
22 *Kensington Gazette*, 12 May, 1939.
23 *Brighton and Hove Gazette*, 20 September, 1941.
24 *Kensington Gazette*, 2 June, 1939.
25 Met. AR, 1939. p. 11.
26 Met. AR, 1945, Table 7; Crim. Stats, 1939–45.
27 PR, 27 September, 1940.
28 HG, 11 April, 1945.
29 Met. AR, 1944, p. 9.
30 SLP, 16 October, 1942.
31 PR, 29 August, 1941.
32 RCG, 22 April, 1942; 11 August, 1943.
33 ibid., 10 February, 1943.
34 Crim. Stats, 1939–45, Table B.
35 Calder, p. 432.
36 *Wembley News*, 9 July, 1943.
37 *Kensington Gazette*, 7 May, 1943.
38 ibid., 7 November, 1941.
39 *East End News*, 16 August, 1940.
40 HG, 21 January, 1944.
41 ibid., 8 March, 1944.
42 ibid., 20 March, 1944.
43 ibid., 28 March, 1944.
44 S. Cohen, *Folk Devils and Moral Panics* (1973 edn), p. 106.
45 *Brighton and Hove Gazette*, 20 September, 1941.
46 PR, 29 August, 1941.
47 Met. AR, 1944.
48 Hill, pp. 75–6.
49 ibid., p. 157.
50 R. Fabian, *London After Dark*, pp. 91–2.
51 *Evening Standard*, 11 January, 1946.
52 Hill, p. 118.
53 HG, 24 February, 1947.
54 ibid., 19 November, 1947.
55 A. Boyle, *Trenchard* (1962), p. 609.
56 HG, 14 May, 1943.
57 *Islington Gazette*, 18 August, 1942.
58 cf. B. Cox, J. Shirley and M. Short, *The Fall of Scotland Yard* (1977).

CHAPTER EIGHT: PROSTITUTION

1   Anon, *Nell or I had no choice. The Diary of an 'Unfortunate'* (1940), p. 14.
2   ibid., p. 29.
3   ibid., p. 89.
4   ibid., p. 126.
5   Sir C. Burt, *The Young Delinquent* (1948), p. 154.
6   Sharpe, pp. 106–7.
7   S. Cousins, *To Beg I am Ashamed* (1954), pp. 241–2.
8   L. Wyles, *A Woman at Scotland Yard* (1932), p. 77.
9   C. H. Rolph (ed.), *Women of the Streets. A Sociological Study of the Common Prostitute* (1955), p. 109.
10 *Paddington News*, 14 May, 1938.
11 ibid., 14 May, 1938.
12 *St Pancras Chronicle*, 17 March, 1939.
13 ibid., 3 February, 1939.
14 *Paddington News*, 15 July, 1939.
15 R. Jackson, *Occupied with Crime* (1967), p. 58.
16 *Paddington News*, 19 February, 1938.
17 ibid., 6 October, 1944.
18 Orwell, *Collected Essays*, I, p. 76.
19 H. Mannheim, *Social Aspects of Crime in England between the Wars* (1940).
20 Rolph, pp. 204–5.
21 ibid., p. 82.
22 *Paddington News*, 9 March, 1940.
23 ibid., 4 July, 1941.
24 ibid., 5 September, 1941.
25 ibid., 10 April, 1942.
26 ibid., 4 September, 1942.
27 ibid., 26 November, 1943.
28 ibid., 23 May, 1941.
29 ibid., 8 January, 1943.
30 ibid., 4 September, 1942.
31 ibid., 10 December, 1943.
32 ibid., 11 May, 1945.
33 *Westminster and Pimlico News*, 3 March, 1944.
34 *Brighton and Hove Gazette*, 29 July, 1944.
35 *St Marylebone Record*, 17 June, 1944.
36 Marthe Watts, *The Men in My Life*, p. 205.
37 ibid., Chapter X.
38 ibid., p. 234.
39 ibid., pp. 178–96.
40 Rolph, p. 26.
41 Watts, p. 196.
42 J. Gosling and D. Warner, *Shame of a City* (1960), pp. 68–150.
43 *Paddington News*, 19 May, 1944.
44 ibid., 10 August, 1945; 22 June, 1945.
45 *New Survey*, vol. IX, *Life and Leisure*, p. 298.
46 *Paddington News*, 1 December, 1944.
47 ibid., 1 December, 1944.
48 Gosling, *Shame of a City*, p. 68.
49 ibid., p. 68.
50 R. Fabian, *London After Dark* (1954), p. 65.
51 ibid., p. 65.
52 Fabian, p. 12.

53   Cousins, p. 249; Rolph, p. 20.
54   Thorp, pp. 108–9.
55   Crim. Stats, 1946, Table C.
56   Birm. AR, 1938–46.
57   *St Marylebone Record*, 17 June, 1944.
58   *Paddington News*, 16 February, 1945.
59   *Brighton and Hove Gazette*, 11 March 1944.
60   *Paddington News*, 16 February, 1945.
61   Webb, pp. 154–63.
62   *Paddington News*, 28 December, 1945.
63   cf. L. Kennedy, *The Trial of Stephen Ward* (1965 edn).
64   H. Montgomery Hyde, *The Other Love* (1970), p. 213.
65   *Paddington News*, 15 July, 1939; 16 March, 1940; 24 October, 1941.
66   Webb, pp. 158–63.
67   *St Marylebone Record*, 11 March, 1944; 17 June, 1944; 24 June, 1944; 26 August, 1944.
68   *Paddington News*, 3 August, 1945; 10 August, 1945.
69   Rolph, pp. 204–5.

CHAPTER NINE: VIOLENCE

1   G. Greene, *The Ministry of Fear* (1963 edn), pp. 73–4.
2   Crim. Stats, 1939–45, p. 11.
3   N. Walker, *Crime and Punishment in Britain* (1965), p. 18.
4   Crim. Stats, 1939–45, Table D.
5   James Spenser, *The Wheels* (1938), pp. 122–4.
6   Hill, *passim*.
7   cf. A Richardson, *Nick of the River* (1955), pp. 152–7.
8   Gosling, *Ghost Squad*, pp. 149–51.
9   ELA, 10 July, 1943.
10   SLP, 20 July, 1943.
11   F. H. McClintock and E. Gibson, *Robbery in London* (1961), xiv.
12   Spencer, pp. 118–19.
13   cf. N. Longmate, *The GI's* (1975), pp. 129–33.
14   *Kensington Gazette*, 10 September, 1943.
15   SLP, 20 July, 1943.
16   e.g. ELA, 7 December, 1945.
17   *Wembley News*, 14 September, 1945.
18   Orwell, *Collected Essays*, III, pp. 72–3.
19   Longmate, pp. 160–1.
20   ibid., p. 161.
21   *Kensington Gazette*, 29 June, 1945; 27 July, 1945; cf. also PR, 19 October, 1945, and PC, 24 November, 1944.
22   *Leicester Mercury*, 3 May, 1944.
23   *Paddington Mercury*, 26 August, 1944.
24   *Leicester Mercury*, 1 June, 1944.
25   *Ilford Recorder*, 5 October, 1944.
26   *The People*, 23 April, 1944.
27   *East End News*, 11 February, 1944.
28   ibid., 21 April, 1944; 12 May, 1944; ELA, 21 April, 1944.
29   SLP, 2 February, 1940.
30   WLP, 10 September, 1943.
31   WLP, 6 March, 1942.

33 *East End News*, 3 December, 1943.
34 ELA, 30 January, 1943.
35 *East End News*, 4 October, 1940.
36 ibid., 25 April, 1941.
37 *Paddington Mercury*, 9 September, 1944.
38 HG, 21 September, 1945.
39 *Kensington Gazette*, 5 April, 1946.
40 *Leytonstone Express and Independent*, 12 February, 1944.
41 *Kensington Post*, 22 April, 1944.
42 Calder, p. 363.
43 Crim. Stats, 1939–45, Table D.
44 EC, 13 February, 1942.
45 Crim. Stats, 1939–45, Table D.
46 *Kensington Gazette*, 30 January, 1942.
47 *Willesden Chronicle*, 24 August, 1945; 28 September, 1945.
48 *East End News*, 23 October, 1942.
49 *Kensington Gazette*, 14 June, 1946.
50 *Leicester Mercury*, 31 March, 1944.
51 Crim. Stats, 1939–45, p. 6.
52 BA, 16 June, 1945.
53 HG, 13 August, 1945.
54 ibid., 16 June, 1944; 30 June, 1944.
55 EC, 3 October, 1941.
56 *Bath Weekly Chronicle and Herald*, 22 April, 1944.
57 ibid., 31 March, 1945.
58 BA, 24 February, 1945; 7 March, 1945.
59 Crim. Stats, 1938, Table XI, XII; 1946, Table 5.
60 *Bath Weekly Chronicle and Herald*, 23 September, 1944.

CHAPTER TEN: JUVENILE DELINQUENCY

1 J. B. Priestley, *English Journey* (1949 edn), pp. 401–3.
2 G. Orwell, *Inside the Whale and Other Essays* (1962 edn), p. 89.
3 H. Nicolson, *Diaries and Letters 1939–1945* (1970 edn), p. 167.
4 ibid., p. 436.
5 *New Survey*, I, p. 193.
6 Manch, AR, 1938; PR, 23 April, 1937.
7 PR, 23 April, 1937.
8 ibid., 5 February, 1937.
9 ibid., 9 June, 1939.
10 ibid., 2 April, 1937.
11 ibid., 5 February, 1937.
12 ibid., 5 February, 1937.
13 Met AR, 1936, pp. 23–4.
14 Manch. AR, 1940; PR, 30 July, 1937; PC, 19 July, 1940.
15 PR, 23 April, 1937.
16 ibid., 9 April, 1937.
17 ibid., 30 April, 1937.
18 ibid., 30 July, 1937.
19 ibid., 30 April, 1937.
20 Met AR, 1936, pp. 23–4.
21 PC, 3 February, 1939.
22 PR, 31 March, 1939.
23 Met. AR, 1937, p. 10.

24 PR, 27 June, 1941.
25 ibid., 23 April, 1937.
26 Burt, pp. 121–2.
27 PR, 9 February, 1940.
28 *Hampshire Telegraph*, 17 May, 1940.
29 PR, 28 February, 1941.
30 H. Mannheim, *Juvenile Delinquency in an English Middletown* (1948), p. 70.
31 PRO. HO 45/20250.
32 Mannheim, *War and Crime*, p. 87.
33 PR, 17 November, 1939.
34 PC, 13 June, 1941.
35 Mannheim, *War and Crime*, p. 88.
36 PC, 19 July, 1940.
37 ibid, 19 July, 1940.
38 PR, 28 February, 1941.
39 SLP, 19 July, 1940.
40 PR, 27 June, 1941; cf. *Ilford Recorder*, 4 February, 1943.
41 PC, 4 April, 1941.
42 PR, 30 April, 1943.
43 ibid., 27 June, 1941.
44 PC, 9 April, 1937.
45 Met. AR, 1936, pp. 23–4.
46 PR, 30 October, 1942.
47 ibid., 5 July, 1946.
48 ibid., 28 February, 1941.
49 H. D. Willcock, *Report on Juvenile Delinquency* (1949), p. 129.
50 PR, 18 April, 1941.
51 PRO. HO 45/20250.
52 PC, 7 March, 1947.
53 ibid., 2 February, 1945, to 16 March, 1945.
54 ibid., 2 February, 1945.
55 PR, 25 March, 1938.
56 PC, 9 April, 1937.
57 PR, 27 September, 1940.
58 *Bath Weekly Chronicle and Herald*, 9 October, 1943.
59 ibid., 27 March, 1943.
60 ibid., 5 February, 1944.
61 ibid., 10 March, 1943.
62 cf. *Brighton and Hove Gazette*, 7 October, 1939.

CHAPTER ELEVEN: THE POLICE AND THE COURTS

1 PC, 10 February, 1939.
2 Crim. Stats, 1933–9.
3 Met. AR, 1938.
4 PR, 23 June, 1939.
5 Crim. Stats, 1939–45, p. 11.
6 BA, 6 February, 1943.
7 Met. AR, 1945, p. 24.
8 PR, 9 May, 1945.
9 *Report of H.M.s Inspectors of Constabulary for the Year ended 29th September 1945*, p. 6.
10 T. A. Critchley, *A History of Police in England and Wales 900–1966* (1967), p. 230.
11 PC, 15 June, 1945; 4 January, 1946.
12 Met. AR, 1945, p. 5.

13   PC, 29 March, 1946.
14   PR, 13 April, 1945.
15   PC, 14 January, 1944.
16   ibid., 24 March, 1944.
17   ibid., 28 April, 1944.
18   ibid., 5 May, 1944.
19   ibid., 26 May, 1944.
20   ibid., 26 May, 1944.
21   ibid., 24 March, 1944.
22   ibid., 5 May, 1944.
23   ibid., 21 April, 1944.
24   PR, 10 May, 1946.
25   PC, 26 May, 1944.
26   ibid., 25 February, 1944.
27   ibid., 21 April, 1944.
28   ibid., 26 May, 1944.
29   *Report . . . Constabulary*, 1945, p. 6.
30   Crim. Stats, 1939–45, p. 5.
31   ibid., p. 5.
32   PR, 6 February, 1942.
33   Crim. Stats, 1939–45, p. 11.
34   Crim. Stats, 1946.
35   PC, 31 May, 1946.
36   PR, 19 October, 1945.
37   ibid., 19 October, 1945.
38   ibid., 16 October, 1942.
39   ibid., 16 October, 1942.
40   ibid., 30 October, 1942.
41   ibid., 20 November, 1942.
42   ibid., 5 February, 1943.
43   ibid., 5 February, 1943.
44   ibid., 21 May, 1943.
45   Crim. Stats, 1946.

CONCLUSION

1   The Chief Constable of Birkenhead; PC, 15 March, 1946.
2   McClintock and Avison, op. cit., pp. 179–80.
3   M. Sissons and P. French, *Age of Austerity 1945–1951* (1964).

Index